In Bed with the Georgians

Dedicated to dollymops in general, and to Dolly Mopp in particular.

Love in her eyes sits dreaming.

In Bed with the Georgians

Sex, Scandal and Satire in the 18th Century

Mike Rendell

PEN & SWORD HISTORY

First published in Great Britain in 2016 by
Pen & Sword History
an imprint of
Pen & Sword Books Ltd
47 Church Street
Barnsley
South Yorkshire
S70 2AS

Copyright © Mike Rendell 2016

ISBN 978 1 47383 774 4

A CIP catalogue record for this book is available from the British Library

Typeset in Ehrhardt by
Mac Style Ltd, Bridlington, East Yorkshire
Printed and bound by Replika Press Pvt. Ltd.

Pen & Sword Books Ltd incorporates the imprints of Pen & Sword Archaeology,
Atlas, Aviation, Battleground, Discovery, Family History, History, Maritime,
Military, Naval, Politics, Railways, Select, Transport, True Crime, and Fiction,
Frontline Books, Leo Cooper, Praetorian Press, Seaforth Publishing and
Wharncliffe.

For a complete list of Pen & Sword titles please contact
PEN & SWORD BOOKS LIMITED
47 Church Street, Barnsley, South Yorkshire, S70 2AS, England
E-mail: enquiries@pen-and-sword.co.uk
Website: www.pen-and-sword.co.uk

Contents

Introduction

Observing the events of 1750, Londoner Richard Hall noted in his journal that an earthquake was felt in the capital on Thursday 8 February – and again on 8 March at 5.30 in the morning, i.e. precisely one month later.

Earthquakes are not, of course, common in the London area. Scientifically-minded people at the time were able to conjecture that immediately below the earth's surface there was a void – a honeycomb of air pockets – and that from time-to-time violent winds, or possibly flames, or water, or maybe all of the above, would rush through these pockets causing quakes on the surface. *The Gentleman's Magazine* was able to inform its anxious readers that there were three types of quake: the 'Inclination', where the earth vibrated from side to side; the 'Pulsation' where it shook up and down; and the 'Tremor' 'when it shakes and quivers every way like a flame'.

But the Church was having none of this scientific mumbo-jumbo. The Bishop of London, Thomas Sherlock, wrote to all his clergymen calling on them to inform their flocks of the true reason for the earthquakes: Divine displeasure at pornography. In fact the word had only recently been coined, from Greek roots meaning 'writing about prostitutes'. Were these quakes not 'immediately directed' against London, the sinful city? After all, nowhere else experienced the tremors. Was it not a reflection of the Lord's wrath at the publication of '*The Memoirs of Fanny Hill*, this vile book, the lewdest thing I ever saw?' as the Bishop put it.

'Have not the histories of the vilest prostitutes been published?' he bellowed from the pulpit, going on to have a swipe at swearing and blasphemy, and at the 'unnatural lewdness' for which God had destroyed Sodom, and for the constant publication of books which challenged 'the great truths of religion'.

Before long, rumours swept the Capital that these two minor quakes were warning signs, precursors of 'the big one' which would surely be unleashed on London exactly one month later. And so it was that on 8 April 1750, large swathes of the population tried to leave the City with their worldly belongings stacked high in wheel-barrows, hand-carts – whatever was available. The result was chaos, a total gridlock which lasted until nightfall, when everyone sheepishly trudged home.

The story illustrates several interesting points about the eighteenth century – the so-called Age of Reason. Many of the long-held beliefs of the day were in fact mere superstitions dressed up as scientific proof. Pornography caused earthquakes; masturbation caused blindness; having sex with a young virgin would cure venereal disease (a sort of 'reverse infection' – the man could catch the goodness from the virgin, and this would drive out the evil). It was generally believed that a woman could spontaneously catch venereal disease from having sex with healthy males, and then infect their male partners. No-one thought that the man was in any way to blame – it was entirely the woman's fault. In treating venereal disease there was no distinction made between syphilis, gonorrhoea or other sexually transmitted diseases – and treatment invariably involved either ingesting or applying mercury, often with fatal results. The medical profession still adhered to the vestiges of the ideas of ancient Greece. Hippocrates in his book *On the Nature of Man* had described the four fluids – humours – which made up the human body, namely: blood, yellow bile, black bile and phlegm. Any imbalance between these humours could cause illness. Writing a century after the birth of Christ, Galen developed the idea of the four humours – characterised by a combination of hot, cold, moist and dry qualities – and identified them with four temperaments – sanguine, choleric, melancholic and phlegmatic. Men were considered to be predominately 'cold' and 'dry' whereas in women 'hot' and 'moist' dominated.

Medical ignorance extended to a staggering lack of knowledge about human reproduction and the menstrual cycle. Folk lore and old wives' tales took the place of family planning. Drinking the water from a local smithy, where red-hot iron and molten lead would have been plunged into butts of water by the blacksmith, was believed to prevent pregnancy. Eating strawberries in pregnancy would cause the baby to be born with birthmarks, and eating lobsters could result in your progeny having claw feet. Beware of being frightened by a hare while pregnant – or your child would be born with a hare-lip. Avoid intercourse on the stairs, or your child would suffer from a hunched back.

Superstition and confidence tricks went hand-in-hand, as in the curious case of Mary Tofts. It was in November 1726 that a story broke in *Mist's Weekly Journal* that a young woman from Godalming had given birth to a rabbit. Or rather, various rabbit parts. The story quickly became famous, not least because the newspaper which Nathaniel Mist published had a reported readership of 20,000 a week, and the public lapped up details of the remarkable story. More rabbits were 'delivered' from under a blanket by the poor young woman, who had secreted the rabbit parts up her vagina, presumably in an attempt to gain fame (and fortune). Doctors examined her, and astonishingly did not dismiss the fakery out of hand. News reached the ear of King George I. Intrigued, the king sent Nathaniel St. André, the surgeon to the Royal household, to check out the story. He appears to have been taken in by the deception, and it was another month before the true story emerged. The medical profession was lampooned mercilessly and William Hogarth produced an etching entitled *Cunicularii, or The Wise Men of Godliman in Consultation* (1726), showing the labour throes of Mary Toft surrounded by St André and the other dupes.

So much for the Age of Reason. The story of the earthquake also illustrates another aspect of life in the 1700s: the constant and often futile battle by the Church to make its voice heard above the torrent of immorality which swept the country. Nowadays our newspapers may be dominated by stories of the antics of wannabees, reality TV stars, super-models and WAGS. They are the celebrities of modern culture, held up as role models, and fashion icons. Two hundred and fifty years ago, that role was held by the courtesans. The name 'celebrity' when used to describe a famous person, may not have been developed until the 1840s, but in the 1750s the high class courtesan emerged as the arbiter of fashion and taste, an aspirational figure for lesser mortals. They were the women who were succeeding in a man's world; they had money, fame and status, and they were celebrities in all but name. The papers were full of their antics, in and out of the bedroom. The world of the 'demi rep' as it was called – half respectable – was not so much criticised as held up for public admiration. Stories abounded of the vast 'signing on' fees charged by these beautiful and often wealthy young women, as they became the subject of bidding wars between rival aristocrats and members of the royal family. Far from shunning the limelight, these women revelled in their fame – they dressed immaculately in the latest fashions from France, they disported themselves in open phaetons drawn by matching horses controlled by liveried horsemen, they went to public places such as the theatre with the sole purpose of being seen by as many admirers as possible. The courtesan represented the pinnacle for those who sold sex for money, but they were supported by a huge pyramid underneath. The favoured few were backed up by thousands – tens of thousands, of women who were available for hire. The streets of London were thronged with prostitutes plying their trade – from the pox-ridden drunken slut, sleeping in a doorway and willing to exchange her favours for the price of a meal and a glass of oblivion-making alcohol, to the well-dressed whore promenading at places like Bagnigge Wells, (Image 1) or the occupants of the fine seraglios, those high class brothels which were nick-named 'nunneries', run by fierce bawds called Lady Abbesses.

It has been estimated that a figure of twenty per cent of all women in London were engaged in the sex trade at one time or another in their lives. They were not necessarily earning their living from full-time prostitution – they may have been servant girls who occasionally made a few shillings satisfying the whims of their randy employers; they may have been women who had no other means of avoiding starvation while seeking new employment; they may have been 'good time girls' who enjoyed sex and who were very happy to be paid for something they found pleasurable. And of course, many were vulnerable young girls, seduced or raped and then abandoned to their fate.

Daniel Defoe, writing in 1725, was certainly of the view that young servant girls made up the majority of London prostitutes, and that they took to prostitution when they were unemployed, as a way of supporting themselves. *'This is the reason why our streets are swarming with strumpets. Thus many of them rove from place to place, from bawdy-house to service, and from service to bawdy-house again.'*

The numbers are staggering, although calculations varied: one report in 1758 estimated that there were 62,500 whores plying their trade in London. The German traveller Johann Wilhelm von Archenholz, writing in 1789, came up with a figure of 50,000, but this was stated to include only full-time prostitutes. By 1839 Michael Ryan was claiming in his book *Prostitution in London, with a comparative view of that of Paris and New York* that there were then about 80,000 prostitutes, operating out of 5,000 brothels, in the London metropolis. He also gives a figure of 400 full-time 'procurers' engaged in London in kidnapping young children for sale into the sex-trade. At the time the age of consent was just twelve years old, but the market for young virgins meant that many children below this age were entrapped as prostitutes, with orphanages providing a constant supply of newcomers. It is clear that girls as young as eight or nine were lured into prostitution by a trade desperate for virgin newcomers.

The eighteenth century saw a massive growth in London's population but this was set against the statistic that, in many years, deaths exceeded births in the capital. The growth was entirely made up of migrants drawn to London from all over England. They came in search of work, and for young girls that often meant the sex trade. Large numbers were lured over from Ireland. Many moved on to other areas of work once they reached their mid-twenties, if, of course, they lived that long. *The Times* of 31 October 1785 famously quoted a figure of 5,000 prostitutes dying every year in London. Of those that survived a few (a very few) lived the dream, with money, fame and glamour. But, for the majority, it was a seedy life of depravity, degradation, poverty and debilitating illness. Not that that ever put off the wave of newcomers entering the City every year, eagerly snapped up by the bawds and procurers who scoured the coaching stations and inns on the main arterial routes coming in from the country.

What follows is the story of sex in the Georgian era. It is the story of the common whore, just as much as that of the high class courtesan. It is also a tale of male bigotry and hypocrisy, of incredible double-standards and appalling examples set by royalty and the ruling classes. It shows the world as it appeared to the people living through that period, through the eyes of the writers, the artists and in particular the satirists who faithfully recorded the foibles, the scandals, the frailties and the criminality of the nation's rulers.

Chapter One

The Sex Workers

In 1758 a book was published by G. Burnet (author unknown) with the long-winded title of *A Congratulatory Epistle from a Reformed Rake to John F...g Esq upon the new scheme of reforming prostitutes*. It contained ten gradations of prostitutes, starting with the most genteel, and working down through to the most miserable of sluts:

Looking at each category in turn:

Women of Fashion, who intrigue.
Demi-Reps.
Good-natured Girls.
Kept Mistresses.
Ladies of Pleasure.
Whores.
Park-Walkers.
Street-Walkers.
Bunters.
Bulk-mongers.

1. **Women of Fashion, who intrigue.** This classification covered bored wives, perhaps married into the aristocracy, who felt sufficiently liberated to have multiple affairs simply because they wanted love, and sex, and could not find it within marriage. As they did not 'sell' sex they cannot really be classed as prostitutes.
2. **Demi-reps.** Girls of a dubious reputation were called demi-reps, short for demi-reputation. They would not have 'lived in' at the brothel or seraglio, but would have been brought in when customers required their services.
3. **Good-natured girls.** These were the unmarried women who would have sex with their admirers in return for a good meal and an evening's entertainment.
4. **Kept mistresses.** An example would be a courtesan paid an annuity, or provided with a house, by a man who was not her husband, and who would be available for sexual favours although not necessarily on an exclusive basis. In France these kept women were known as '*dames entretenues*', and the practice of keeping a mistress was termed '*la galanterie*'. In England, a whole new language developed in line with the French – men were no longer adulterers, they were 'gallants' and 'affairs' became 'intrigues'.
5. **Ladies of Pleasure.** These would be attractive, well-spoken prostitutes able to discuss current affairs with their admirers, perhaps play a musical instrument, and who would live in lodgings or high class brothels.
6. **Whores.** Living in down-market brothels, operating from bagnios, or making a living by picking up custom in the taverns and theatres such as the ones around Covent Garden.

7. **Park-walkers.** These would attract custom by walking through parks such as Ranelagh and New Spring Gardens (later Vauxhall Gardens). Well-dressed, they would attract male attention by a touch on the elbow or a provocative tilt of a fan.
8. **Street-walkers.** Openly accosting men in the street, and either servicing their clients in public places, (when they might be termed 'threepenny stand-ups') or in garrets or rooms above taverns.
9. **Bunters.** These were the diseased whores, the lowest of the low. Unclean, often physically scarred by mercury poison and open syphilitic sores, bunters would be found near the docks, willing to exchange their favours for the price of a drink.
10. **Bulk mongers.** Homeless beggars, living rough and often in the final stages of disease.

The same book goes on to urge readers to accept that the higher class sex-workers were just as likely to corrupt the morals of the nation as the lowly street-walker:

If low, mean, Whores are a Bane to Society, by debauching the Morals, as well as Bodies, of Apprentices, and Lads scarce come to the Age of Puberty; if they frequently infect them with venereal Complaints, which almost as often terminate in as fatal Consequences; if they sometimes urge these youths to unwarrantable Practices for supporting their Extravagance in Gin; do not those in a more dazzling Situation produce still worse Consequences, by as much as they are above the others? Are not youths of good Family and Fortune seduced by these shining Harlots, who more frequently than their Inferiors in Rank, propagate the Species of an inveterate Clap, or a Sound-pox?

Later, the blame is put fairly and squarely on women for corrupting men, rather than the other way round:

There is a Lust in Woman that operates more strongly than all her libidinous Passions; to gratify which she sticks at nothing. Fame, Health, Content, are easily sacrificed to it. Fanny M...y and Lucy C....r have made more Whores than all the Rakes in England. A kept mistress that rides in her Chariot, debauches every vain Girl she meets – such is the Presumption of the Spectator, she imagines the same Means will procure her the same Grandeur. A miserable street walker who perhaps has not Rags enough to cover her Nakedness, more enforces Chastity – I had almost said Virtue – than all the moral Discourses, and even Sermons that ever were wrote or preached.

Put simply, the writer felt that society had less to worry about with the girl in *The Whore's last shift* shown as Image 9 than with the high-class prostitute in her finery, such as in Image 1 entitled *A Bagnigge Wells Scene, or no resisting Temptation.* The latter print was published by Carington Bowles in 1776 and shows two well-dressed prostitutes plying their trade at the popular watering hole. They are dressed in the latest fashions, they are smart and respectable – something a young girl might aspire to look like. In *The Whore's last shift* published just three years later, the title is a pun on the word 'shift' – the whore has had her last customer of the day, and is washing her flimsy garment, i.e. shift, in a cracked chamber pot. No-one would call it an aspirational image.

Caricaturists loved to parody the extremes, such as with the contrasting images of 'the great impures' of St James's and of St Giles shown as Image 6. It was created by Thomas Rowlandson in 1794, and demonstrates the differences between the glamorous courtesans of St James and the rough and ready good-time girls from St Giles. Either way, the 'happy hooker' image, the 'tart with a heart' having a good time, was well and truly established by the eighteenth century. However, both the high-class woman and the street worker were seen as having one thing in common – they operated for money. *Dividing the Spoil* shown as Image 7 shows that whereas the St James's ladies ripped off punters at the game of Faro by operating a crooked deck of cards, and then shared out the ill-gotten gains, they were no better than the whores down the road in St Giles's, who shared out the proceeds of picking pockets and stealing watches from their foolish customers.

Certainly if you were a household drudge, rising at five to sweep out and re-lay the fires, spending all day on your hands and knees, you must have thought 'I'm in the wrong job' if you saw a courtesan drive by in her phaeton drawn by four matching greys, especially once you realised that it would take you several years to earn what 'Fanny M…y' or 'Lucy C…r' could make in a couple of days simply by lying on her back thinking of England. Imagine someone in one of the needle trades, such as the humble milliner, working on a splendid head-dress made of fine silks and plumed with ostrich feathers, expecting the creation to be collected by a duchess or countess, and then discovering that it was to be worn by someone who was themselves once a milliner. William Hogarth was one of many who suggested that the ranks of prostitutes were mostly made up of recruits from the Provinces, who would come up to London and there fall prey to wily brothel keepers. Thus Hogarth's first plate in the six-part series called *The Harlot's Progress* (see Image 8) shows the notorious procuress Mother Needham ensnaring the young fresh-faced girl called Moll Hackabout. However, the temptation to 'have a go' was all too easy and, in practice, many entered the profession knowingly and willingly.

It is interesting to remember that admission to what became known as the 'Cyprian Corps' allowed for both upward and downward movement – more usually the latter, as sickness took its inevitable toll. At the start of her career, an attractive girl could aim for the stars. Her value, as a virgin, was perhaps fifty times the amount she would command as 'used goods' but a clever bawd would show the girl how to 'restore her virginity' many times over. It was commonplace to insert a small piece of bloodied meat, or a sponge soaked with blood, inside the vagina so that a lover would mistake the signs of bleeding for the breaking of the long-ago ruptured hymen. The author Nicholas de Venette, in his 1712 book *The Mysteries of Conjugal Love Reveal'd* gave advice to brides who were no longer chaste and who wished to deceive their husband, to the effect that they should insert lambs blood into the vagina on their wedding night. For the more adventurous, surgeons were already performing operations to 'tidy up' the labia by means of a labiaplasty. Simpler, non-surgical, procedures involved the application of water impregnated with alum, or other astringents.

At the outset, a young girl might hope to catch the eye of an aristocratic gentleman. It is interesting in this context to see the images in the caricature by Richard Newton entitled *Progress of a Woman of Pleasure*. It appears as Image 4 and 5.

The first picture shows the girl in country garb arriving in town, where she has been placed in 'the house of a Great Lady in King's Place'. King's Place was the home of the legendary bawd Charlotte Hayes, who is featured in Chapter Three. Scene two shows the lady in question at the start of her career, under the caption 'I see you now waiting in full dress for an introduction to a fine Gentleman with a world of money'. The third scene shows her 'in high keeping' accompanying her Adonis to the Masquerades. But our heroine has a character flaw – she cannot hold her drink and she loses her temper too readily.

The fourth image shows her flinging a glass in the face of her keeper. She is turned out and her only consolation is that her hairdresser has promised to marry her, but he offers her an annuity of only £200 a year. Furious, she complains that for that money she could get the smartest Linen Drapers Man in London, and chucks him out as being a dirty rascal.

By now she is forced to move to Marylebone, where she exhibits herself in the Promenade in Oxford Street – in other words she has slipped down the list from kept woman to street walker. The downward spiral continues – she scorns a customer who offers her a crown (five shillings), insisting that she wants five guineas (more than twenty times the amount offered). She starts knocking back the brandy to hide her disappointment with life, earning a few shillings dancing at a sleazy emporium in Queen Anne Street East. She gets involved in a brawl, earning herself a warrant and two black eyes.

Before long, she is selling her favours to an apprentice boy who has stolen half a crown from his master's till. She moves into a sponging house (i.e. she is confined there on account of her debts) pawns a silver thimble to pay for breakfast, and becomes a servant of a woman who was formerly *her* servant, only able to afford a bunch of radishes and a pint of porter for her dinner. She is drunk on cheap gin. The journey into oblivion ends up with her slumped on the doorstep of the house of 'this female monster' who has turned her out into the street in case she gets lumbered with the expense of a funeral.

The whole progress is far more 'fun' that Hogarth's *Harlot's Progress* – it doesn't moralise or suggest that whoring was inherently immoral, merely that failing to hold your liquor and assaulting your customers is bad for business. The non-censorious viewpoint is perhaps not surprising given that the brilliant Richard Newton was aged 19 when he drew it – he died of 'gaol fever' two years later in 1798, and his caricatures suggest that he was well acquainted with the seedier side of life and probably knew many prostitutes personally. The images are delightfully drawn caricatures, far removed from the serious tone of the meticulously staged Hogarth scenes in '*The Harlot's Progress*'. The modern equivalent would be the busty cartoon figure of Jessica in '*Who framed Roger Rabbit*'.

What then was the attitude of the second oldest profession (i.e. the Law) to its senior profession? Prostitution was never illegal under Common Law and prosecutions could only be brought if the offence was linked with disorderly conduct, public indecency, or some other crime. 'Keeping a bawdy-house' was an indictable misdemeanour at Common Law but there were often difficulties in proving the identity of the proprietor of the premises, and the sort of evidence needed to prove the offence was generally only available from someone who had actually attended the premises, that is to say as a paying customer. Bawds simply had to factor in the cost of employing lawyers to defend them against prosecution in the charges they passed on to their customers.

Periodically, reform societies pushed for prosecutions to be brought. The records of the 'Societies for Promoting a Reformation of Manners', in their thirtieth account of the *Progress made in the Cities of London and Westminster*, stated:

> the said Societies have in pursuance of their said design from 1 December 1723 to 1 December 1724 prosecuted divers sorts of offenders viz:
> Lewd and Disorderly Persons 1951
> Keeping of Bawdy and Disorderly houses 29

They also claimed to have prosecuted 600 people for breaking the Sabbath, 108 for swearing and cursing, and twelve for drunkenness, adding: 'The total prosecuted in and near London for debauchery and profaneness for the thirty three years past was 89,333'. Various Vagrancy Acts had been passed, particularly in 1609 and 1744, but these did not make prostitution an offence. In 1752 Parliament passed an Act against the keeping of Disorderly Houses, but this did not in itself criminalise sexual solicitation e.g. by street walkers. The Act was primarily aimed at the public nuisance caused when premises were used for the illegal sale of alcohol, or as gambling dens, or for unlicensed dancing and rowdy entertainment. Unusually, the 1752 Act made it a legal requirement that publicly funded prosecutions were to be brought if two or more parishioners were prepared to act as informants. Previously, any such prosecutions would have had to have been privately funded. However, few parishioners would volunteer to give evidence that they had entered a brothel, let alone be tarred with the name of 'informer'. The brothel owner was, after all, a neighbour and generally bawds employed bullies and other 'enforcers' to make sure that complaints from the public never got to court.

What made prosecutions even harder was that a brothel owner had the legal right to transfer the case to the Court of Kings Bench. Doing so meant that the prosecutor lost all chance of recovering legal fees from the Crown. Faced with the expense, few prosecutions were made and as the 'Society for the Suppression of Vice' noted in 1803: 'as the law now stands, the punishment for the offence of keeping a brothel, one of the most heinous and mischievous that can occur in society, is attended with such difficulty as almost entirely to deter from prosecution'.

It was not until the 1818 Disorderly Houses Act was passed that the 'King's Bench escape route' was blocked. It also removed the problem of having to identify the proprietor – the offence was committed by 'any person … who shall appear, act or behave him or herself as master or mistress, or as the person having the care, government, or management of any such house'.

Whereas running a brothel could give rise to legal penalties, prostitution remained lawful. Nevertheless the crusading Justice of the Peace Sir John Fielding tried to use Common Law to prosecute prostitutes simply on the grounds that they were a public nuisance. Various cases against prostitutes appear in the petty sessions records of the City of London and Fielding urged constables that it was their duty to bring charges against 'night walkers'. It therefore made sense for brothel keepers and whores to 'look after' the constable, the night watchman and the beadle, either by offering financial bribes to leave them alone, or by rewarding them 'in kind' for their protection. Clearly these benefits were regarded as perks of the job. A wealthy prostitute had nothing to fear, because she paid her protector to look the other way. The impoverished whore at the bottom of the pile needed to watch out 'lest she be carried to *Bridewell*, where, instead of being reclaim'd, she is harden'd by her indelible Shame in her miserable State of Wickedness' (from *Satan's Harvest Home*, 1749).

In 1828 a case was heard against Samuel Hall, charged with indecent assault on a street-walker. *The Times* of 13 June 1828 reported:

> *that the watchmen, as a body, were a worthless and depraved set of fellows. Not only did they levy contributions on the pockets of the unfortunate women who walked the streets at night, but it was a fact they reduced them to such a state of terror, that they durst not refuse them any favour they might demand.*

Petty crime was closely linked with prostitution; an assignation with a prostitute often led to an accusation of theft of personal belongings such as silk handkerchiefs, pocket watches, snuff boxes and so on. But theft of an item exceeding one shilling in value was classed as 'grand larceny' (a criminal offence carrying the death penalty). In 1820 the distinction between petty larceny (involving goods worth less than one shilling) and grand larceny was abolished and replaced with a single offence of simple larceny. Avoiding the death penalty could still leave a convicted felon at risk of being whipped or sentenced to a spell in the pillory (especially in the first half of the Georgian era) and deportation, initially to the American colonies (between 1720 and 1776) or, after 1787, to Australia. Throughout the Georgian period convicted felons could expect to be sent to a house of correction – called the Bridewell – where beating hemp was a common penalty for women.

By the turn of the century public pressure to end the nuisance of noise, drunkenness and petty thieving that was linked to prostitution led to a spate of prosecutions. On 27 January 1816, *The Times* reported that 'fifteen more of those wretched females whom the Lord Mayor has determined to expel from the streets' were arrested. They were found guilty of causing a public nuisance and were sentenced to a month in Bridewell. Pending trial, these unfortunates would have been incarcerated in appalling conditions, either in watch-houses where they could expect to have to pay exorbitant fees to their gaoler for basic food, or in the city prisons known as the Poultry Compter and the Wood Street Compter. Arguably, conditions there were better than at the Roundhouse prison in St Martin's Lane, Westminster, where, in 1742, the keeper William Bird was convicted of murder when four women prisoners died. Horace Walpole described the incident in a letter to Sir Horace Mann:

> *There has lately been the most shocking scene of murder imaginable; a parcel of drunken constables took it into their heads to put the laws in execution against disorderly persons,*

and so took up every woman they met, till they had collected five and six or twenty, all of whom they thrust into St. Martin's roundhouse, where they kept them all night, with doors and windows closed. The poor creatures, who could not stir or breathe, screamed as long as they had any breath left, begging at least for water ... in the morning four were found stifled to death, two died soon after, and a dozen more are in a shocking way. In short, it is horrid to think what the poor creatures suffered: several of them were beggars, who, from having no lodging, were necessarily found in the street, and others honest labouring women.

It was not until Parliament passed The Vagrancy Act of 1824 that prostitution was targeted — and then only if the offence involved 'behaving in a riotous or indecent manner.' A conviction was only possible if the behaviour was truly outrageous, and therefore it was not prostitution *per se* which Parliament was seeking to control, merely riotous or indecent behaviour.

Women were faced with few choices: one was to engage in a life of prostitution with all the risks of legal harassment and disease; another was marriage with its resulting loss of independence. Few poor women could hit the jackpot of marriage to a wealthy husband, but it occasionally happened as evidenced by two anecdotes told by that inveterate old gossip-monger, Horace Walpole. Writing to George Montagu on 3 September 1748, he tells the tale of a smitten young man, forced to marry a girl way below his social class before she would let him have her between the sheets:

Did you not know a young fellow that was called Handsome Tracy? He was walking in the Park with some of his acquaintance, and overtook three girls; one was very pretty: they followed them; but the girls ran away, and the company grew tired of pursuing them, all but Tracy. He followed to Whitehall gate, where he gave a porter a crown to dog them: the porter hunted them – he, the porter. The girls ran all round Westminster, and back to the Haymarket, where the porter came up with them. He told the pretty one she must go with him, and kept her talking till Tracy arrived, quite out of breath, and exceedingly in love. He insisted on knowing where she lived, which she refused to tell him; and after much disputing, went to the house of one of her companions, and Tracy with them. He there made her discover her family, a butter-woman in Craven Street, and engaged her to meet him the next morning in the Park; but before night he wrote her four love-letters, and in the last offered two hundred pounds a-year to her, and a hundred a-year to Signora la Madre [i.e. her mother]. Griselda made a confidence to a stay-maker's wife, who told her that the swain was certainly in love enough to marry her, if she could determine to be virtuous and refuse his offers. "Ay," says she, "but if I should, and should lose him by it." However, the measures of the cabinet council were decided for virtue: and when she met Tracy the next morning in the park, she was convoyed by her sister and brother-in-law, and stuck close to the letter of her reputation. She would do nothing, she would go nowhere.

At last, as an instance of prodigious compliance, she told him, that if he would accept such a dinner as a butter-woman's daughter could give him, he should be welcome. Away they walked to Craven Street: the mother borrowed some silver to buy a leg of mutton, and they kept the eager lover drinking till twelve at night, when a chosen committee waited on the faithful pair to the minister of May-fair. The doctor was in bed, and swore he would not get up to marry the King, but that he had a brother over the way who perhaps would, and who did. The mother borrowed a pair of sheets, and they consummated at her house; and the next day they went to their own place. In two or three days the scene grew gloomy; and the husband coming home one night, swore he could bear it no longer. "Bear! bear what?" – "Why, to be teased by all my acquaintance for marrying a butter-woman's daughter. I am determined to go to France, and will leave you a handsome allowance." – "Leave me! why you don't fancy you shall leave me? I will go with you." – "What, you love me then?" – "No matter whether I love you or not, but you shan't go without me." And they are gone! If you know any body that proposes marrying and travelling, I think they cannot do it in a more commodious method.

On another occasion Walpole writes to say:

Lord Marchmont had married a second wife, a Miss Crampton. The circumstances attending this marriage are thus related by David Hume, in a letter to Mr. Oswald, dated January 29, 1748:- "Lord Marchmont has had the most extraordinary adventure in the world. About three weeks ago he was at the play, when he espied in one of the boxes a fair virgin, whose looks, airs, and manners had such a wonderful effect upon him, as was visible by every bystander. His raptures were so undisguised, his looks so expressive of passion, his inquiries so earnest, that every person took notice of it. He soon was told that her name was Crampton, a linen-draper's daughter, who had been bankrupt last year. He wrote next morning to her father, desiring to visit his daughter on honourable terms, and in a few days she will be the Countess of Marchmont. Could you ever suspect the ambitious, the severe, the bustling, the impetuous, the violent Marchmont of becoming so tender and gentle a swain …!"

These two examples of 'love at first sight' may or may not have been true, but they serve as a reminder of how important it was for a girl to get a ring on her finger before she succumbed to the blandishments of a man who was her social superior.

Chapter Two

The Alphabet of Sex, and More Besides

Abortion: Historically it was thought that life began when a mother first felt her baby kick – known as 'quickening'. This would usually happen between the sixteenth and twentieth week of pregnancy. At Common Law it was not illegal to have an abortion, provided it took place before the mother was 'quick with child.' A woman wanting a termination would have been faced with two choices – either by means of a surgical intervention in order to cause a miscarriage, or by taking plants known to have an abortifacient property. She might try plant extracts such as savin, obtained from a type of juniper, sometimes mixing it with black hellebore (highly toxic). She might try oil of hyssop (risky, as even a few drops were known to cause seizures and convulsions). Another favourite was Pennyroyal essential oil, even though it was highly poisonous and could be fatal to the mother as well as the child.

In 1803 Parliament passed the Malicious Shooting and Stabbing Act, which provided for a penalty of fourteen years' transportation for performing an abortion on a woman who was not yet 'quick with child' – and the death penalty if she was. The distinction lasted until 1837 when the death penalty was removed, and the distinction between late and early abortions was abolished.

Adultery: see Crim. Con.

Aphrodisiacs: Whether it was Casanova recommending fifty oysters at a sitting before snuggling up under the sheets, or tucking into stilton and red wine, the eighteenth century was full of ideas to boost a flagging appetite. Madame du Barry, the mistress of King Louis XV, set down her recipe for what might nowadays be termed 'lust and lurrv' based upon … cauliflower soup. Others swore by chicken broth ('Take four cocks…') or recommended a nice quince jelly to get the juices going.

Bagnios: Originally, the term meant a bath house, but by the eighteenth century the term was often applied to a brothel. Sometimes they were genuine public baths at which men and, separately, women could bathe. More usually they were houses arranged with numerous bedrooms, where prostitutes plied their trade. Image 2 gives a view of the Turks Head bagnio, in a print published in 1787. Entitled *Retail traders not affected by the shop tax* it shows a trio of prostitutes waiting to invite male customers inside. Above the lintel are the words 'Neat Lodgings for Men', while the cat in the window is a symbol of female sexual desire.

Bigamy: Marrying a second spouse while the first spouse was still living was a crime, but one which was not always clear-cut. Marriages were not required to be registered, and because divorce was only for the wealthy, couples frequently split up and went their separate ways, later entering a second marriage in blissful ignorance as to whether the original spouse was still alive. In addition, there was much confusion as to the validity of some earlier marriages, especially those entered into prior to Hardwicke's Marriage Act of 1753.

Birth Control: Although the medical profession did not fully understand the menstrual cycle and exactly how insemination took place, women may have been using their own attempt at the rhythm method, no doubt using the pretext that it was 'not appropriate' to have sex on particular Saints Days when these coincided with times when she considered herself most at risk. A woman might also insist on *coitus interruptus*. Equally she might put her faith in a herbal abortifacient such as tansy, dittany or yarrow, all recommended by Nicholas Culpeper in his *Complete Herbal* published midway through the seventeenth century. The seeds of Queen Anne's Lace, mentioned 2,000 years earlier by Hippocrates, were understood to prevent the egg attaching to the lining of the womb. The seeds would first have been harvested in the autumn, dried, then ground in a pestle and mortar and taken immediately after intercourse.

By the eighteenth century various cervical suppositories were in use (intended to seal the entrance to the cervix) as well as mechanical barriers. Casanova was apparently a keen advocate of inserting half a lemon to act as a barrier – and others would use a piece of marine sponge soaked in liquid believed to have spermicidal qualities, notably when made from Peruvian Bark (i.e. quinine) and olive oil. Lemon juice and vinegar were also favoured, either on a sponge, or diluted and used as a douche after intercourse.

Condoms (otherwise Cundums): These had been around for centuries, made from sheep intestines, but were mainly regarded as a protection for the wearer against the Pox, rather than because of concerns about getting a female pregnant. They were openly sold in shops such as The Green Canister in Half Moon Street in Covent Garden.

Casanova called them 'the English riding coat' while the diarist James Boswell records various instances when he used 'armour', otherwise calling it 'a machine.' They could be bought, singly, for a few pence, with one end tied up in coloured ribbon, but the intended wearer had to allow time to nip off and soak the condom in water before use, in order to make it supple. Well into the twentieth century some condoms were regarded as re-usable. Early models, being made of porous animal tissue, were highly ineffective as a form of birth control. The French writer Madame de Sevigne, writing in 1671, had described the condom as a 'spider's web against danger'.

Cosmetics: Known as 'paint', the wearing of make-up, particularly 'French rouge', was considered reprehensible by male writers. Prostitutes were especially considered likely to use make-up in order to enhance their sexual power. Paint was considered to be the tool of the devil, encouraging those female characteristics of vanity, pride, and duplicity. Jonathan Swift wrote a poem entitled *The Lady's Dressing Room* in 1732 in which he ridiculed the tricks of the trade used by women to deceive and mislead males. In practice much of the make-up used in the eighteenth century was based on white lead and carmine – both highly toxic ingredients. Thomas Rowlandson's *Six Stages of Mending a Face* appears as Image 11 and is a particularly harsh criticism of female trickery and deception. The bald-headed crone transforms herself (with wig, glass eye, false teeth and cosmetics) into an attractive young maid. The poor male of the species never stands a chance…

Crim. Con. (short for 'criminal conversation'): The common law tort of criminal conversation – which in effect was based on adultery – was abolished in 1857. It was an action, conducted at the Court of the Kings Bench at Westminster Hall, brought by a husband against a third party for compensation for breach of fidelity with his wife. An aristocratic cuckold could bring a suit demanding astronomical damages – sometimes as much as £20,000 – against a person debauching his wife. Grosvenor v Cumberland in 1769 shocked the nation because it involved the royal family, and is mentioned in Chapter Six. The actual evidence of the adulterous act was usually presented in the form of statements made by witnesses such as servants. Their testimony was often circumstantial, with much reference to squeaking bedsprings, crumpled sheets, and figures departing from bedrooms in the early hours of the morning. The public lapped up the trial reports, and books based on crim. con. cases were often titillating, voyeuristic, insights into the lives of the rich and famous.

Having obtained an award of damages the cuckolded husband could then decide whether to get a formal separation, or even a divorce.

Images 12 and 13 show how the satirists viewed crim. con. trials, with *Crim. Con. Temptations* setting out the measure of damages likely to be awarded according to whether the married female was a servant, a woman of low morals, a lady, and so on. *Cross examination of a Witness* mocks the value of hearsay evidence, with the lawyer asking the witness whether the lady cried out 'murder' or 'further'.

Cross-dressing: In an era which was so heavily biased against women, it is not surprising that many women dressed as men in order to avoid prejudice and stereotyping. There were a number of instances of women succeeding in a man's world – in the armed forces, as doctors, as artists. Sometimes dressing as a man was a subterfuge used to try and mislead other women into marriage.

In July 1777, a woman going by the name of Ann Marrow was convicted at Guildhall for 'going in man's cloaths, and personating a man in marriage, with three different women … and defrauding them of their money and effects'. She was ordered to stand in the pillory and serve six months in jail. The infuriated crowd were so enraged that they pelted her with objects, leaving her blind in both eyes. A similar case involved a woman called Mary Hamilton, otherwise Charles Hamilton, who was alleged to have married no fewer than fourteen different women as she travelled around the country. Astonishingly some of the wives were unaware of the deception, one of them describing in court how she was deceived by 'something of too vile, wicked and scandalous a nature' (in other words a dildo). Mary was found guilty of fraud and in 1746 was sentenced to be publicly whipped in four different towns in Somerset; her story was written up by Henry Fielding under the title of *The Female Husband*.

Charlotte Charke, a daughter of the poet laureate Colley Cibber, was a well-known actress and writer who gained infamy as a transvestite using the name Charles Brown. She went on to write one of the first autobiographies written by a woman, published in 1755 as *A Narrative of the Life of Mrs. Charlotte Charke*.

The Museum of London has a print entitled *Mils Grahn alias Theodora de Verdion* dated 1804, showing a person in a gentleman's outfit. The text explains that 'Dr. de Verdion was a woman from Berlin who dressed as a man. She worked in London as an exchange broker, secretary and a teacher of languages.'

The sculptress Anne Damer, mentioned in Chapter Eight, was renowned for her male attire, while the diplomat Chevalier d'Éon intrigued London society for many years by appearing at all times as a woman.

Cross-dressing was often encountered at masquerades, where the opportunity to escape from sexual stereotyping was too good to miss (see Masquerades).

Dildos: In the seventeenth century most dildos originated in Italy, where they were known as *dilettos*, with expensive models crafted from ivory, or even silver. By the 1700s dildos from France, where they were known as *consalateurs*, became popular. Leather or wooden dildos could be bought openly in shops such as 'The Green Canister' off Covent Garden. Also known as a travel godmiche, they were available in a variety of sizes. The Science Museum has one example in the form of an erect penis made of ivory, capable of being filled with warm liquid which could be 'ejaculated to order' via a plunger mechanism. Later models featured a compressible 'scrotum' for the same purpose.

Divorce: Whereas the ecclesiastical courts could grant an order for divorce '*a mensa et thoro*' this was more like a judicial separation, enabling the parties to live apart, but not to re-marry. The only way of terminating a marriage (apart from death) was by a private Act of Parliament. This was slow, expensive and involved a very public exposure of the state of the marriage in front of all the Members of Parliament. The number involved was incredibly small – just over three hundred divorce bills were passed in the entire period from 1700 up to the passing of the Matrimonial Causes Act in 1857, and, of those, only four were cases brought by women. Divorce was a rich man's privilege.

Flagellation: The French reckoned that English males had a propensity for being flogged – and for flogging women – as a means of getting aroused. Flagellation features in a number of satirical prints, including Image 14 showing a man with his buttocks bared, being soundly thrashed by a woman wielding a birch twitch.

The undoubted high priestess of flagellation was Mrs Theresa Berkley who operated out of 28 Charlotte Street, Portland Place. She was a 'governess' specialising in beating the living daylights out of wealthy patrons (known as 'flogging cullies') and was a veritable master of the art of inflicting pain for pleasure. It was said that she 'possessed the first requisite of a courtezan, viz., lewdness; for without a woman is positively lecherous she cannot keep up the affectation of it, and it will soon be perceived that she moves her hands or her buttocks to the tune of pounds, shillings, and pence'. Her speciality involved the use of a wooden frame called the Berkley Horse. The punter would be tied in such a way that he (or even she) could be lashed in the chosen part of the body with the medium of choice – birch twigs, nettles, furze, holly or leather straps.

Hurwood's *The Golden Age of Erotica* makes it clear that Theresa was prepared to be flogged herself – if the money was right – and quotes one source as saying:

For those whose lech it was to flog a woman, she would herself submit to a certain extent; but if they were gluttons at it, she had women in attendance who would take any number of lashes the flogger pleased, provided he forked out an ad valorem duty. Among these were Miss Ring, Hannah Jones, Sally Taylor, One-eyed Peg, Bauld-cunted Poll, and a black girl, called Ebony Bet.

When she died in 1836 Theresa left her very considerable estate, including her paraphernalia of torture, to her brother, a missionary. He was so shocked at discovering the source of her wealth that he renounced his inheritance and returned post-haste to Australia. The assets in the estate, amounting to £100,000, passed to the Crown.

Foundling Hospital: The philanthropic sea captain Thomas Coram opened the first refuge for abandoned children in Hatton Gardens in 1741. The purpose was to provide for the 'education and maintenance of exposed and deserted young children'. The Trustees had to cope with a flood of applicants, especially once great numbers of children from outlying country parishes started to be brought in. A ballot system was operated to determine admission. Applicants for admission had to be under twelve months old, and the intention was to give each child a good education, in which religious instruction was paramount, with a view to the person gaining an apprenticeship once old enough to leave. The hospital moved to larger premises at Bloomsbury in 1745. For thousands of unwed mothers it was the only prospect of securing food, lodging and a reasonable education for their unwanted offspring.

Game of flats: A slang phrase used to describe lesbian acts, so called because playing-cards were otherwise known as 'flats' and the sliding of two cards together was likened to females rubbing their genital areas together. See Lesbianism.

Harris's List of Covent Garden Ladies: The first printed version of the directory appeared in 1757, ostensibly based on the earlier handwritten list kept by John Harrison – otherwise known as Jack Harris – who was chief waiter at the Shakespeare's Head Tavern in Covent Garden and who gloried in the title of 'Pimp General of All England.' The early printed editions are thought to have been the work of an impoverished hack called Samuel Derrick, who presumably paid Jack Harris a fee to acquire the list. Each edition started with a defence of prostitution, before listing over 150 prostitutes operating in the Covent Garden area, with their age, address, physical attributes, sexual specialities and so on. The entries were salacious, and appear to have been designed to arouse and titillate the male reader rather than just operating as a simple directory.

There were many passages describing 'snowy white orbs' 'tufted groves' and 'fonts of pleasure'. The entries were often embellished with descriptions of the girl's drinking habits, whether she used profane language – and whether she had good teeth. In some cases the list also gives an account of how the lady became involved in prostitution, some having been raped, others seduced and abandoned, others widowed, while others 'in high keeping' were presumably bored and looking for more action, and more money, than they were getting from their protector.

The list sold in considerable quantities, with the German traveller von Archenholz writing in 1791 that 'eight thousand copies are sold annually'. No basis was given for the figure, but clearly the pocket-sized directory was extremely popular. Some nine editions are known to have survived from a period of over thirty-five years, with different authors and different publishers. The sequence came to an end in 1795 when prosecutions were brought against the publisher James Roach. The court took a decidedly dim view of what was described as 'a most indecent and immoral publication' saying that 'an offence of greater enormity could hardly be committed'. Roach was fined £100 and sentenced to a year's imprisonment in Newgate, and that was the end of Harris's List. Image 15 shows the frontispiece for the 1773 edition, as well as a caricature by Richard Newton (Image 16) showing a punter arriving at a brothel with a copy of the List in his pocket, undecided as to which of the three whores he should favour with his custom.

Infanticide: 'Lying over' upon an unwanted child was not uncommon, but hard to prove. Equally, an unwanted baby might be farmed out to a wet-nurse who would allow it to starve to death. Writing in 1727, Thomas Coram, who went on to found the Foundling Hospital in 1741, had campaigned against the 'daily sight of infant corpses thrown on the dust heaps of London.'

Jelly houses: These were not so much brothels as pick-up joints, dedicated to lust and liquor, where clients could develop their appetite for the forthcoming encounter by building up their strength and mutual ardour – by eating jelly. The couple would then go off and find a room where their passion could be assuaged... .

Jelly, made from animal gelatin, was renowned for its restorative properties. In addition, 'Jelly-box' was a slang word for the vagina. In Andrewes' *Strangers Guide for London*, published in 1800, there was the advice that 'Procuresses … are to be met with at the jelly-houses, milliners, and perfume-shops'. The book links the activities at the jelly house with those at bagnios (public) and bawdy-houses (private).

Legitimacy: For titled families, legitimacy was all-important, both in terms of protecting their title and of ensuring that wealth was inherited within the family. If a couple married subsequent to the birth it did not legitimise the child under English law. An illegitimate child would not have a claim on his or her parent's estate under intestacy rules. As William Blackstone's *Commentaries on the Laws of England* pointed out, an illegitimate child could 'inherit nothing, being looked upon as the son of nobody ... incapable even of a gift from [his or her] parents.'

The eighteenth century saw a dramatic increase in illegitimate births – but it has to be said that if there was no money or title involved, it made very little difference to the parties. With divorce beyond the reach of ordinary families, couples often split up and went their separate ways, and never took the trouble to re-marry if they subsequently had more children. It has been suggested that illegitimate births rocketed from three per cent of all births in 1750 to around twenty per cent a hundred years later. The stigma of being an unwed mother was particularly strong – especially with those from the working classes, and this meant that many poorer women, especially household servants who perhaps had been seduced, made pregnant and then abandoned, resorted to infanticide (see earlier).

Lesbianism: this was never a criminal offence, but was liable to arouse considerable public wrath and intolerance if openly displayed. On the other hand relationships such as that of 'the Ladies of Llangollen' (where Eleanor Charlotte Butler and Sarah Ponsonby lived openly together for over fifty years, shared the same sleeping arrangements and dressed in men's clothing) were objects of curiosity. They had set up home together rather than being forced into arranged marriages and the public appears to have taken the view that, as they kept themselves to themselves and were not a public nuisance, their 'odd behaviour' was capable of being tolerated. Others, such as the 'Sapphic poet' Anna Seward published outpourings of eternal love for her enamorata, Honora Sneyd – and no-one batted an eyelid, although they lived openly together for a number of years. There are several references to what we would term lesbianism in Harris's List (see earlier) including one for Miss Wilson of 11 Green Street, Cavendish Square who 'frequently declares that a female bed-fellow can give more real joys than ever she experienced with the male part of the sex'. The List goes on to refer to the 'many ... pranks which she has played with her own sex in bed (where she is as lascivious as a goat) ...' In practice the word 'lesbian' was not in general use until the following century (named after the island of Lesbos, where the Greek poetess Sappho was born). 'Sapphic' and 'tribadism' were terms more commonly used in the eighteenth century.

Lock Hospital: In July 1746 a philanthropist called William Bromfield started a charity to treat venereal disease. The trust acquired a house near Hyde Park Corner, and it opened as a hospital in January 1747. Before that date the 'lock hospitals' had specialized in the treatment of leprosy – 'lock' being the name for the pieces of rag or cloth used to cover the lesions and sores exhibited by the leprosy patients, from the old French word 'locque'. It did not derive from the practice of locking the patients away and out of the public gaze. The hospital treated over 300 patients in its first year and even though it turned out that the treatment (mercury) was as bad as, if not worse than, the disease, it was at least a first step in trying to treat an epidemic which swept through all classes of London society. Patients, once discharged, were not eligible to be readmitted as it was assumed that any re-infection was evidence that the patient had not mended his or her ways.

Forty years later it was decided that a refuge should be opened, exclusively for fallen women who had been treated at the Lock Hospital. 'The Lock Asylum for the Reception of Penitent Female Patients' (also known as 'the Lock Rescue Home') opened in 1792 at 5-6 Osnaburg Row and was moved to Knightsbridge in 1812. There, repentant females were taught needlework and other domestic skills to enable them to find 'suitable' paid employment.

Magdalen Hospitals: The first Magdalen Hospital for the Reception of Penitent Prostitutes, to give it its full title, was founded in late 1758 in London's Whitechapel. Women who had 'fallen' i.e. prostitutes, were given menial chores such as doing laundry and mending clothing. The women had to be under thirty, and priority was given to younger women and those who had been 'on the game' the shortest time. Above all, they had to have repented and exhibited a desire to mend their ways. Religious services were held twice a day, and were compulsory. In 1772 the institution moved to new premises at Blackfriars Road, St George's Fields, and was renamed the Magdalen Hospital. In time the movement spread worldwide, and was still active in some countries into the twentieth century.

Masquerades: The second half of the Georgian period saw a huge popularity for masked balls or masquerades – whether at fashionable places like The Pantheon, or The Rotunda at Ranelagh Gardens, or at private houses. Horace Walpole, writing to Sir Horace Mann on 18 February 1782, complained:

> *I write to you more tired, and with more headache, than anyone but you could conceive!*
> *I came home at five this morning from the Duchess of Norfolk's masquerade .... I must*

tell you how fine the masquerade of last night was. There were five hundred persons, in the greatest variety of handsome and rich dresses I ever saw, and all the jewels of London – and London has some! There were dozens of ugly Queens of Scots, of which I will only name to you the eldest Miss Shadwell! The Princess of Wales was one, covered with diamonds, but did not take off her mask: none of the Royalties did, but everybody else did.

Walpole had attended the masquerade dressed as an old woman. Afterwards he said that he was so awkward at trying to undress unaided, that he had stood for an hour in his stays and under-petticoat before his footman came to his assistance.

People from across the class spectrum could mix freely, and cast aside their inhibitions behind masks and exotic outfits. You could expect cross-dressing, shepherdesses, allegorical figures, clowns, harlequins and above all, well-dressed whores on the look-out for customers. Thomas Rowlandson depicts a group of harlots getting themselves ready for the fray in *Dressing for a Masquerade* (Image 17). One is going in male attire, another as a nun, while another wears a mask. Meanwhile, *The Beauty Unmaskd* reveals that not all disguises were misleading. (Image 19)

Midwives: In previous centuries mid-wives were mostly female. Very often they were simply women who assisted in labour but without any training, and with no specialist knowledge of female anatomy. The tools of the trade were often barbaric, and with no concept of hygiene it was little surprise that there were many stillborn births. Rickets was commonplace, making giving birth difficult because of inadequate development of the pelvis.

In general, male midwives were viewed with suspicion – from their female counterparts because they were encroaching on a traditionally female preserve, and from doctors in general because it was 'beneath their dignity'. As late as 1827 *The Lancet* featured a letter from a well-known surgeon by the name of Sir Anthony Carlisle in which he describes midwifery as 'a humiliating office' suitable only to women. Others saw it as improper and immoral for a male to be present – that it was in some way lewd and likely to increase immorality and marital breakdown. In the 1779 pamphlet entitled *Thoughts on the times: but chiefly on the profligacy of our women, and its causes*, Francis Foster criticized male midwifery because it involved 'placing the citadel of female virtue directly in the hands of the enemy.'

Death of a mother in childbirth was common. A figure of six deaths in a thousand births has been quoted, but the mortality rate was far higher than this if the birth took place in a hospital, because of the highly infectious nature of puerperal fever. It is also worth remembering that throughout the eighteenth century there was a one in three chance that an infant would fail to reach its second birthday.

Greater scientific and anatomical studies brought midwifery more in line with general medicine, and books such as William Smellie's *A Treatise on the Theory and Practice of Midwifery*, first published in 1752, eventually helped put things on a more scientific footing.

Molly houses: The name given in the eighteenth century to premises operating either as a gay club or tavern (where homosexual men could meet up and socialise) or as a male brothel. A 'molly' was the name given to an effeminate or homosexual male. The most famous molly house was Mother Clap's, which was open for two years from 1724 to 1726 in the Holborn area of London. Her premises were raided in 1726 and three men (Gabriel Lawrence, William Griffin, and Thomas Wright) were charged with the capital offence of sodomy. They were hanged at Tyburn on 9 May 1726. The evidence at their trial suggested that thirty to forty men were in the habit of congregating at Molly Clap's house, where beds were set out in every room. There was also a Marrying Room or Chapel, complete with double bed, where couples could take part in a form of 'marriage ceremony'.

Paedophilia: This was rarely noted or talked about. Throughout the eighteenth century, the age of consent for sexual relations was just twelve years. There were, however, many instances of girls, and boys, as young as eight or nine being engaged in the sex trade – and indeed of being introduced to it by a whoring mother, anxious to earn a premium from an eager customer.

Posture Molls: Generally refused to be treated as whores – they were there to titillate and excite. The posture moll would start her act by dancing naked on a polished pewter platter set down in the middle of the room, and then lie on her back, drawing her knees up towards her chin while clasping both hands together, and then invite the men to ogle and inspect. For added frisson she would either flagellate or be beaten by the men, getting them to a point of arousal where they would then go off and take their pleasures with one of the whores of the house. A posture moll, about to begin her act, is shown by Hogarth in Plate 3 of *A Rake's Progress* (see Image 20). The ogling dirty old men also appear in Thomas Rowlandson's *The Cunnyseurs* shown as Image 21.

Ranelagh Gardens: Opening in 1742 as an upmarket challenge to Vauxhall Gardens, Ranelagh was a fashionable place to see and be seen. The site in Chelsea was dominated by a Rotunda (until it was demolished in 1802), and became famous for its masked balls and musical performances such as the one by the infant Mozart in 1765. The gardens were a favourite place for prostitutes to stroll along plying their trade, with the historian Edward Gibbon commenting that Ranelagh Gardens were 'the most convenient place for courtships of every kind – the best market we have in England'.

Rape: Rape was a capital offence until 1841. Getting a conviction for rape meant proving that actual penetration took place – not always easy if the incident was only witnessed by the couple in question and it was 'his word against hers'. In some cases witnesses may not have wanted to give evidence if this was likely to result in a death sentence. The Old Bailey records suggest that in many decades of the eighteenth century only five per cent of cases led to a conviction. The lesser offence of an assault with intent to rape, a misdemeanour, was therefore often alleged in cases prior to 1841.

Sodomy: This catch-all covered either anal or oral intercourse, whether between a man and another man, a man and a woman, or a man and an animal. In all cases it was necessary to prove that both penetration and ejaculation had occurred. The crime could only be proved if there were two witnesses, and since the crime applied to both the 'active' and the 'passive' partner this often meant that if one of the parties acted as witness he could himself be open to prosecution. As a result of this difficulty, many men were prosecuted with the reduced charge of assault with sodomitical intent.

Buggery was regarded by Blackstone as an 'infamous crime against nature' and 'that horrible crime not to be mentioned among Christians'. It was a capital offence, described as being 'the horrid sin of buggery, contrary to the order of Human Nature'. Writing in 1774 William Hickey describes the case of a Captain Jones of the Royal Artillery 'who was taken up on a charge of having committed an offence with a boy, the apprentice and nephew of a man who kept a small toyshop in Parliament Street Westminster'. Solely on the word of the boy, the Captain was convicted and sentenced to death. Fortunately for him, the lawyer Edward Burke heard of what appeared to be a travesty of justice. Burke secured a pardon, conditional upon Jones agreeing to go into permanent exile.

In general, the Georgians became increasingly prudish about reporting sodomy cases – the reports of the Old Bailey trials were censored after 1780. Knowing that sodomy was a capital offence, extortionists would threaten to reveal details of sodomitical acts unless money was paid, and therefore what information there is about trials is generally revealed in associated proceedings – for extortion and fraud, for instance.

Vauxhall Gardens: Pleasure gardens, originally known as Spring Gardens, situated south of the River Thames, near the Vauxhall Bridge. They opened as Vauxhall Gardens in 1785 and became famous for their concerts, masquerades – and places for private assignations. Admission originally cost one shilling – increased in 1792 to half a crown (2/6d) and audiences of tens of thousands of people met to walk the gardens and to experience the spectacle of thousands of oil lamps being lit at the same time, by teams working in sequence throughout the gardens. In the days before electric lighting it was a sight which would have filled the onlookers with awe. However, not everything was bathed in light, and it was also a favourite place for prostitutes to engineer pick-ups, and to satisfy their clients down dark alley-ways.

Venereal disease: As mentioned, the medical profession made no distinction between syphilis and gonorrhoea, or any other form of STD. There was a generally held view that it was a disease which could occur spontaneously in women of low morals, whereas men could only catch it from a woman who was already infected. It rather supported the view that female immorality and lewdness lay at the root of all problems… .

The 'cure' was often worse than the disease, since it invariably involved the use of mercury in one form or another. Pills and ointments containing mercury could cause blindness, paralysis, skin ulcers and 'saddle nose' where the bridge of the nose rots away. Teeth would fall out, and there was always a risk of neurological damage.

Dr Buchan's Domestic Medicine, the eighteenth century handbook of medicine in the home, advised patients with the Great Pox to avoid extreme heat, spicy foods and in particular to abstain from horse-riding. As for medicines the Good Doctor says: 'It more frequently happens, that we are able only to procure an abatement or remission of the inflammatory symptoms, so far as to make it safe to have recourse to the great antidote *mercury*… .'

He continues:

Mercury is often not at all necessary in a gonorrhoea; and when taken too early, it does mischief. It may be necessary to complete the cure, but can never be proper at the commencement of it. When bleeding, purging, and fomentations … have eased the pain, softened the pulse, relieved the heat of urine, and rendered the involuntary erections less frequent, the patient may begin to use mercury in any form that is least disagreeable to him.

If he takes the common mercurial pill, two at night and one in the morning will be a sufficient dose at first. If calomel be thought preferable, two or three grains of it, formed into a bolus with a little of the conserve of hips, may be taken at bed-time, and the dose gradually increased to eight or ten grains. One of the most common preparations of mercury now in use is the corrosive sublimate. I have always found it one of the most safe and efficacious medicines when properly used.

Virginity: Men were always prepared to pay more for de-flowering a virgin. Clever bawds knew ways of 're-virginising' their girls, or 're-arranging the crumpled blossom of the rose' as it was euphemistically called.

Women's rights on Marriage: A women could own property in her own name up until the moment she was married, when her assets passed automatically to her husband. She was his property – and her property became his. In legal parlance she changed from being a 'feme sole' to a 'feme covert'. Coverture had been introduced in England after the Norman Conquest, and meant that a married woman had virtually no legal rights whatsoever – she could not own land, nor even enter into a contract. She was not entitled to receive a wage or salary in her own right – it belonged to her husband – but she could have 'pin money'. She was 'covered' i.e. protected by her husband and, in return for her assets, a wealthy woman would expect to be awarded a pension under her husband's will.

On her husband's death a widow suddenly achieved full legal status. The law remained in force until the various Married Women's Property Acts were passed in the nineteenth century.

Chapter Three

Of Brothels and Bagnios, Madams and Molls

The majority of London prostitutes traded their wares in full public view – on the streets and in the parks. They operated singly or in pairs, attracting attention from passing males with a suggestive wink, a tap on the shoulder, or a tip of the fan. Having negotiated a deal it would then be consummated in the open air. Most of the encounters with street walkers recorded by the diarist James Boswell resulted in sexual activity in parks, down alleyways, or by the river (see Chapter Nine). For men wanting to move indoors, and perhaps add conversation and a drink to the encounter, there

were innumerable taverns willing to make rooms available by the hour – or there were the bagnios. Originally public bath-houses, they proliferated in areas such as Covent Garden. They were not brothels in the sense that whores were not living in, but the proprietors were always willing to send out for female company. Most consisted of a series of individual rooms, where a couple could drink, take light refreshments, and add a measure of acquaintanceship before or after fornication.

Brothels were always to be found in the areas of London where housing was cheap and over-crowded – such as the dockland area to the east of London, with its high population of sailors. During the previous century, what was known as the Ratcliffe Highway – the area lying immediately to the north of the waterfront at Wapping – became notorious for its brothels catering to the needs of sailors returning from long voyages overseas and, as Britain's merchant navy tripled in size during the eighteenth century, the demand for prostitutes similarly multiplied. The area of St Giles, situated on the road between Holborn and Tyburn, had originally been a small village, but numbers swelled throughout the Georgian era so that by 1830 some 30,000 people were living in the parish, often with as many as fifty inhabitants to a four-bedroom property. St Giles became notorious, with perhaps the worst slums to be found anywhere in

London, and caricaturists often made the point that this was where the rougher end of the spectrum of harlotry was to be found. Better-dressed prostitutes may have favoured newly popular places such as Bagnigge Wells, in St Pancras. Others operated from the myriad of run-down and overcrowded lodgings in Southwark known as rookeries. St James was always popular with prostitutes in Westminster, but all of these places paled into insignificance compared to the epicentre of whoredom, Covent Garden.

Covent Garden, with its close link to the London theatres, was where the vice trade really flourished. Here, dozens of bagnios or Turkish baths jostled for trade alongside the taverns, the jelly houses and the brothels. The magistrate Sir John Fielding called Covent Garden 'the great square of Venus', saying: 'One would imagine that all the prostitutes in the kingdom had picked upon the rendezvous'. Cartoonists loved to show the scene, as in Image 23 where a young man ('a lobby flesh-monger') negotiates terms for 'a prime piece'. It has the sub-title *Buying fruit at Covent Garden Market for an evening's entertainment*.

There were, of course, brothels employing prostitutes, some of whom lived on the premises. Others were drafted in as the occasion required. These brothels were run by a Madam – a bawd who had laid out the expense of furnishing rooms with basic furniture, and of clothing her whores (sometimes known as 'molls') in fine silks. In practice, 'moll' was a word which started off as a diminutive form of the name 'Mary', developed into a generic name for a girl, and ended up as a nick-name for a prostitute. The molls were required to sign promissory notes for the use of the clothing, at hugely inflated prices. Any effort to leave without repaying the loan would have meant the Debtors Prison, and many of the brothels employed bully boys to ensure that both the whores and their customers behaved themselves. There were frequent outbreaks of violence, such as the riots in London on 1 July 1749. Three sailors from 'The Grafton' had visited a brothel in The Strand and had their possessions stolen, including their watches and a considerable quantity of money. They vowed revenge, and headed for Wapping to get reinforcements. They returned later that night with forty sailors and thoroughly trashed the brothel, setting it on fire. They were careful not to steal any items – they simply destroyed the prostitutes' furniture and belongings. Imbued with euphoria caused by their instant popularity (the neighbours gathered to cheer the destruction of the brothel) the sailors returned over the following nights to continue their crusade against neighbouring bawdy-houses, bringing with them a number of enthusiastic if drunken followers. One of these was the unfortunate Bosavern Penlez, a young apprentice who had spent most of the day getting thoroughly inebriated. Encountering the rioters, he seized upon the confusion to help himself to a bundle of linen from the house of one Peter Wood. Penlez was caught, tried and hanged at

Tyburn in October 1749 – even though he was not one of the main architects of the rioting.

The German writer von Archenholz described the hammams which proliferated around Covent Garden as:

… a certain kind of house, called bagnios, which are supposed to be baths; their real purpose, however, is to provide persons of both sexes with pleasure. These houses are well, and often richly, furnished, and every device for exciting the senses is either at hand or can be provided. Girls do not live there but are fetched in chairs when required… A girl who is sent for and does not please receives no gratuity, the chair alone being paid for.

Something of the raucous, chaotic, world which was Covent Garden in the 1770s is shown in the comments by William Hickey in his 'Memoirs', written in the first decade of the nineteenth century but not published until 1925. He was not bragging, but nor was he embarrassed in painting a picture of what it was like, with the brothels cheek-by-jowl. He describes how a rowdy group of friends usually:

…adjourned to Bow Street, Covent Garden, in which street there were then three most notorious bawdy houses. The first was kept by a woman whose name I have forgotten; it was at the corner of a passage that led to the theatre. The second was at the top of the street in a little corner or nook, and was kept by an old Irish woman, named Hamilton, with whom I was upon remarkable good terms of which she gave me most convincing proof in many times offering me money…. I however did not scruple turning her partiality towards me … by enjoying any particularly smart or handsome new piece, upon them becoming inmates with her, and she never failed giving me due notice when such was to be the case….The third brothel was kept by Mother Cocksedge, for all the Lady Abbesses were dignified with the respectable title of Mother. In those days of wonderful propriety and general morality, it will scarcely be credited that Mother Cocksedge's house was actually next, of course under the very nose of that vigilant and upright magistrate Sir John Fielding who, from the riotous proceedings I have been witness to at his worthy neighbour, must have been deaf as well as blind, or at least, well paid for affecting to be so.

Hickey goes on to explain that:

In these houses we usually spent from three to four hours, drinking…. and romping and playing all sorts of tricks with the girls. At a late, or rather, early hour in the morning, we separated, retiring to the private respective lodgings of some of the girls, there being only two that resided in the house, or to our homes, as fancy led, or according to the state of finances. My pocket being generally well-stocked, I often went to Nancy Harris's, or some other fresher and therefore more attractive female.

That then was Covent Garden – close to the theatres and therefore a popular haunt of young blades eager to pick up one of the large number of aspiring actresses 'waiting for a new part to come along.' Few of the whores lived in and a riotous time was had by all. An example of the exuberance of life, and its consequences, is shown in the 1739 print by Louis Philippe Boitard entitled *The Covent Garden Morning Frolick –* see Image 24.

It shows Betty Careless, one of the most famous whores of the 1720s and 30s, being carried home in a sedan chair after a night on the town with Captain 'Mad Jack' Montague. Mad Jack was a sea-farer, eccentric to the point of insanity, and he is shown sitting on the roof of the chair, with his sword broken, and being accompanied by a group of ne'eer-do-wells including Betty's own personal link-boy Laurence Casey, otherwise known as Little Cazey. The job of the link-boy was to carry a flaming torch ahead of the sedan chair, lighting the way. Typically paid a farthing for his trouble, link-boys were also notorious for causing trouble. Little Cazey was no exception and ended up being transported to America for stealing a gold watch from a gentleman. Betty Careless ended up in the Poor House, and Mad Jack, younger brother of the Earl of Sandwich, died at the distinctly young age of 37 after a somewhat chequered career in the Royal Navy.

Not all of the houses frequented by the whores and their customers were brothels. There were also the meeting places where sexual activity did not actually take place, but where the throngs emerging from the theatres and other places of entertainment would gather to drink, and make their choice for their late-evening's entertainment. An example of this was the notorious Coffee House run by Tom and Molly King in Drury Lane. It flourished for twenty years from 1725, frequented by bawds and their 'nymphs' as well as by men from all ranks of society. It opened when most of the taverns were closing, and entertained its customers until day-break, or until the last of the customers had been partnered off, or had passed out. Tom King died in 1739 having amassed a large fortune which had enabled him to buy an estate near Hampstead, but his widow preferred the more convivial life of the city to the peace and quiet of the country. By now a bloated alcoholic, and frequently in trouble with the law, she kept going until her death in 1747 at the age of 51.

Another famous bawd was Elizabeth Keep, aka Fawkland. She managed three brothels, next door to each other in St James's Street, each with a dozen girls. The younger ones, aged between 12 and 16, occupied the Temple of Aurora. As they grew older the girls progressed to the luxurious Temple of Flora. In time the older girls moved through to the third, known as the Temple of Mystery, where they practised all manner of perversions and catered to even the most jaded appetites. Flagellation and sado-masochism were all available – at a price to make the eyes water.

It was this layer of high class brothels and seraglios (where very considerable expense was taken to provide a convivial atmosphere) which marked out the eighteenth century. In Hogarth's *Harlot's Progress*, shown as Image 8, the pox-ridden Elizabeth Needham is seen in the process of ensnaring the young Moll Hackabout, recently come up from the country. Hogarth shows Mother Needham as a rather ugly woman, badly marked by the pox, but in writing about her he used the description 'a handsome old Procuress … well dressed in silk'. She was ruthless, and harsh – once ensnared, her girls could never escape her clutches. Equally, when illness or old age caught up with them, Mother Needham had no further use for her girls and would throw them out on the street. Her brothel, in Park Place, St James was a most exclusive and fashionable address, and she enjoyed great popularity and success. Fate intervened in 1724 when her premises were raided. Two gentleman of distinction were found having sex with two of the girls, and although the men were bound over to keep the peace, Mother Needham was sentenced to hard labour at Tothill Fields Bridewell. As the Daily Journal of 21 July 1724 recorded at the time 'This being the first time Mrs Needham ever received publick correction, since her being at the head of venal affairs in this town, 'tis thought will be the ruin of her household'. In practice she bounced back for a while, but pressure from the Society for the Reformation of Manners led to her premises being raided again in 1731. This time she was fined one shilling for keeping a disorderly house, but in addition was sentenced to stand in the pillory on two separate occasions. Despite paying for 'protectors' to save her from the indignation of the mob, she was pelted so hard that she suffered injuries from which she died a few days later. Her demise gave rise to a derogatory rhyme in the Grub Street Journal:

Ye Ladies of Drury, now weep
Your voices in howling now raise
For Old Mother Needham's laid deep
And bitter will be all your Days.
She who drest you in Sattins so fine
Who trained you up for the Game

Who Bail, on occasion would find
And keep you from Dolly and Shame
Now is laid low in her Grave.

('Dolly' was a cant word for hemp – in other words Mother Needham would pay to protect her girls from being sent to prison to beat hemp).

Mother Needham was not of course the first bawd to try and move 'up market'. Before her there had been Mother Wisebourne, who had a reputation for running the most expensive brothel in London. Her 'star attraction' was the renowned harlot Sally Salisbury, born Sarah Pridden in 1699. Sally attracted the likes of the Prince of Wales (later, George II), Viscount Bolingbroke, and the Dukes of Buckingham, Richmond and St Albans. Mother Wisebourne was especially adept at 're-virginising' her girls so that she could charge a hefty premium on their services. When Mother Wisebourne died, Sally transferred her business to the house of Mother Needham – or at least until Sally was jailed for stabbing one of her lovers, ending up in prison and dying of syphilis in 1724.

Mother Needham's role as chief procuress was eventually filled by a woman known as Mother Douglas. Edinburgh born, she had become a prostitute when young, and quickly found herself entertaining men of wealth and fame. No doubt they helped her acquire premises in Covent Garden when she was in her mid-thirties. The house she bought in the Little Piazza, Covent Garden had previously belonged to Betty Careless. Betty had tried her hand at running a brothel (rather than being a harlot) but she had no head for business, and drink had taken its toll, so she sold up and retired. When Jane Douglas bought it, she immediately redecorated it in the latest style. She prospered in her opulent surroundings, and in 1741 moved to larger premises at the nearby Kings Head. These too were richly refurbished, and stuffed with fine furniture and fabrics. Her clientele were decidedly up-market – princes and peers, as well as Army officers – and she revelled in her notoriety. But being at the top of one's profession was never a secure position, and the clientele proved fickle. Five years on and she was no longer pre-eminent. Drink had taken its toll, and eventually the lease of the house was transferred to a relative in 1759. She died, bloated and in much pain, in 1761 and is remembered as one of the inspirations for the bawd called Mother Cole, created by John Cleland in the notorious *Fanny Hill.*

It became fashionable to display conspicuous wealth – a fashion picked up on by procuresses like Jane Goadby, who ran one of the 'Kings Place Nunneries' at St James's Place. Not for her a back-street and somewhat anonymous knocking shop – rather an up-market Town House, beautifully decorated and furnished, in which her male customers could find a home-from-home. Here, men could be wined and dined, and benefit from convivial conversation in elegant surroundings. They could relax and escape family pressures, before availing themselves of the company of their chosen partner. Jane Goadby had been inspired by a visit to the high-end brothels of Paris, and she sought to replicate the luxurious, sensuous surroundings in her own establishment. Her house was no hole-in-the-corner dive; it was where the most fashionable courtesans of the day could be enjoyed by the most wealthy. The young Elizabeth Armistead was one of the Goadby protegées – and she quickly became the lover of the Duke of Ancaster, the Earl of Derby, Viscount Bolingbroke, the unbelievably wealthy General Sir Richard Smith and later, the Prince of Wales.

Elizabeth Armistead may also have been associated with another notorious madam by the name of Elizabeth Mitchell – and certainly when Sir Joshua Reynolds painted Elizabeth in 1771, his daybook describes his sitter as *Mrs. Armistead at Mrs. Mitchell's, Upper John Street, Soho Square.* Mrs Mitchell had originally run a brothel in Berkeley Street, and later went on to acquire an establishment in King's Place which had been set up by the bawd Charlotte Hayes. Of all the madams who helped establish the demi-monde as the 'Toast of the Town', it was Charlotte who came nearest to achieving respectability. She had been a child prostitute, born around 1725, and had followed the usual path of wildly fluctuating fortunes, flush with money one minute, and destitute in a Debtor's Prison the next. But it was while she was incarcerated for debt that she had the good fortune to meet an Irish con-man and horse-racing *aficionado* called Dennis O'Kelly. Together they went into partnership, with Charlotte providing the business nous and acumen. O'Kelly, through his racing connections, had friends in high places and he introduced his friends to the brothel which Charlotte opened in Great Marlborough Street. Soon her girls were entertaining Dukes and Earls, and the Hayes-O'Kelly partnership became extremely profitable. O'Kelly went on to acquire the country's leading race horse, by the name of Eclipse. The horse won every single race for which it was entered, not just by a narrow margin but by such a huge distance that after eighteen races it was retired in 1770 because no-one would bet against it. Instead, O'Kelly put Eclipse to stud, charging fifty guineas a time, and the poor horse ended up being carted about to different stables around the land in the country's first horse box until it expired, exhausted, after nineteen years 'on the road'. The experience of the poor horse was echoed by many of Charlotte Hayes' girls – they too charged fifty guineas for their services, and they too were lucky if they lived to see old age.

Charlotte's skill lay in grooming her girls so that they could entertain her wealthy customers not just by their good looks and sexual allure, but with their wit and conversation. In his memoirs William Hickey writes about a girl called Emily Warren, who was being kept in high keeping by his friend Bob Potts. Potts had gone to India, leaving Emily behind, and Hickey lost no time in seducing her. He describes how he first met the girl in 1776:

> *then an unripe and awkward girl, but with features of exquisite beauty. That experienced old matron Charlotte Hayes, who then kept a house of celebrity in King's Place, where I often visited, had just got hold of her as an advantageous prize, and I have frequently seen the little sylph, Emily, under the tuition of the ancient dame learning to walk, a qualification Madam Hayes considered of importance, and in which her pupil certainly excelled, Emily's movements and air being Grace personified.*

Hickey goes on to explain that Sir Joshua Reynolds 'whom all the world allowed to be a competent judge' had painted Emily's portrait many times, declaring that 'every limb of hers was perfect in symmetry, and altogether he had never seen so faultless and finely formed a human figure'. Hickey describes how Emily lent him her distinctive yellow vis-à-vis, and how he was stopped several times by:

> *fashionable people who, knowing the carriage and liveries, halload the coachman to draw to the side, concluding the much-admired Emily was within, instead of which they found an ugly male stranger. Amongst these disappointed heroes were his Grace of Queensbury, Lord Carlisle, Charles Wyndham, Harry Greville and Colonel Fitzpatrick, against whom my fair friend afterwards had a hearty laugh.*

A friend of Bob Potts he may have been; entrusted to look after Emily he most certainly was, but that did not stop Hickey enjoying her favours, or, as he himself put it 'I passed a night that many would have given thousands to do'. He bemoaned the fact that he was convinced that she was totally void of feeling and was as cold as ice, but adds that she could neither read nor write, having been procured by Charlotte Hayes as a 12-year-old while begging for assistance for her blind father. If that is correct, then Emily must have been grateful to the old bawd for grooming her so well that she was able to set up on her own as a high class whore.

Charlotte may have eventually married her partner Dennis O'Kelly, and certainly they continued to prosper. She put a manager in to run her premises at Number two King's Place and took over Number five. It too became a huge success, and as a result 'Mr and Mrs O'Kelly' were able to run two prestigious estates, Clay Hill outside Epsom, and later Canons Park at Edgware, former home of the Duke of Chandos. The Duke of Cumberland and the Prince of Wales were regular visitors to their homes, giving them a sort of dubious respectability. Their joint assets would have made them multi-millionaires today, but incredibly Charlotte ended up in the debtors' prison in 1798, her 'husband' having died thirteen years earlier. Her legacy was the way she helped transform whoring into something almost aspirational. Proudly she had walked her charges through the park, or taken them to be paraded through Brighton, Bath and Oxford to drum up new customers. Her 'nuns' may not have achieved respectability, but through her they attained money, status, and admiration. She looked after their health, and she helped make them what we would now term 'celebrities'.

* * *

Before leaving the Madams who helped redefine harlotry, moving it upmarket and giving it glamour, it may help to try and set aside prejudices about exploitation and the commercialisation of sex. These women managed to succeed in a man's world. They ran successful businesses at a time when women did not otherwise feature in business. They brought to those businesses taste and style and a sense of fashion. Nowadays they would perhaps be fashion designers or hosting makeover programmes on television. They were entrepreneurs who helped make the courtesan's lifestyle aspirational. They could be ruthless, but they were successful. For the whore in a low-class brothel of course there was nothing whatsoever aspirational in their lifestyle. However, it was the Madams who introduced a new top layer to whoredom, and they deserve recognition for changing the face of society.

Chapter Four

Courtesans and Harlots

The vast majority of eighteenth century sex workers lived anonymous lives, died, and were buried in unmarked graves. But a few, a very few, ascended to the heights of public celebrity. They became household names, their passing was noted and even mourned. Why? Not, one suspects, because they were any more adept at their trade than others, nor that they were necessarily more attractive. But they generally had that little extra something – style, chutzpah, call it what you will, that distinguished them from their 'Cyprian sisters'. A brief look at a handful of these stars of their profession reveals much about public attitudes towards paid sex.

FANNY MURRAY, 1729–1778

Fanny had an unpromising start in life – she was born in Bath around 1729 to the wife of an itinerant musician called Rudman. Both parents were dead by the time she was 12 and she eked a living as a flower-seller on the streets of Bath near the Abbey and outside the Assembly Rooms. She was an attractive young girl and unfortunately she caught the eye of a philanderer called Jack Spencer. He was noble-born – the grandson of Sarah, Duchess of Marlborough – and no doubt he saw the seduction of a 12-year-old orphan as a bit of fun. He had his wicked way with her, and promptly left. His place was taken by a Captain in the army called Ned Harvey, but he too deserted her, leaving her at the mercy of all the unscrupulous rakes and pimps about town. Enter a rather strange hero – none other than the ageing roué Beau Nash, for long known as 'the King of Bath' by virtue of being the Master of Ceremonies at the Assembly Rooms. No matter that at 66 he was over fifty years her senior – he invited her to become his mistress and for a couple of years she was his devoted help-mate. He helped her acquire a veneer of good manners, but without crushing her sparkle and sense of fun. He showered her with clothes and presents, and enjoyed showing her off to his friends. As she grew up she became even more of a beauty, and reports speak of her dimpled cheeks, her perfect white teeth, her coral lips and her chestnut-brown hair. Just as importantly, she was also growing more curvaceous by the day. But the odd couple were never likely to stay together for long and, after two years, she left Nash, and Bath, and headed for London.

She became a 'dress-lodger', which meant that she was under the control of a bawd. She would have been supplied with fine clothes, in return for something which many whores, before and since, found to be a life of servitude. In general, they were never able to repay the extortionate charges for their clothing. But Fanny was different and somehow managed to pay off her debts, escape from the brothel, and acquire lodgings of her own.

It was there that she came to the notice of Jack Harris (as in 'Harris's List of Covent Garden Ladies' – see Chapter Two). Harris had been building up a hand-written list of girls-about-town, and he was happy to include young Fanny, describing her as 'a new face.... Perfectly sound in wind and limb. A fine Brown girl, rising nineteen next season. A good side-box piece, she will show well in the Flesh Market', and commending her as 'fit for high keeping with a Jew merchant.... If she keeps out of the Lock she may make her fortune and Ruin half the Men in Town'.

She rocketed to fame and by the end of her teens was widely acknowledged as the 'Toast of the Town', so much so that she is widely credited as being the inspiration for Fanny Hill, the central character in John Cleland's *Memoirs of a Woman of Pleasure* published in 1749. Her impressive physique was noted in songs which were composed by the bucket-load throughout the 1750s. One such included the lines:

> *What paint with her Complexion vies*
> *What jewels sparkle like her Eyes*
> *What Hills of Snow so white as Rise*
> *The Breasts of Fanny Murray?*

She became an arbiter of fashion – the person everyone else wanted to copy. If she wore her broad-brimmed cap crooked, everyone wanted to do the same and it became known as the Fanny Murray cap. As an article in *The Centinel* of 30 July 1757 put it:

> *If Fanny Murray chuses to vary the fashion of her apparel, immediately every Lucretia in town takes notice of the change, and modestly copies the chaste original. If Fanny shews the coral centre of her snowy orbs—miss, to outstrip her, orders the stays to be cut an inch or two lower; and kindly displays the whole lovely circumference.*

Race horses, ships and even cocktail drinks were named after her. Prints made her a national pin-up, and Fanny-mania was no different to today's preoccupation with television reality stars such as the Kardashian sisters. She had become the mistress of John Montagu, the Fourth Earl of Sandwich. He had her nude portrait painted, and later hung it in his hall alongside the naked charms of Kitty Fisher, who was to succeed Fanny as toast of the town and lover of the Fourth Earl. He introduced her to fellow members of the Hellfire Club, established by Sir Francis Dashwood and originally based in the George and Vulture public house. Subsequently the club met at Medmenham Abbey, where Fanny would take part in orgies in her capacity as a 'nun', which was the term given to females attending the club. Her name was associated with a host of other well-known and well-heeled young men, including barristers, soldiers, politicians and apparently even members of the royal family. Eventually she fell for the charms of a wealthy young baronet called Sir Richard Atkins, a tall gangling individual nick-named 'Supple Dick' by the actor Sam Foote. She was living with him by 1748, but she constantly complained of his parsimony and of his failure to indulge her with the sort of gifts which he showered on his other lady-friends. The often-told story of the bank-note sandwich has been attributed to various other courtesans, but in all probability started with Fanny, who allegedly felt insulted when Sir Richard gave her a twenty pound note. She stuffed it between two slices of buttered bread and ate it. According to Horace Walpole, who always appears to have been on hand to record a *bon mot*, she derided Sir Richard, shouting out 'Damn your twenty pounds, what does that signify?'

Her on-off relationship with the baronet continued, but not at the expense of her liaisons with numerous other men-about-town, including the beau Robert 'Handsome' Tracey, the highway robber John Maclean, and a man prone to repeated outbreaks of bigamy by the name of Captain Plaistow. In 1756 Sir Richard persuaded Fanny to accompany him and his friends on a yacht trip to the Mediterranean, but he caught a fever and died before the voyage got under way, leaving Fanny, at 27 years of age, in dire straits. Her youthful good looks were fading, her creditors were pushing for payment and her gallants deserted her in her hour of need. She was carted off to the sponging house (a temporary holding place for debtors) and her inevitable downward spiral into poverty and degradation must have been staring her in the face. But fortune favours the brave, and she decided to pen a letter to the son of the man who had first debauched her. Unlike his late father, *this* Mr Spencer was exceedingly honourable and generous, settling an annuity of £200 on Fanny. He also did her the great favour of introducing her to a friend of his, an actor called David Ross. The two fell in love, and to the amazement of everyone, got married. Fanny really had turned over a new leaf and appears to have remained a faithful and devoted wife throughout their marriage.

It cannot have been easy for Mr Ross as there were constant reminders of his wife's notorious past. In 1758 the *Memoirs of the Celebrated Miss Fanny Murray* was published, purportedly being her autobiography and raking up many details of her highly promiscuous past. It is unlikely that she actually wrote the book herself but it is memorable for being one of the very first 'kiss and tell' whore's memoirs. Worse was to follow when, in 1763, her name cropped up in connection with the trial of John Wilkes. His *Essay on Woman* was, after all, dedicated to her, and began with the words 'Awake, my Fanny…'. As mentioned later, salacious extracts were read out before the shocked Houses of Parliament, and the press immediately began raking over stories about the woman who had inspired such scandalous and blasphemous verses.

She made one further triumphant appearance in public, when she was one of the belles of the ball at a masquerade held in October 1767 in honour of a visit by the King of Denmark. She attended the ball as 'Night', in a costume which the *Gentleman's Magazine* stated was 'of thin black silk studded with silver stars, and fastened to the head with a moon very happily executed'. She was one of the ladies pictured arriving at the ball in a barge at the riverside entrance to The Mansion House. Simple, but sensational, she was noticed by everyone.

She died, aged 49, on April Fools' Day 1778 at her home just off The Strand. She had been married for twenty blameless years, but will forever be remembered for the years of immorality which preceded them.

NANCY PARSONS, 1735–1814

Next on the demi-monde throne was Nancy Parsons, who was the daughter of a Bond Street tailor, and was probably born around 1735. As a teenager she appears to have been drawn to prostitution, charging clients a guinea a time, and according to one of her boasts, was able to earn 100 guineas in a week, which is quite some work-rate. She was considered beautiful, as well as shrewd, and it wasn't long before she fell for a West Indian slave merchant called Mr Horton. She accompanied him to Jamaica, and may possibly even have married him, but when he died she returned to England and resumed her horizontal athleticism with a series of eager young men. She could claim the acquaintance of various members of the peerage and numerous politicians, including William Petty, second Earl Shelburne, but her willingness to hop from one lover's bed to the next earned her Horace Walpole's rebuke that she was 'one of the commonest creatures in London, one much liked, but out of date'. Her portrait appears as Image 25.

Her affair with Lord Grafton is mentioned in more detail in Chapter Seven. Suffice to say that after she had got used to sitting alongside the Prime Minister, she wasn't going to go back to anyone lacking a title – or a fortune – when he chucked her over. By 1769 Nancy had moved on to John Frederick Sackville, third Duke of Dorset, accompanying him on his continental tour which commenced the following year.

Given that he was not involved in politics, their affair did little to engage the interest of the general public. Horace Walpole, however, waggishly remarked that she was 'the Duke of Grafton's Mrs. Horton, the Duke of Dorset's Mrs. Horton, everybody's Mrs. Horton'. They split up in 1776 when the Duke took up with Elizabeth Armistead (see later) and Nancy moved swiftly on to Sir Charles Maynard, who had recently become the second Viscount Maynard. He was just 24 years old, whereas she was past her fortieth birthday, and no doubt keen to get a ring on her finger before age dulled her charms.

She married her viscount in September 1776 and Walpole noted that she 'deserved a peerage as much as many that have got them lately'. The couple went to live in Italy, and settled in Naples. But her appetite got the better of her and her particular 'seven year itch' involved Francis Russell, fifth Duke of Bedford. He was just 19, and joined the pair of them in a curious *ménage à trois* in Nice. Eventually she drifted apart from her husband – and her young lover – to lead a solo existence in Italy and then France, before dying near Paris in 1814.

KITTY FISHER, 1738–1767

When Nancy put down the crown as 'Toast of the Town', her place was taken immediately by young Kitty Fisher. She had probably been born in 1738 and, although she did not live to see her thirtieth birthday, her career burned like a shooting star. She was considered beautiful and charming, and having her portrait painted by several members of the new Royal Academy – including nine times by its President Sir Joshua Reynolds – helped seal her status as Number One 'pin-up girl'. When Nathaniel Hone painted her (see Image 26) he showed her alongside a cat toying with a goldfish in a glass bowl. They form a rebus based on her name – the cat for Kitty, the goldfish for Fisher – while the glass bowl reflects the image of the window opposite. The reflection clearly shows figures peering in to have a look at the famous sitter. Hone was showing that Kitty was herself in a goldfish bowl, her life constantly on public view.

Originally a milliner by trade (often a euphemism for a whore) she specialised in affairs with wealthy young men and quickly became a fashion icon. Meeting her in London in 1763 Giacomo Casanova refers to '… the illustrious Kitty Fisher, who was just beginning to be fashionable. She was magnificently dressed, and it is no exaggeration to say that she had on diamonds worth five hundred thousand francs.' He was informed that he might have her then and there for ten guineas, but he declined because the girl did not speak any foreign languages. Apparently, Casanova liked to hear his ladies talk to him in French or Italian before having his wicked way with them, and on another occasion bemoaned to Lord Pembroke that the problem with the girls he met in London was that the prettiest spoke only English, adding: 'Never mind, we shall understand each other well enough for the purpose I dare say'.

Described as 'the most pretty' extravagant, wicked little whore that ever flourished' by one commentator, Kitty's sexual allure and brazen behaviour captivated London. In her hey-day she was charging a hundred guineas a night, and her lovers included Admiral Lord George Anson, in charge of the navy, as well as General John Ligonier, head of the British army. Then there was Edward, Duke of York, but he rather blotted his copybook by offering a paltry fifty pounds, and was promptly thrown out of bed.

Kitty scandalized Society by having a full retinue of liveried servants – an unheard-of piece of ostentation. She was a keen horsewoman, heralding a succession of whores determined to learn how to drive a coach-and-four. *A Lesson Westward* (Image 18) parodies this development, by showing a young prostitute being given a riding lesson, scattering a family of pigs and a passer-by.

Never one to miss the equivalent of a photo-opportunity (she loved to be seen, and was a self-publicist without equal) she took to riding in Hyde Park, and in their turn the public took to coming along to watch her ride by. One day she engineered a fall in front of a group of gallant soldiers. Cue a dramatic rescue of a damsel in distress, along with much thigh on display. Exit Kitty in a smart sedan chair which just happened to be waiting nearby. The press the next day were full of stories of how Kitty was a fallen woman twice over, and hinting that her fall from the horse was nothing compared with her fall from grace. She retaliated with a letter which defended her reputation, but in doing so laid her open to mockery and ridicule. However, on the basis that all publicity is good publicity, she became even more infamous.

Image 10 shows her displaying her charms, sprawled at the feet of the eager onlookers. Several men have quickly gathered at the scene of her misfortune as another on horseback leaps a fence exclaiming, 'Oh my Kitty, oh my Kitty, oh my Kitty.'

> Lord Mount-Stuart, eldest son of the E. of Bute.—to the eldest daughter of the late Lord Windsor.
>
> 9. Henry Goodwin, of Essex-street, Strand, Esq;—to Mrs Cromebridge of Maidstone.
>
> Miss Kitty Fisher,—to a gentleman of fortune.

Kitty was lively, witty and extremely cheeky. This made it all the more surprising when, at the age of 28, she announced that she was marrying John Norris, a man without a title, fortune or significant talent. He was, however, infatuated with Kitty

Image 1. A Bagnigge Wells scene. Two whores, dressed to the nines, ply their trade at the fashionable Islington spa. (See pp. viii and 3)

Image 2. Retail Traders not affected by the shop tax. Everything, but everything, was for sale at Covent Garden. (See p. 10)

Image 3. A St Giles's Beauty. (See p. 24)

Images 4 and 5. Progress of a Woman of Pleasure. (See pp. 4 and 71)

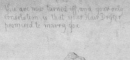

AN of PLEASURE.

Image 6. St James's & St Giles's. (See p. 3)

Image 7. Dividing the Spoil. (See p. 3)

Image 8. A Harlot's Progress. (See pp. 3, 28 and 59)

THE WHORE'S LAST SHIFT.

Image 9. The Whore's Last Shift. (See p. 3)

Image 10. The Merry Accident' with Kitty Fisher showing rather a lot of leg, deliberately. (See p. 38)

SIX STAGES OF MENDING A FACE
Dedicated with respect to the Right Hon.ble Lady Archer

Image 11. Rowlandson's Six Stages of Mending a Face, from bald hag at top left to beguiling temptress at bottom left. Six Stages of Mending a Face. Moll is befriended by the procuress Mother Needham. (See p. 12)

Image 12. Crim. Con. Temptations. (See p. 13)

Image 13. Cross-examination of a Witness. (See p. 13)

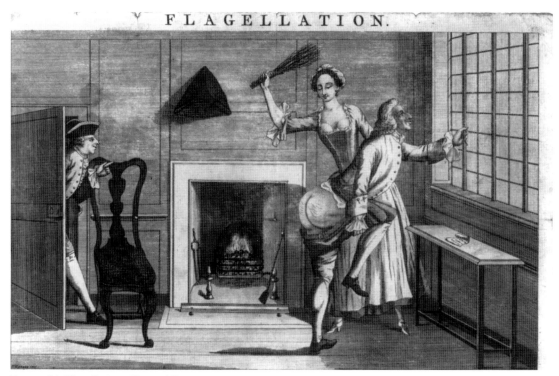

Image 14. Flagellation. (See p. 14)

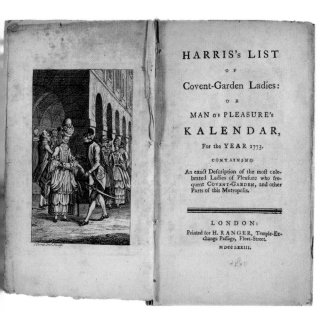

Image 15. Harris's List. (See p. 16)

Image 16. Cupid's London Directory. (See p. 16)

Image 17. Dressing for a Masquerade. The whores select their chosen outfits. (See p. 19)

Image 18. A Lesson Westward. (See p. 38)

Image 19. The Beauty Unmask'd. (See p. 19)

and the pair eloped to Scotland to get married, away from the possible objections from John's father, MP for Rye. She settled at her husband's home – now Benenden School – and became a popular local figure in the four months that Fate decreed she had left. Her husband's wedding present to Kitty was a black mare, and she delighted in the simple pleasure of riding, apparently never missing the constant adulation and praise which had marked her recent life.

Whether it was smallpox, or consumption, or the effect of ingesting lead from heavy make-up, her health deteriorated and her doting husband decided to take her to the Hot Wells in Bristol to 'take the waters' and effect a cure. She died on the journey and the heartbroken Mr Norris took her body back to Benenden and buried her in her finery, with her jewellery and her best gown. Her fame and memory lingers on, in the nursery rhyme 'Lucy Locket':

> *Lucy Locket lost her pocket,*
> *Kitty Fisher found it;*
> *Not a penny was there in it*
> *Only ribbon round it.*

NELLY O'BRIEN, 1738–1767

An exact contemporary of Kitty was Nelly O'Brien. Little is known about her upbringing, but she shares the limelight with Kitty because she too was painted on more than one occasion by Sir Joshua Reynolds, and became the subject of mezzotint copies bought by the public in their hundreds. Men bought the prints so that they too could 'have a piece' of a beauty who was otherwise unattainable except for the extremely rich; women bought the prints because they illustrated the very latest fashion trends, and were the fore-runners of fashion plates.

Nelly had been a minor actress and, like many on the stage, had used her skills to attract the attention of wealthy admirers. One was the naval hero Augustus Keppel (later Admiral Keppel and First Viscount Keppel). He brought Nelly to the Great Newport Street studio used by Reynolds in 1762. Here she had her portrait painted, commissioned and paid for by George Richard St John, Second Viscount Bolingbroke. By then she had been the mistress of 'Bully' Bolingbroke for some months. He was unhappily married to Lady Diana Spencer (the first one) and both he and his wife were extremely active in extra-marital affairs. Ironically Reynolds was commissioned to paint a portrait of Lady Diana at much the same time as he was painting Nelly, which must have led to some interesting scheduling in the artist's diary if embarrassing encounters in the outer office were to be avoided…. The Bolingbroke marriage was dissolved in 1768 after a crim. con. case involving Topham Beauclerk. Lady Diana would subsequently go on to marry Beauclerk, but her divorce was a major scandal of the time.

Nelly gave birth to Bolingbroke's child in 1764 before drifting into an affair with Sackville Tufton, Eighth Earl of the Isle of Thanet. She bore him two children, Alfred in 1765 and Sackville in 1766. She presumably felt 'secure' as Tufton's mistress (he was unmarried) and so must have been devastated when the Earl suddenly kicked her out of the house he had provided for her, and announced that he was getting married. The announcement came at a time when Nancy was heavily pregnant. She miscarried, and died in agony when complications set in. There is a burial record for St Ann's, Blackfriars with an entry made four days after Christmas 1767 – 'Eleanor O'Brien aged 29.' If that is the same Nelly O'Brien, it meant her life-span mirrored Kitty Fisher precisely, both dying in the same year, aged 29.

GERTRUDE MAHON, 1752–1808 – aka the Bird of Paradise

> The Bird of Paradise, by the late secession of business, in her rival Perdita, has very much enlarged her profits; in consequence of which she has got a new chariot, new furniture, and other pageants.

When Kitty Fisher resigned from her role as Queen of Tarts there was no shortage of applicants ready to step up to take her place. None really attained her fame and status until Grace Dalrymple Elliott – mentioned later. But there was a host of women keen to head the list of 'Great Impures', as this fun-loving group of libidinous women was called. The Press delighted in reporting on the plumages of these glamorous ladies and named them after birds – *The Rambler* magazine set out a list of 'The most fashionable Votaries of Venus' and listed the Avians as being Gertrude Mahon (the Bird of Paradise); Polly Greenhill (the Greenfinch); Sally Wilson (the Water Wagtail); Mrs Irvine (the White Swan); and not forgetting Maria Corbyn (the White Crow). Image 29 is entitled *The Bird of Paradise* and shows the lady in her finery and enormous headdress.

Gertrude Mahon was a veritable pocket Venus at just 49 inches tall. From a fairly privileged, if chaotic, background (both her parents had been married before, and neither seemed to have the vaguest idea of how to bring up a young daughter) she had to cope when her father, James Tilson, went off on his own to Cadiz to take up the post of consul – and died in under a year. It was 1764, and Gertrude was 12 years old. Her mother, who had previously been married to the Earl of Kerry, was more interested in pampering her cage birds and lap-dogs than in giving guidance to the impressionable Gertrude, and besides, there was little money despite the aristocratic connection, as Mr Tilson had lived way beyond his means.

At the age of 17 Gertrude went off the rails – falling head-over-heels for an itinerant Irish musician called Gilbreath Mahon. What little money he earned from fiddling he lost at cards, but nothing would put off the coquettish little Gertrude. She eloped with him to Dover, hoping to get married in France, but her mother sent a pair of Bow Street Runners to intercept them. They were stopped, but the enterprising Gilbreath Mahon invited the posse for a libation and promptly drank them both under the table. The couple sailed off to France, got married, and within a year Gertrude had a daughter. That was just about all she did get – Mr Mahon went off with another woman, leaving Gertrude penniless. Worse was to follow when her mother died in 1775.

She did what she had to do to survive – she used her charm, her brilliant complexion, her tiny frame and her dark eyes to entice a string of men into her bedroom. She was especially active at masquerades and balls, where she was often to be seen as a close companion of Grace Elliott – nick-named 'Dally the Tall' – towering over her. Perhaps it was the height difference which prompted the diminutive girl to wear increasingly vertiginous and brightly coloured plumed headdresses – hence her soubriquet 'The Bird of Paradise.' Together this unlikely pair appeared on the arm of Lord Cholmondeley at the grand masquerade at The Pantheon held in January 1776. *The Morning Post* was happy to conjecture that His Lordship shared the bedroom delights of both companions, long and short.

Other, more louche, gatherings saw her enmeshed in an ever-more disreputable crowd of admirers. Through a friendship with the disgraced Henrietta, Countess Grosvenor, she was introduced to a Captain John Turner and quickly moved in with him. He soon suspected that she was sharing her favours with his brother – time for her to move on. Or, as the *Morning Post* of 19 April 1777 put it:

> the Bird of Paradise broke through the upper part of her cage two days ago, flew from her military keeper and perched on the shoulder of Sir John L..d as he was driving his phaeton and four through Knightsbridge, who carried her home to Park Place. The forsaken captain is disconsolate.

Her rescuer was a baronet called John Lade, aged just 17, with an inheritance of £50,000. The infatuation did not last longer than it took to spend the entire inheritance

– two years – at which point the couple went their separate ways, forcing Gertrude to turn to the notorious Lord March (see chapter Seven) for assistance.

The Press revelled in making avian puns – she was seen at Brighton 'wetting her plumage.' On another occasion it was reported that 'The Bird of Paradise is seen hopping about in rather a disconsolate manner. We fear she has had too much saffron administered in the waters of her cage lately.' On another, she was described as a bird of prey, and another spoke of the time when 'The Bird of Paradise appeared at Vauxhall in glittering plumage, her waist not a span round, her stature four feet one inch, with black hair truly Mahomedan, delicately arched eye-brows smooth as mouse skin, and soft pouting lips.'

In 1780 she appeared on stage at Covent Garden, and was generally well-received. Her love of bright clothing, and in particular her choice in millinery, made her a popular figure, never out of the limelight. Aged 29, she decided she wanted to go after a bigger prize – the heir to the throne. No matter that the Prince of Wales was a mere 17 years old; she stalked him at the opera, in Hyde Park, and wherever she could gain advance notice of his whereabouts. In time he duly made her acquaintance, but it was rumoured that he was not prepared to pay for her services and in time she turned her attention in other, more profitable, directions.

Gertrude drew attention to herself by driving a vis-à-vis (see Image 30). This fashionable conveyance involved the two occupants sitting facing each other. It was in the summer of 1782 that Gertrude took to driving her small covered phaeton along the Hampstead Road. Coachmen quickly dubbed her 'Lady Hard and Soft' and the records show that she was wealthy enough to own two carriages and six horses, and employ eight servants. The good times, when she headed the demi-monde, lasted perhaps eleven years, but fame did not last. She moved constantly around England, with a spell in Bath and another in Margate, before going to the continent, and then over to Ireland, with a succession of lovers. She was still appearing on stage into the 1790s, but by then the Press had lost interest in this most colourful of birds, and when she died it was without trace or obituary.

GRACE DALRYMPLE ELLIOTT, 1754–1823 – aka 'Dally the Tall'

Grace Elliott did not come out of the same drawer as the other Toasts of the Town – and her life took a decidedly different turn. She was born in 1754, and her father was a prominent Scottish lawyer. Her parents split up before she was born and when she was 11 years old, Grace was sent to a French convent to finish her education. She was witty, vivacious, and sophisticated, as well as being regarded as good looking. She was also willowy and tall, cut a most elegant figure, and no doubt young suitors collected round her like bees around the proverbial honey-pot when she returned to live with her father in London at the age of 17. It was all the more surprising that she elected to marry a very much older man – Dr John Elliott was fourteen years her senior. He was rich, dedicated to advancing his career in the medical profession, but he was also short, unattractive and not especially attentive to the needs of a young wife. She soon got bored. She embarked on numerous affairs, culminating in one particularly reckless and public liaison with the married roué Arthur Annesley, eighth Viscount Valentia. The papers were full of gossip about her indiscreet behaviour and in 1774, her husband applied to the ecclesiastical courts for a legal separation, sued in crim. con. and was awarded damages of £12,000. He then applied to Parliament for a divorce. The marriage had lasted five years.

Her family were highly embarrassed at her conduct and packed her off to a French convent to reflect on her wicked ways, but almost immediately she was 'rescued' by Lord Cholmondeley. He provided her with 'high keeping' and for a number of years she was his mistress, although this was not an exclusive arrangement for either party. In her case, Grace had affairs with the Prince of Wales, with George Selwyn and with Charles William Wyndham (brother of Lord Egremont). When she gave birth there was much speculation as to which of the lovers had fathered the child. She claimed it was the Prince, called the baby Georgiana Augusta Frederica Seymour, and had his name entered on the christening certificate. But whereas *The Morning Post* of January 1782 reported that the Prince accepted paternity, he never did so openly and the child was brought up in Lord Cholmondeley's household. Indeed when Georgiana died in 1813, leaving a young child, that child was also brought up by Lord Cholmondeley and his family. Arguably, that was simply a measure of how far Lord Cholmondeley, one of the Prince of Wales set, would go to in order to protect his royal friend from scandal.

For Grace, this time marked a watershed in her life. She could, like her companion Gertrude Mahon at so many masked balls, sink into libidinous obscurity and die before reaching old age. Or she could use each affair as a stepping stone to new protectors, networking her way through a succession of wealthy patrons both in England and in France. She chose the latter route and in 1784 ended up as the mistress of the Duc d'Orleans. Come the Revolution and it appears that she and her lover were on opposite sides – he supported the revolutionaries and abandoned his title; she was staunchly royalist and was a firm friend of Madame du Barry, the *maîtresse en titre* of Louis XV.

All her royal friends lost their heads during the Reign of Terror. She narrowly escaped the same fate, and instead languished in a series of French prisons until her release in 1794. If her own memoirs are to be believed, she bravely acted as an informer to the British government during her French sojourn. Grace remained in

France, occasionally returning to England, and the fact that the Prince of Wales started paying her an annuity of £200 in 1800 suggests that this may have been linked with her agreement to live abroad. She died aged 69 in 1823 and was buried in the sprawling Père Lachaise Cemetery in Paris. Her memoirs were published as the *Journal of my life during the French Revolution* by her grand-daughter in 1859, and although some of the events recounted are inaccurate, or are composites of actual events, they do reveal a brave and fascinating woman, who lived life on her own terms. Her portrait appears at Image 27.

FRANCES ABINGTON, 1737–1815 – aka 'Prue'

Born Frances Barton to a father who was either a mercenary soldier, or a cobbler, Frances was put to work selling flowers in the streets near Covent Garden, earning her the name 'Nosegay Fan'. By her early teens she was using her fine singing voice as a street singer, and then became a child prostitute operating from a brothel. At around fifteen, she appears to have got a job working for a French milliner in Cockspur Street – important in her later life because there she acquired a smattering of French and Italian, as well as learning about fashion in general, and hats in particular. Being fashion-conscious added to her strong sense of ambition and helped propel her on to the stage.

In 1755 she made her stage debut at The Haymarket, and came to the attention of David Garrick, who had a soft spot for the elfin-like chanteuse. He enticed her away to the Drury Lane Theatre, where she quickly became famous for her comedic roles especially as Miss Prue, in the play *Love For Love* (see Image 28, showing the coquettish 'Prue', thumb to lip, looking back suggestively at the viewer over the back of her chair).

She travelled to Dublin, and promptly married a trumpet-playing music teacher, but the marriage was a disaster and Fanny quickly turned to other liaisons. Multiple affairs culminated in one with the Irish MP Francis Needham. She accompanied him back to England in 1765 but he died the following year. She received a legacy under his will and went back on the stage. Her fame and impish face made her a favourite of Reynolds, who painted her portrait on half a dozen occasions. However, acting was a precarious profession, and she continued to bolster her income as a prostitute. She is believed to be the Miss Abington appearing in the 1773 edition of Harris's List of Covent Garden Ladies.

At the height of her fame she had been renowned for her dress style and sense of fashion. No sooner that she wore a particular type of headdress in *High Life Below Stairs* than it was universally copied and became known as the Abington cap. Then, as now, if an outfit was seen on a fashion icon, it appeared in shops on the High Street a matter of a few days later. The theatre companies pandered to this fame, since people would come to the theatre just to see what she was wearing, and gave her a dress allowance accordingly, i.e. over and above her salary as an actress.

She retired from the stage in 1790 but came out of retirement seven years later for a final two-year stint on the boards. She retired at the age of 60 and spent her last seventeen years in comparative wealth, thanks to having invested Needham's legacy wisely. She died in 1815.

SOPHIA BADDELEY, 1745–1786

As an actress, what Sophia lacked in talent she made up for in good looks; as a courtesan she lacked for nothing, either in the quality or the quantity of her conquests. Indeed it seems that aristocrats everywhere admired and lusted after her. She had been born in 1745 in London as Sophia Snow. Her father was an army trumpeter. At 18 she eloped with an actor working at the Drury Lane Theatre called Robert Baddeley and two years later she too appeared on that stage, in a variety of Shakespearean roles. Her acting was terrible, but in spite of this, audiences loved her.

Her singing voice made her a particular favourite with the crowds at Ranelagh and Vauxhall Gardens. After seven years her marriage broke down – small wonder given that her husband encouraged her to accept the advances of a wealthy Jewish friend called Mendez. Sophia sought solace and support from a variety of male admirers. She had an affair with the actor Charles Holland, and when he died she lived with his doctor, a Dr Hayes, for nine months. Then there was Lord Grosvenor, George Garrick, William Hanger and the Duke of York. Lord Ancaster described her beauty as 'absolutely one of the wonders of the age'. While likening her to a basilisk, he commented: 'No man can gaze on you unwounded…whose eyes kill those whom they fix on.'

Sophia's problem was money – she lived way beyond her means. She thought nothing of spending a fortune on hot-house flowers, on jewellery, and on fine clothes. In due course she was forced to flee to Dublin, and later Edinburgh, to escape her creditors. Possibly she should have been a bit more discerning with her choice of lover – she caused great consternation by having affairs with both Lord Coleraine and his younger brother John and, when John left her, she was so devastated that she took an overdose of laudanum. She survived, but was left addicted to laudanum for the rest of her life.

She also had a long affair with Peniston Lamb, 1st Viscount Melbourne. In 1769 he had married Elizabeth Milbanke, a woman who had, to say the least, 'put it about a bit' and of her six children, only one was definitely sired by his lordship. The others may well have been a result of her liaisons with the Prince of Wales and Lord Egremont. Elizabeth was therefore presumably not too perturbed when her cuckolded husband took up with Sophia Baddeley. At one stage Sophia became pregnant but suffered a miscarriage. She turned down a proposition from the Duke of Northumberland ('not attractive enough') and embarked on an affair with a particularly worthless individual called Stephen Sayer. When he got her pregnant, he left her for another woman – who had more money. Sarah returned to the stage and began an affair with a Mr Webster and had two children by him. Unfortunately Mr Webster then died, leaving Sophia to take up with the late Mr Webster's manservant. Two more children followed.

At the age of 40 she appeared on stage for the last time. The following year, 1786, she died of consumption, her looks and money all gone. It is likely that she was buried in Edinburgh. The following year saw the publication of her memoirs, recounted by her friend and companion Elizabeth Steele. In the memoirs, which run to four volumes, she describes the domestic violence and sexual double standards which Sophia encountered throughout her life. Much has been made of the fact that Sophia and Elizabeth openly lived together as companions. The fact that Elizabeth was apt to dress in a man's clothes, (she also carried a pistol) has led some to assume that theirs was a lesbian relationship.

Sophia's life at the top of the pile as a courtesan had lasted just four years, from 1771 to 1774. The subsequent rapid decline and early death was a hallmark of many of her Cyprian colleagues.

ANN CATLEY, 1745–1789

Ann's father was a coachman, her mother took in laundry and as a young girl Ann would sing songs in taverns in the areas around London's Tower Hill. When she was 13 years old she was seduced by a young linen draper, became apprenticed to a Mr Bates, and started singing on the London stage. There she came to the attention of a low-life by the name of Sir Francis Blake Delaval, who bought out her apprenticeship in return for her agreeing to become his mistress. She was seventeen years old, and her horrified father immediately applied to the courts to declare the arrangement immoral and contrary to public policy. Sir Francis, besotted with the young girl, happily paid damages, and lavished gifts on Ann including diamond rings, while at the same time giving her a weekly allowance and providing her with her own accommodation.

Unfortunately for his Lordship, she delighted in pursuing intrigues behind his back, each time accepting 'bribes' in the form of gifts and large sums of money. Amongst others, she became the lover of a wealthy Portuguese merchant, who showered her with jewellery.

Highly-sexed and with no concerns about the feelings of others, she made no secret of her affair with the Duke of York and in due course Delaval extricated himself from the arrangement of being her protector and provider. The final straw came when he went to Wetherbys's, a well-known house of ill-repute, and was by mistake shown up to the room in which Ann was entertaining a young client. The furious Delaval insisted that she move out of her apartment immediately, and she went to live above a milliner's shop in Covent Garden. Once there, she obtained regular employment as a singer in the theatre. She then moved for a few years to Dublin, where she pursued a lucrative career both in and out of bed, and on and off the stage. Returning to the London stage she very nearly ensnared an elderly gentlemen into marriage – terms had been agreed (namely a lump sum payment of £1,000, plus an annuity which she would receive for life). The old man thereupon wrote to his son with the news that he would soon be acquiring a step-mother. The son came to his father's house and was somewhat at a loss to find Miss Catley, whose favours he too had been sharing … that was the end of that relationship.

Finally, she succumbed to the charms of General Francis Lascelles, moved in with him, had several children and in due course was rumoured to have got married. Theirs was a tempestuous relationship not helped by her serial infidelities. She eventually died of consumption, aged 44. Under her will – for which a Grant of Probate was obtained – her estate of £5,000 was left to her children. This may well be an indication that she never did marry Lascelles, or everything would have belonged to him and she would not have had any estate to leave.

'THE ARMISTEAD' 1750–1842

Of all the courtesans of the eighteenth century, Elizabeth Armistead was perhaps the most remarkable – remarkable for the extent of her glittering clientele, remarkable for living to the age of 91, remarkable for finding true love with one of the most charismatic and rakish politicians of the period. She did not have an auspicious start – she was born Elizabeth Bridget Cane in 1750. Little is known of her parents, but in her teens she was having to support herself in the only manner she knew – horizontally. By the time she was 19 she was working in a high-class brothel, but whether it was for the notorious bawd Jane Goadby or her rival Elizabeth Mitchell is not clear. However, what is apparent is that this energetic young lady with a warm personality and an impressive physique was extremely popular, and she was soon in high keeping thanks to a large number of ardent followers. In all probability one of her early supporters was a Mr Armistead, and she became famous by the use of that name. Others referred to her as 'The Armistead' – the joke being that she was named like a boat because she was boarded by so many people. She had her portrait painted by Sir Joshua Reynolds, and, as the *Town & Country Magazine* went on to report, she could 'claim the conquest of two ducal coronets, a marquis, four earls and a viscount'.

Certainly her client list included the Prince of Wales, the Duke of Dorset, the Duke of Ancaster, the Earl of Derby, Viscount Bolingbroke, Lord George Cavendish and the fabulously wealthy nabob General Sir Richard Smith. The Earl of Cholmondeley, Lord Robert Spencer and Lord Coleraine were also benefactors. Through her talents she acquired enough wealth to buy herself at least two properties, in Bond Street and in Clarges Street, and quickly became the Toast of the Town. She was pre-eminent in her field for an astonishing ten years during which time she was a fashion icon, a centre of gossip, and an inspiration to many. And then in 1783 she fell for the charms of Charles James Fox, the Whig politician renowned for his six o-clock stubble, his gambling addiction, his womanising and his drinking. They had known each other, platonically, for perhaps ten years. Curiously, their affair only started after Fox had become involved with Mary Robinson, Elizabeth's close rival. Fox was quickly smitten with his new conquest. Theirs was a love-match which astonished Society, a case of the Beauty and the Beast. But love it was, and it stood the test of time, as well as derision from some quarters, and a lack of acceptance into 'polite society'. At one stage Elizabeth tried to break off the affair and in the autumn of 1783 Fox wrote to her:

> *You shall not go without me wherever you go. I have examined myself and know that I can better abandon friends, country and everything than live without Liz. I could change my name and live with you in the remotest part of Europe in poverty and obscurity. I could bear that very well, but to be parted I cannot bear.*

Elizabeth relented and even sold her properties to pay off Fox's gambling debts, set up home with him at St Ann's in Surrey, and introduced him to the delights of gardening and country living. For ten years they lived discreetly as mistress and keeper, with Elizabeth resisting suggestions that they marry because of the scandal that it might cause. She eventually gave in to his entreaties, on condition that the union was kept under wraps, and after they married in 1795 the wedding was kept secret for seven years. It was not until 1802, when the couple embarked for Paris to meet the Emperor Napoleon that Fox decided to go public. There was a brief period of gossip and tut-tutting, but the fuss quickly died down, largely thanks to Elizabeth's charm, good nature and tolerance. Her husband was undeniably besotted with her, writing: 'You are all to me. You can always make me happy in circumstances apparently unpleasant and miserable … Indeed, my dearest angel, the whole happiness of my life depends on you.'

Charles James Fox died at Chiswick on 15 September 1806, leaving his widow to soldier on alone for over thirty-five years. Respect for her was enormous – she was awarded an annual pension of £1,200 and in 1823 her former lover, now King George IV, gave her an annuity of £500. That annuity was continued by the King's brother William IV when he succeeded to the throne – and indeed by Victoria when she became Queen in 1837. Throughout those years she was untouched by scandal, never once attempted to 'kiss and tell', and died beloved by the local community.

> *Jan.* 24. The Perdita now labours under a fevere fit of the rheumatifm, occafioned, it is faid, by *want of exercife*; fhe having had very little bufinefs in her way, to tranfact for fome time.

MARY ROBINSON, 1757–1800 – aka 'Perdita'

Mary, universally known as Perdita after her most famous stage role, was one of the most talked about actress-courtesans of the era. Her affair with the Prince of Wales, and her 'signing on fee' of £20,000, is mentioned in Chapter Six along with her fifteen year relationship with the dashing rake Banastre Tarleton (see Chapter Nine). She was born in Bristol into a dysfunctional family called Darby – father was a naval captain who preferred to live with his mistress rather than with Mrs Darby. Mrs Darby and the young Mary moved to London, and at sixteen Mary agreed to marry an articled clerk called Thomas Robinson, who was believed to have 'expectations of a large fortune'. The fortune never materialised, and Thomas turned out to be a philandering womaniser who made no effort to disguise his many affairs. Mary ended up supporting him, escaping to Wales to avoid creditors, before giving birth to a child called Mary Elizabeth in 1774.

Mary was as bad at managing finances as her husband, proving herself more than happy to live beyond her means, and buying expensive clothes in order to be seen at fashionable places such as Ranelagh and Vauxhall Gardens. Within months their profligate behaviour resulted in the entire family ending up in the Kings Bench prison for debtors. There, Thomas installed a mistress while Mary looked after the young baby, earning a pittance copying legal documents. She also found time to write poetry, and having submitted a volume of 'Poems' to Georgiana Duchess of Devonshire, obtained her support and encouragement to persevere with her literary efforts.

In 1776 she got a part on the stage after befriending David Garrick and the playwright Richard Brinsley Sheridan, and for four years learned her craft as an actress while enjoying various flings. Then the Prince of Wales entered her life, and as will be seen she became the most famous, most talked about woman in London. As one of the grandest of *'les grandes horizontales'* every change of outfit was duly noted and reported on. As the *Morning Herald* mentioned on 12 June 1781:

> *Fortune has again smiled on Perdita; on Sunday she sported an entire new phaeton, drawn by four chestnut-coloured ponies, with a postilion and servant in blue and silver liveries. The lady dashed into town through Hyde Park turnpike at four o'clock, dressed in a blue great coat prettily trimmed in silver; a plume of feathers graced her hat, which even Alexander the Great might have prided himself in.*

In particular the papers loved to report on the alleged rivalry between Perdita, Dally the Tall and the Bird of Paradise. The *Town & Country* magazine regularly passed on tittle-tattle, as did *The Rambler Magazine* with comments such as:

> *January 14: The Perdita now labours under a severe fit of the rheumatism, occasioned it is said, by the want of exercise, she having had very little business in her way, to transact for some time. The Bird of Paradise, by the same secession of business in her rival Perdita, has very much enlarged her profits; in consequence of which she has got a new chariot, new furniture, and other pageants.*

The rivalry showed one thing – a very small circle of high-class courtesans serviced an equally small circle of aristocratic rakes. Being seen with the most famous woman of the moment was something which the young, and not so young, blades aspired to, a sort of 'Pass the Parcel' game played for rather high stakes.

After one prolonged visit to Paris, she returned to England bringing with her all the prevailing French influences in fashion and style. As the *Morning Herald* of 7 December 1781 had predicted, she was expected to return with ideas 'which could not fail to set the whole world a-madding'. Later, on 9 January 1782, the same paper gushed:

> *Last night the divine Perdita visited the opera...She was dressed in white satin, with purple breast-bows, and looked supremely beautiful. Her head-dress was in a stile*

which may be called the standard of taste; her cap, composed of white and purple feathers entwined with flowers, was fastened on with diamond pins.

By the following season she was wearing what became known as the 'Robinson hat for Ranelagh' along with the 'Perdita Hood', the 'Perdita Hat' and the 'Robinson Gown'. She caused a sensation when she turned up at the opera in March 1783 sporting gold embroidered stockings. In all matters of taste and style, she reigned supreme, and what Mary Robinson wore one day was immediately picked up by the 'frail sisterhood' i.e. leading courtesans, the next. Milliners and costumiers had every reason to be thankful to Mary – she was decidedly good for business.

After her affair with the Prince of Wales ended and she had taken up with Banastre Tarleton, Mary increasingly devoted time to writing – poems, odes, and sonnets, and then novels. Some of these sold in considerable numbers, mainly because of the perceived autobiographical nature of the works, and ran to numerous editions as well as being translated into French and German. She was an admirer of the works of Mary Wollstonecraft and in 1799 published *A Letter to the Women of England, on the Injustice of Mental Subordination.* In it she showed her disillusionment with the institution of marriage. Later, she started writing her autobiography but she died on Boxing Day in 1800 before it was finished. Her daughter subsequently published it as *Memoirs of the Late Mrs. Robinson, Written by Herself, With Some Posthumous Pieces.*

HARRIETTE WILSON née Dubouchet – 1786–1845, one of four whoring sisters. Harriette Wilson was perhaps the best-known courtesan of the Regency era. She was born in 1786 to a watch-maker by the name of Dubouchet, who kept a shop in Mayfair and who had come to London from Switzerland. He adopted the surname of 'Wilson' in 1801. Harriette was rumoured to have had fourteen siblings. Of the five girls who reached maturity one, and only one, chose not to join the Cyprian Corps. She was dubbed 'The Paragon'. Of the others, Harriette disliked her sister Amy, who appears to have found it impossible to resist the temptation to steal whoever Harriette was sleeping with. Another sister, called Sophia, earned Harriette's dismissive assessment as being 'unintelligent and lacking wit'. In Harriette's words Sophia

had begun her career before other girls even dream of such things. She had intruded herself on a cobbler at thirteen, thrown herself into the arms of the most disgusting profligate in England at fourteen, with her eyes open, knowing what he was; then offered herself for sale, at a price, to Colonel Berkeley, and when her terms were refused with scorn and contempt by the handsome and young man, then throws herself into the

arms of age and ugliness for a yearly stipend, and at length, by good luck, without one
atom of virtue, became a wife.

Her husband was Lord Berwick, who had initially wooed her as a potential mistress by offering an annuity of £500, and had then decided to marry the girl, more-or-less out of spite since it was quite apparent to all that Sophia hated her paramour most assiduously. But a Lady she became, at the grand age of 17 years, leaving Harriette and her younger sister on the game.

Sister Fanny had barely entered her teens when she started her career as a courtesan. Compared to her, Harriette was a slow-starter. As she enigmatically remarked in the opening section of her memoirs:

I shall not say how and why I became, at the age of fifteen, the mistress of the Earl of
Craven. Whether it was love, or the severity of my father, or the depravity of my own
heart, or the winning arts of the noble Lord which induced me to leave my paternal roof
and place myself under his protection, does not now much signify…

Other wealthy patrons followed, and she ended up with an impressive list of clients including the Prince of Wales, the Lord Chancellor and four future Prime Ministers. She and Fanny cut a swathe through the cream of London's 'well endowed' men, with one often picking up where the other left off. In 'The General out-generalled' shown as Image 31 Harriette is seen leaning out of the bedroom window alongside the Duke of Argyll, while the Duke of Wellington is dancing around on the pavement demanding to be let inside.

When she was 35 years old, Harriette astonished everyone by retiring from harlotry. She got married to a man called Rochfort, and hopped on a boat to France. And then decided that it was pay-back time. She published her memoirs one instalment at a time, ending each one with a list of the famous names to be included in the following instalment (unless the persons named paid up…). Yes, it was blackmail, but it was a very open and straight-forward form of blackmail. Her targets were principally men who had promised her money in her retirement, or an annuity, but had gone back on their word. The strategy used by Harriette was extremely effective, and the public were enthralled with her under-the-bedclothes revelations. Harriette supposedly made £10,000 out of the venture, which gave a fascinating insight into the mind of a woman who had scaled the heights of her chosen profession. The Earl of Craven was dismissed as a monumental bore, and a figure of fun because of the cotton night cap he wore to bed. Wellington had no small-talk and was described as looking like a ratcatcher. But she saved her vitriol for her chief target, the Duke of Beaufort. He had promised her an annuity in exchange for her agreeing to break off her liaison with his heir, the Marquis of Worcester. The annuity failed to materialise, and the Duke, like many others, paid the price for his duplicitous and niggardly behaviour.

Elsewhere she gives this view on a woman who fornicates: 'There are but two classes of women ... she is a bad woman the moment she has committed fornication; be she generous, charitable, just, clever, domestic, affectionate ... still her rank in society is with the lowest hired prostitute.' The book ran to thirty-one editions in the first year alone. It was a best-seller translated into many languages and sold throughout Europe, making Harriette a wealthy but much-despised woman. In time the public lost interest. Harriette came back from Paris and lived for a while in Knightsbridge before disappearing from view and dying in Chelsea in 1845 at the age of 59.

* * *

What these summaries show is that at the top of the tree, for those courtesans who dominated the second half of the Georgian era, life was often short but never dull. They occupied a sort of parallel universe, a demi-monde where they were never entirely acceptable in polite society, and yet were held out as fashion icons, and as the representation of good taste, fashion and style. Above all, they were successful business women – they made sex pay, and it gave them a lifestyle way beyond anything they might have aspired to in any other line of work. It reached the point where wealthy men would vie with each other to be able to boast of having whoever was the Toast of the Town in 'high keeping' – rather like a modern-day footballer parking a Bentley Mulsanne outside his house even though he does not have a driving licence. Being seen out at the opera with a leading courtesan had enormous caché, and for the women at the top, these liaisons were highly profitable.

It is no coincidence that their fame occurred at a time when the public were, for the first time, able to see exhibitions of portraits in art galleries. Both the Society of Artists (from 1761) and the Royal Academy (from 1769) held annual summer exhibitions open to the public. The pictures were hung without differentiation as to the rank of sitter, so the harlot might appear next to the royal princess, without any indication which was which (save in the catalogue). Viewers therefore saw the portraits without any preconceptions – they saw them as *fashionistas* in all their finery, setting trends especially in their choice of clothes, the way they styled their hair, and the ornaments and jewellery they wore to complete their ensemble. Although the original paintings would then disappear from view, passing to whoever commissioned them, the printers swiftly produced mezzotint copies, giving a far wider audience the chance to appreciate the fashion sense of the sitters. These mezzotints – from the Italian mezzo ('half') and tinta ('tone') – were particularly good at demonstrating fine detail. The process allowed soft gradations of tone and rich and velvety blacks, and although the plates wore out quickly, the different tones made for very realistic facial representations. The portraits were collected in sets and kept in portfolios. They were also hung separately on the walls of countless homes, bringing 'pin-ups' into the domestic arena.

At the same time, new and more outspoken satirists came to the fore. This coincided to some extent with the ludicrous fashions of the 'macaronis', with their high wigs, effeminate manners and elaborate dress – they were easy to satirise. Print shop owners, such as the husband-and-wife team the Darly's, saw a regular trade in sets of prints, retailing at a couple of pence a copy in monochrome, and perhaps sixpence to a shilling in colour. Mary Darly had produced the first book on caricatures in 1762 with her *A Book of Caricaturas* and the couple went on to open a number of print shops in The Strand and Fleet Street under the name of 'The Golden Acorn'.

Carington Bowles was the most famous of a dynastic family of print publishers operating in London throughout the eighteenth century. He had moved to premises in St Paul's Courtyard by 1767, and for thirty years had been publishing highly detailed and attractive prints, many focusing on females and fashion. Image 34 is a Carington Bowles print of an elegant gentleman being accosted by two smartly dressed prostitutes, who have already relieved him of his silk handkerchief.

What was a minor craze became a commercial sensation, with print shops appearing across London, each one churning out a complete range of material from political lampoons to fashion satires. The British Museum catalogue shows some 5,500 prints dated between 1760 and 1800, of which over three hundred were mezzotint satires.

Chapter Five

Sex and Satire in Print

Satire really hit its stride in the eighteenth century. What had started with bawdy ballads making crude comments about randy philanderers, progressed to ground-breaking performances like *The Beggar's Opera* lampooning the corruption and excesses of the ruling classes. The often general satire (as opposed to personal attacks) of Jonathan Swift gave way to the somewhat intellectual criticisms by people like Pope and Steele and then on to the much more accessible and personally vitriolic attacks of the Grub Street hacks. They in turn helped promote a raucous and outspoken Press which showed a voyeuristic interest in the bed-hopping exploits of the great and the good – but even this paled into insignificance compared with the explosion of satirical caricatures linked to the appearance of the Print Shop on the streets of London, particularly after 1770. Not only was the satire highly personal, it echoed a fascination which the public had developed into the private and not so private lives of the rich and famous. These caricatures brought the 'celebrities' into the public domain – their foibles and peccadilloes were now known not just to the educated classes but to the Great British Public. No matter that they may not have been able to read and write – suddenly they knew what the famous people looked like, and they voraciously devoured any salacious and titillating information about them. Crowds jostled around the windows of the Print Shops, eager to see the latest offering from men like Gillray, Newton, Cruikshank and Rowlandson. It was all very different from the prevailing atmosphere at the start of the Georgian era.

The closing years of Queen Anne's reign had seen a large growth in periodicals often highly critical of society in general and the government in particular. Joseph Addison and Richard Steele had launched *The Spectator* in 1711, specialising in poking gentle fun at contemporary *mores* and foibles. Later came one of the great watersheds in satire, the bursting of the 'South Sea Bubble' in 1720. It was the country's first major stock market crash. The public had been duped into buying shares on the basis of lies, flim-flam and hype. When the crash came it was clear that many people had profited illegally, and corruption went right up to the top of government and to the monarch himself. Worse still, with the economy in ruins, the leader Robert Walpole decided that it was not in the public interest to have a prolonged period of navel-gazing (in other words, he presided over a cover-up which left many of the perpetrators unpunished). It provided William Hogarth with a target for one of the first caricatures he ever published, in 1721, entitled *Emblematical Print on the South Sea Scheme*.

It shows the gullible British public on the financial merry-go-round (including a whore and a clergyman) alongside a representation of the Monument. However, the inscription shows not that it commemorated the Great Fire, but the destruction of the City of London in 1720. It was typical of the satire of the time – slightly ponderous, and with little attempt to show identifiable people. It focussed on corruption and greed, themes regularly dealt with by writers such as Jonathan Swift in *Gulliver's Travels*. Swift was a master of both Horatian and Juvenalian styles of satire (Horatian – named after the Roman writer Horace, who chided and poked fun at human frailties and Juvenalian, named after the Roman Juvenal, who favoured a more contemptuous and critical style). Juvenalian satire was acerbic, harsh and often heavy in sarcasm and irony. Horatian satire was generally more humourous and gentle.

In 1713 Swift and Alexander Pope had helped form the Scriblerius Club. They were joined by John Arbuthnot, who first introduced the character of John Bull as representing the symbol of Britishness. Another member was the playwright John Gay, and together this quartet doggedly attacked Robert Walpole and corruption in government, as well as making fun of the new acquisitiveness which was beginning to dominate society. Pope's *The Dunciad* alienated many other writers of the day by satirising literary hacks. Grub Street really was a street, in London's Cripplegate Ward. It attracted writers (such as the young Samuel Johnson) who were happy to espouse more-or-less any opinion just so long as they were being paid to express it. Many of the outpourings from Grub Street were thinly veiled attacks on greedy politicians, concentrating on financial improprieties rather than sexual proclivities. When *The Grub Street Journal* was published in 1731 (it ran under one guise or another until 1737) it lampooned ideas on theology, medicine, the theatre and justice. Although it lampooned lawyers, clerics and actors, by and large it did not make fun of the private lives of the targets.

It had, however, become common for writers to pepper the text with 'gutted' names. 'Ox....' instead of 'Robert Harley, Earl of Oxford' may have fooled nobody, but gutted names became a hallmark of satirists throughout the century. It was without legal significance – a case in 1713 had established that gutting the name was no defence to a prosecution for libel. The case involved a printer called William Hurt, who had published a piece of political criticism entitled *The British Embassadress's Speach to the French King* and contained lewd suggestions about Queen Anne and the Duke and Duchess of Salisbury. Jonathan Swift had described the highly defamatory piece as 'the

Cursedest Libel in Verse … that ever was seen'. At the trial, Lord Chief Justice Parker made it clear that as long as common sense identified the 'victim' from the cut-down version of the name, gutting it – or 'emvowelling' as it was known at the time – was no defence, and Hurt was sentenced to a spell in the prison, pilloried and fined heavily. It did not however diminish the practice of using gutted names – if anything it became even more extensively used. It helped draw in the audience – they felt 'in on the secret' and satirists saw it as a necessary and useful badge of their trade. Images 62 and 63 show two drawings which appeared in the *Town & Country Magazine*, scandalously pairing off those in the public eye who were considered to be having affairs. One of the images uses descriptions ('A female Pilot' to describe Nancy Parsons) and the other shows emvowelling, with Lady Waldegrave and the Duke of Gloucester appearing as 'Lady W' and Duke of G'.

In time newspapers became highly skilled at 'innuendo by juxtaposition'. An innocent and entirely accurate sentence (for example, stating that the Prince of Wales had attended a masquerade the night before) would be followed by a sentence, equally correct, stating that such-and-such an actress was appearing on stage. The sentence immediately following would make a reference to the 'Cyprian Corps' or 'the frail sisterhood'. In the minds of the readers all three sentences would be read together to say: 'The Prince of Wales has fallen for the charms of this actress and has made her his mistress'.

Above all, it was a time when gossip emerged as a national pastime. As the playwright Sheridan was to remark: 'Satires and lampoons on particular people circulate more by giving copies in confidence to the friends of the parties than by printing them'.

Satirists also used allegorical stories, laced with innuendos, but a case in 1728 proved that this too was no defence to an allegation of seditious libel. The case involved *Mist's Weekly Journal*, a publication which had printed an allegorical story which poked fun at the Royal Family. The Attorney General laid down this test: would the generality of readers take it as the obvious and natural meaning that it was directed at the King? If so, the libel had been proved. Similarly, rebus-like devices were often used to identify the person involved. A boot would signify Lord Bute, a picture of a fox Charles James Fox, and a pair of ostrich plumes the Prince of Wales. None of these devices, from gutted names to visual puns, gave protection against prosecution, but in text and in etchings they helped define the satirists work, from Pope to Gillray. In practice the only thing which mattered was whether a judge and jury were convinced that a libel had been made against an identifiable individual. Why were more prosecutions not brought? Because the accusation of libel focused on the fact of defamation – in other words, the court case looked as much at the reputation of the 'victim' as at the intention of the accused in the dock. Few people wealthy enough to be able to afford litigation would want to expose their reputation to such minute scrutiny. If you wanted to avoid washing your dirty linen in court, you kept out of the libel arena.

Increasingly, writers introduced characters who were sexually promiscuous. Daniel Defoe published *Moll Flanders* in 1722. Partly based on the life of Moll King, mentioned in Chapter Three, Defoe is believed to have befriended Moll when she was in Newgate prison. His book relates the tale of a female who was at various times a con artist, a common thief and a kept woman who journeys through life, eventually triumphing against all odds. In the end, she and her husband repent of their wicked ways. In 1724 Defoe published his final novel, *Roxana, the fortunate mistress* – a story of the moral and spiritual decline of a high society courtesan. The central character is in many ways a proto-feminist, deploring marriage because it strips women of their legal rights ('the Marriage Contract is … nothing but giving up Liberty, Estate, Authority, and every-thing, to the Man'). It also shows that women cannot have full sexual freedom on a parity with men, because of the risk of pregnancy. Indeed the central character's own downfall is largely brought about because one of her offspring tracks her down and decides to expose her. Such repentance as she shows is largely nullified by the fact that she has become extremely wealthy as a result of her having seduced a number of well-heeled (and generous) benefactors. Far from being 'a tart with a heart' she is a calculating prostitute who pays the price for abandoning her children.

1728 saw the premiere of John Gay's *Beggar's Opera* – a hugely popular and influential satire (see Image 35). It did not just lampoon the prevailing taste for Italian opera, it ridiculed Robert Walpole (identified in the play as Bob Booty). It railed against corruption and the incompetence and greed of politicians as well as drawing a comparison between the crimes committed by the lower orders with those of their social superiors, but contrasting the different way that the Law dealt with each. It ends with the comment 'the lower People have their Vices in a Degree as well as the Rich, and are punished for them,' implying that the rich get away with their vices and are in effect above the law. *The Beggar's Opera*, with its sixty-nine popular songs taken from existing folk tunes, ballads and well-known melodies, made a hero out of Macheath (the highwayman) while Lavinia Fenton, who played the first Polly Peachum, became an overnight success. More of her, and the besotted Duke of Bolton, in Chapter Seven.

When Gay tried to follow up the success with a sequel (*Polly*) in 1729 the Prime Minister Robert Walpole leant on the Lord Chamberlain to have the play banned because it was even more overtly critical of the government than *Beggar's Opera*. It did not appear on stage for another fifty years. The powers of the Lord Chamberlain's office were strengthened even more after the passing of the Licensing Act in 1737. Not only could the Lord Chamberlain veto any play he did not like, but theatre owners could be prosecuted for putting on a play, or part of a play, unless they had obtained prior approval. This censorship was greatly resented by playwrights, especially as the banning orders were generally used for political purposes i.e. to prevent criticism of the government. The legislation remained on the Statute Book until 1843, when it was replaced by the slightly less draconian Theatres Act.

In 1732 Jonathan Swift published his poem *The Lady's Dressing Room* – a scatalogical but humourous tale of a man sneaking in to look through his lover's dressing room. In the poem Swift denounces the vanity of women in general, and is highly critical of false beauty aids and cosmetics. He was also poking fun at men – and their unrealistic expectations. But Swift also displays an underlying belief at the time, that women were to blame for corrupting men and leading them astray. It is no different to some of Thomas Rowlandson's pornographic prints of a century later, showing elderly men being seduced by a naked and glamorous young lady (see Image 22).

Hogarth published his series of six prints under the heading *A Harlot's Progress* in 1732. The first in the series is shown as Image 8 and shows a young girl from the country called Moll (or Mary) Hackabout who comes to London and is lured into prostitution by the notorious bawd Elizabeth Needham. Lord Charteris, known as the Rape-Master General and described further in Chapter Eight, looks on in the background, fondling himself in anticipation.

Subsequent scenes show Moll's descent into poverty, disease and an early death, and they also offer a very early instance where the characters are identifiable. One of the prints shows the magistrate Sir John Gonson; another, the medics Dr Richard Rock and Dr Jean Misaubin (both of whom specialised in promoting cures for venereal disease). Satire was becoming personal, and in case the public did not recognise the targets, Hogarth added their names on pieces of paper. He followed up this highly moralising and ever-so-worthy tale with a companion set of eight called *A Rake's Progress* (1736) charting the downward spiral into debt and madness of Tom Rakewell. Image 20 shows one of the images in the set. Drink, gambling and whoring lead Tom to being incarcerated in the Fleet Prison, and ultimately, in Bedlam. In 1743 Hogarth followed up his finger-wagging with the six part *Marriage à-la-mode* in which he lampoons the idea of marrying for money, and again shows the 'hero' as he succumbs to whoring, catches venereal disease and ends up being murdered.

Such was Hogarth's influence and popularity that he helped get the Engraving Copyright Act onto the statute books in 1734. This gave artists a measure of protection from being ripped off, and cover was extended to other forms of plagiarism in 1775, to prints in 1777, and finally to sculptures in 1814.

Many of Hogarth's engravings were only prepared once he had raised sufficient money by subscriptions, but he helped develop a market for popular printed culture. Meanwhile, the lack of effective libel laws, coupled with a return to adversarial two-party politics at the start of George III's reign, encouraged a strong and vibrant Press.

A book that gives an insight into the finance of sex was *Chrysal – the adventures of a guinea* published in 1760 and running to twenty-four editions by 1800. It follows the life of a gold guinea coin as it is passed around throughout society. On several occasions it is used to buy the services of prostitutes. The guinea is often cited as the 'coin of choice' for a woman selling her virtue, and Image 33 shows a whore weighing the gold coin on her scales. It has been clipped and therefore is underweight, and the rake will not have his pleasures tonight.

Readers of *Chrysal* would have been able to identify the elderly Field Marshall, who wishes to have sex with a ten year old girl, as being John, Earl Ligonier, Commander of the British forces. The old lecher was notorious for his paedophilia, resulting in the *Town & Country Magazine* in 1760 remarking that 'as the Old Soldier increases in years, the age of his mistresses diminish and now he is near eighty, he gives it as his opinion that no woman past fourteen is worth pursuing'. Other identifiable individuals in *Chrysal* are the Duke of St Albans, Lord Anson and Lord Deloraine, all infamous for their immorality and debauchery.

A later writer who liked to poke fun at the foibles and pretentiousness of the English aristocracy was Fanny Burney. Her four novels *Evelina*, *Cecilia*, *Camilla* and *The Wanderer* appeared during the period between 1778 and 1814 and in many respects she paved the way for Jane Austen and her witty observations on sexual politics, the role of women, and the perils of playing fast and loose. Neither writer was commenting on specific individuals, but both helped to ridicule prevailing attitudes in that particular echelon of society. To that extent they were following on from the tradition developed by Richard Brinsley Sheridan in *The School for Scandal*, mocking society for its hypocrisy and preoccupation with gossip. The play was first performed in London at the Drury Lane Theatre on 8 May 1777, a comedy of manners which lampooned the gossip-mongers.

Throughout the eighteenth century writers had to worry about the twin prongs of libel and obscenity, both of which were used to curb artistic and literary freedoms during the Georgian period. Obscene books, poetry and prints had started to become widespread after the Restoration, often with material copied from the French. A popular example was *L'Escole des Filles*, copied into English as *The School of Venus* (1655). The diarist Samuel Pepys admits to reading a copy in 1668 describing it as a 'mighty lewd book, but yet not amiss for a sober man once to read over to inform himself in the villainy of the world'. Read it he did – and promptly threw it on the fire in case his wife saw it. The plot involves a discussion between a sexually experienced woman and an innocent young maid, and details the pleasures to be enjoyed. The underlying viewpoint is that 'women are gagging for it' and that the poor man has very little choice but to rise to the occasion and do his duty.

In 1668 prosecutions were brought against Joseph Streater and Benjamin Crayle for selling 'several obscene and lascivious books' (of which *The School of Venus* was one) and were fined forty shillings and twenty shillings respectively. Nevertheless, versions of the book remained in print, and records show it was still being sold, to men and women alike and by both male and female booksellers, well into the middle of the eighteenth century.

One famous writer of obscene verse was the Earl of Rochester, the man who said of his drinking companion and fellow-lecherer King Charles II:

> *His scepter and his prick are of a length;*
> *And she may sway the one who plays with th'other…*
> *Restless he rolls about from whore to whore,*
> *A merry monarch, scandalous and poor.*

Other poems written by the Earl were altogether more explicit. Writing of a new type of dildo available from Italy, he suggests that English ladies will prefer it to their husbands, with the words 'This signior is sound, safe, ready, and dumb; As ever was candle, carrot, or thumb.' Poems such as a *Ramble in St James Park* are almost unprintable but an idea of his crudity can be seen from *Regime d'viver*

> *I Rise at Eleven, I Dine about Two*
> *I get drunk before Seven, and the next thing I do,*
> *I send for my Whore, when for fear of a Clap,*
> *I spend in her hand, and I spew in her Lap.*

After the whore has robbed him and departed, the poem continues:

> *I storm and I roar, and I fall in a rage,*
> *And missing my Whore, I bugger my Page*
> *Then crop-sick, all Morning, I rail at my Men*
> *And in Bed I lye Yawning, till Eleven again.*

By the reign of Queen Anne there was a strong anti-Catholic satirical tone to much of the earlier lascivious and titillating texts – titles such as *A Full and True Account of a Dreaded Fire that Lately Broke Out in the Pope's Breeches* (1713) emphasised the hypocrisy of priests who paid lip-service to chastity while having their wicked way with their female parishioners at every opportunity. It is hardly surprising that Roman Catholics were often portrayed as debauched sex-maniacs – it was simply part and parcel of the anti-papist groundswell which was to put George I on the throne as the first of the Hanoverians.

Into this scene stepped the unloved and unlovely Edmund Curll. In 1707 he had published *The Works of the Right Honourable the late Earl of Rochester* and then moved on to publish a variety of pirated and unauthorised works, specialising in 'biographies' of famous people who had just died. There was no attempt to be truthful or accurate – the only consideration was getting the biography out on to the street as soon as possible. Gradually he built up a reputation not just as a huckster but as a peddler of indecent literature – 'curllecisms' as they were called. In 1725 he brought out a book called *A Treatise on Flogging* (about the joys of using whips in the bedroom) and *Venus in the Cloister* about a nun who seduces a young initiate. Curll was dragged before the courts, but the problem was that it was unclear what offence he had committed. Obscenity in itself was not a crime. In the end the judges invented the new offence of 'publishing an obscene libel', fined him £100, and sentenced him to a spell in the pillory. He got off lightly – he made sure a pamphlet was circulated to those attending his time in the pillory, in which he claimed that he was being punished for defending the memory of the much-loved late Queen Anne (rather than for printing and distributing obscene material). The crowd refrained from pelting him, and when his time was up, carried him shoulder high to a local hostelry.

Curll was embroiled in a long-running dispute with Alexander Pope, largely because he kept publishing works by Pope (both fake and genuine) without permission. Pope's *The Dunciad* contained many attacks on Curll, who responded with *The Popiad* and used the publicity to promote his catalogue of works. From 1741 onwards Curll published a number of erotic books under the umbrella title of *Merryland* – a euphemistic reference to topographical features while actually describing the female anatomy in salacious detail.

In 1735 *Kick him Jenny* had been published – a rollicking tale of a man called Roger who is in the middle of making love to Jenny the maid, behind a locked door, when her Mistress spies what is going on through the keyhole:

> But as he drove, the Coaſt being clear,
> Stopt ſhort he was, in mid Career.
> My Lady ſaw it thro' the Hole,
> And furious Anger fill'd her Soul.
> Hot, to prevent the wicked Whoredom,
> She thunder'd like to beat the Door down.
> By all that's good, cry'd ſhe, I'll ſtick him,
> Kick him—why kick him, *Jenny*, kick him—

Sir John, the householder, is altogether more encouraging of the young swain and offers conflicting advice:

> When gay Sir *John*, who lov'd the Sport,
> And would not have the Lad retort,
> Mad at his Wife, he cou'd have ſtuck her,
> Aloud cry'd ——— her, *Roger*, ——— her.
> Kick him, as loud, the Dame went on;
> ——— her, ſtill louder, cry'd Sir *John*:

Erotic writing received a huge boost in November 1748 when Part One of John Cleland's *Memoirs of A Woman of Pleasure* came out in print. The second part was published three months later. The book is more generally known as *Fanny Hill*, and was a sensation. For the first time ever, a book was written in the style of a novel, but incorporating pornographic descriptions as part of a believable story. The tale is about an innocent young maid arriving in London and, as in Hogarth's *A Harlot's Progress*, the young girl is lured into a brothel. The procuress is a Madam by the name of Mrs Brown. Fanny is led down the path of sexual experimentation by her new friend Phoebe and has all manner of sexual encounters, including lesbianism, flagellation and orgies, and discovers that sex, with or without being in love, can be great fun. She attends drag balls; she gets pregnant and has a miscarriage; she beds a number of extremely well-endowed lovers both young and old; and finally meets up with the one true love from whom she was separated for several years, confesses all, and gets married to him.

The Church was horrified: this was no Hogarthian moral tale which said 'live a wild and promiscuous life and you will end up impoverished, diseased and dead' – instead it was an explicit, highly salacious, story which said that you can eat your cake and still have it. You can have a great sex life, have a lot of fun along the way, find true love as a result of your sexual adventures between the sheets, get married and live happily ever after.

For nearly a year the authorities took no action but in November 1749 charged Cleland with 'corrupting the King's subjects.' Faced with a spell in prison and a heavy fine, Cleland renounced the novel and it was officially withdrawn, but immediately pirated editions appeared. For over 200 years no official unexpurgated version was printed, but that is not to say that it disappeared – it simply went underground. When William Wilberforce helped found the Proclamation Society in 1787 it had as its aim the suppression of 'all loose and licentious Prints, Books, and Publications, dispersing Poison to the Minds of the Young and Unwary, and to punish the Publishers and Vendors thereof' and a number of booksellers and publishers were prosecuted. In 1788 Londoner John Morgan was charged with having published a book called *The Battle of Venus* – described in court as 'a certain nasty filthy Bawdy and obscene Libel'. The court sentenced him to a year in prison and a spell in the pillory for having attempted to 'corrupt the morals of all the youths of this kingdom and to bring them into a state of wickedness lewdness debauchery and brutality'. A year later a James Hodges was hauled before the Kings Bench to answer charges that he had published Cleland's *Memoirs of a Lady of Pleasure*, in an edition which featured a number of sexually explicit engravings showing 'Men and Women not only in the Act of Carnal copulation in various attitudes and position but also with their private parts exposed in various other lewd and indecent attitudes and Postures'. Those explicit illustrations set a bench-mark for subsequent caricaturists – such as Thomas Rowlandson., and helped set the stage for highly scatological engravings by satirists like James Gillray and Richard Newton.

Pressure from moral reforming groups led to a number of obscenity prosecutions in the second half of George III's reign, but the methods used by the prosecution were highly questionable, often using blatant entrapment. Public disquiet at these methods came to a head after the Society for the Suppression of Vice charged an itinerant Italian print-seller by the name of Baptista Bertazzi with distributing obscene prints. An undercover agent, paid by the Society, had persuaded Bertazzi to obtain obscene material on the pretence of wanting to re-sell the material to a third party. Bertazzi obtained the prints, was promptly arrested, and in his subsequent trial in 1802 details of the fraudulent and immoral tactics used by the Society came to light. Moral crusaders such as William Wilberforce distanced themselves from the methods used, and public support for further prosecutions quickly faded. Nevertheless, in its annual report in 1825 the Society for the Suppression of Vice was able to assert that it had prosecuted fourteen authors for 'infidel and blasphemous' material in the previous seven years.

Freedom of the Press had long been considered a cornerstone of 'Britishness' – it helped distinguish the country from its continental neighbours. There had been a number of attempts by the government to curb this freedom, but whenever Parliament debated the topic there were fierce arguments in favour of the right to free speech (even where what was being said or depicted was clearly libellous). As the playwright and Member of Parliament Richard Brinsley Sheridan said in 1798:

The press should be unfettered, that its freedom should be, as indeed it was, commensurate with the freedom of the people and the well-being of a virtuous State; on that account even one hundred libels had better be ushered into the world than one prosecution be instituted which might endanger the liberty of the press of this country.

Libel proceedings were, however, brought against authors and artists, but in many cases the heavy-handedness of prosecutions backfired. In its place the government of the day started to rely on bribery to try and control journalistic attacks. When *The Times* newspaper first made an appearance, under the guise of *The Daily Universal Register* in 1785, it was little more than a scandal sheet but the proprietor John Walters quickly realised that he could make money – £300 a year – in return for agreeing to publish stories favourable to the government. However, Walters was no fawning lackey and he also published scandalous stories about famous public figures such as the Prince of Wales – and was rewarded for his efforts with a £50 fine and a two-year spell in prison.

The heavy-handed approach was exemplified by the prosecution of John Wilkes. In 1752 Wilkes had befriended Thomas Potter, the son of the Archbishop of Canterbury. Potter was more than your run-of-the-mill debauched rake, since his private life included acts of bestiality, and he had started to pen a satire on Pope's *An Essay on Man.*

When Potter died in 1759 Wilkes inherited the manuscript and modified it to become *An Essay on Woman.* Pope had started his 'Essay' with the words:

Awake, my St John! Leave all meaner things
To low ambition, and the pride of Kings.
Let us (since Life can little more supply
Than just to look about us and to die)

The parody version used this as its opening stanza:

Awake, my Fanny! Leave all meaner things;
This morn shall prove what rapture swiving* brings!
Let us (since life can little more supply
Than just a few good fucks, and then we die)

(*swiving – i.e. copulation).

At the time, many regarded it as the filthiest poem ever written. In 1763 Wilkes had a dozen copies printed off for the amusement of his friends in the Hellfire Club. There is no evidence that he intended it for wider, public, consumption but Wilkes was already in trouble with the authorities because of an article he had written for the *North Briton* – a blatant attack on the government of Lord Bute. Bute was from Scotland (the *North Briton* referred to in the title) and edition 45 of the *North Briton* directly attacked Lord Bute and, by association, George III for his speech to the opening of Parliament. Wilkes contended that Bute and the King had betrayed the best interests of Great Britain in agreeing the terms of peace with France in the treaty of Paris, but his outspoken criticism led to him being seized and charged with seditious libel. He was one of a large group of people charged, but Wilkes was able to argue successfully that his case was covered by parliamentary privilege, on account of the fact that he was MP for Aylesbury. He then tried to sue the government for breaching his civil rights.

Infuriated at being wrong-footed, the government were determined to bring Wilkes down. As it happened, one of the members of the Hellfire Club was Lord Sandwich, a notorious whore-monger and libertine. He was the Secretary of State at the time and in that capacity had bribed or bullied the printer of the poem to hand over a copy for inspection. Quite possibly the poem was then modified by government hacks in order to make it even more blasphemous and obscene. Sandwich felt particularly incensed by the poem *An Essay on Woman* because Wilkes had been a long-term thorn in his side and had played an infamous practical joke on him at the Hellfire Club. Furthermore, Wilkes had cheekily dedicated the poem to the courtesan Fanny Murray, one of Lord Sandwich's many lovers. Sandwich offered to drop proceedings against Wilkes if Wilkes would drop his case against the government. Wilkes refused and, on 15 September 1763, Sandwich read out the entire poem before the peers assembled in the House of Lords, one of whom commented that he 'never before heard the devil preach a sermon against sin'. The charge before their Lordships was that the poem libelled the Bishop of Gloucester. All of their Lordships would have known full well that the poem was in part written by Potter, at a time when he was bedding the Bishop of Gloucester's wife. To be cuckolded by Potter was one thing; to have that fact broadcast before your colleagues in the House of Lords must have been totally humiliating. But the House was horrified at the blasphemous final lines – probably not written by either Potter or Wilkes, and more likely to have been inserted in order to gain maximum opposition to the poem. Swept up by the carnival nature of the occasion, Parliament found Wilkes guilty of libel and expelled him from the House.

Horace Walpole felt that the plot:

... so hopefully laid to blow up Wilkes was so gross and scandalous, so revengeful and so totally unconnected with the political conduct of Wilkes, and the instruments so despicable, odious, or in whom any pretentions to decency, sanctimony or faith were so preposterous that, losing all sight of the scandal contained in the poem, the whole world almost united in crying out against the informers.

Wilkes fled the country in December 1763 in order to avoid punishment for his 'crime' and remained in exile in France until his triumphant return in 1768. He was elected as MP for Middlesex, and was promptly thrown into prison for having evaded justice by going into exile. Enraged at finding their hero in prison, the supporters of Wilkes rioted and in the ensuing fracas seven people were killed and fifteen injured in what was known as the St George's Fields Massacre. Wilkes remained in prison until 1773, and on his release was appointed a sheriff of London, being made up to Lord Mayor the following year. In time he abandoned most of his radical connections and ended up as a supporter of William Pitt the Younger.

The whole story of the proceedings based on *An Essay on Woman* merely showed the futility of legislating against lewd, satirical and libellous publications. Perhaps it explains in part why those in power generally took no action against the owners of print shops selling scurrilous prints, which mushroomed in London from 1770 onwards. Put simply: bribery was a more effective weapon than prosecution. It cost less, kept the offensive material off the streets, and did not lead to public disorder or offend public ideas of decency and morality.

Nevertheless, a charge of seditious libel – in other words a libel calculated or likely to cause public disorder and undermine the government – was a draconian measure used by the Crown on several occasions, and it was a serious threat to the much vaunted freedom of speech enjoyed by the British Press. Sedition had always been a crime at Common Law, and charges were brought in 1792 against Thomas Paine for his work *The Rights of Man*, in which he set forth the idea that the public have a right to overthrow the government of the day if it ceases to act in the public interest. Given what was happening in France at the time of the French Revolution, this was incendiary stuff, and Paine was found guilty, fleeing to France to escape punishment. His printer William Holland was not so lucky, and ended up spending a year in Newgate, leaving the young caricaturist Richard Newton to run the print-shop for him and to publish his drawings. The Sedition Trials were followed by the 1794 Treason Trials, in which some thirty radicals were rounded up, imprisoned in the Tower of London, and faced trials where the penalty was to be hanged, drawn, and quartered. Thanks in part to the brilliance of the lawyer Thomas Erskine, the first three radicals (Hardy, Tooke and

Thelwall) were acquitted and the remaining treason charges were dropped, to great public acclaim.

It did not however mean the end of attempts by those in authority to curb free expression, and one famous case involved the Prince of Wales shortly after he became Regent. A sycophantic eulogy had appeared in the *Morning Post* in which the Prince had been praised as a paragon of virtue and good taste, describing him as the 'glory of his people', and a champion of the arts. He was, in the eyes of the Tory newspaper, an 'Adonis in loveliness'. Leigh Hunt and his brother Robert had launched a journal called *The Examiner* some years before, and on 22 March 1812 the paper retaliated against the praise heaped upon the Prince by describing him as 'a violator of his word, a libertine over head and ears in debt and disgrace, a despiser of domestic ties, the companion of gamblers, and demireps, a man who has just closed half a century without one single claim on the gratitude of his country or the respect of posterity!'

The Examiner also included a poem about the Prince which contained the words:

> *Not a fatter fish than he*
> *Flounders round the polar sea.*
> *See the blubber at his gills*
> *What a world of drink he swills!*

The fact that the allegations were true was immaterial – that, in itself, was not a defence. The Prince was outraged, especially at the description of him as 'a fat Adonis of Fifty', and both Leigh Hunt and his brother (as printer) were tried for libel, convicted, sent to prison and fined heavily.

By then, more and more newspapers had appeared in London with the main purpose of spreading gossip and scandal. In 1720 there were a dozen London newspapers. By 1776 there were fifty-three, and the appetite for news, or more accurately gossip, was insatiable. Publications such as *The Rambler's Magazine* (not to be confused with Samuel Johnson's *The Rambler* from thirty years earlier) started in 1783 with the alternative title of *The Annals of Gallantry, Glee, Pleasure and the Bon Ton*. In practice it was little more than a collection of titillating and voyeuristic extracts from the leading crim. con. trials of the day. In turn this encouraged the emergence of the *Bon Ton Magazine – or Microscope of Folly and Fashion*, which hit the streets in 1791. This was followed by collections of the 'juicy bits' from famous crim. con. trials, such as the anthology edited by R. Gill entitled *A collection of trials for adultery, or a General History of Modern Gallantry and Divorce* (1799 and 1802). These trial reports, often illustrated with obscene prints, helped develop a separate genre of erotica – and the public developed a fascination for the minutiae of the private lives of their social superiors and an obsession with their sexual exploits.

Extract from the trial (at DOCTORS COMMONS) *of* Mrs. ANN NISBETT, *wife of* WALTER NISBETT, Esq; *for adultery with* THOMAS TOTTY, Esq; *a captain in the navy, and commander of his majesty's ship the* Sphinx. *This curious trial is just published, and may be had complete, price* 2s. 6d.

Meanwhile, print shops became magnets for people from all social backgrounds eager to see and read what was happening. For those who were illiterate, there was always someone available who would explain the exhibits, and images of print shop windows appear under the hand of many different artists. Gillray in *Very Slippy Weather,* shown as Image 36, portrays an elderly gentleman – possibly Gillray himself – falling down on the wet pavement outside the print shop run by Hannah Humphrey. A small group of onlookers take no notice, because they are eagerly looking at the prints on display in the window.

One contemporary view of the print shops is shown by Horace Walpole when writing to his friend George Montagu. As he said, 'There is nothing new but what the pamphlet shops produce; however it is pleasant to have a new print or ballad every day'. A later observer of the London scene remarked that 'the enthusiasm is indescribable when the next drawing appears; it is a veritable madness. You have to make your way in through the crowd with your fists …'

The general public loved the new images and liked nothing more than being able to laugh at the portrayal of the antics of the rich and famous.

JAMES GILLRAY, 1756–1815

Into this world of voyeurism and salacious gossip leapt James Gillray, born around 1756. His first caricatures appeared in 1779 and he quickly developed into a most prolific and scabrous commentator on the follies of the age. Gillray produced hundreds of caricatures in his lifetime, many of them acerbic and scurrilous. They were offered for sale in the print-shop of Miss Hannah Humphrey, with whom Gillray lived. After 1806 he started to lose his eyesight and the year afterwards began to decline mentally, in time becoming insane. He attempted suicide by flinging himself from an upstairs window in 1811, an event described in *The Examiner* with the words "On Wednesday afternoon Mr. Gillray the caricaturist who resides at Mrs Humphrey's, the caricature shop in St. James's Street, attempted to throw himself out of the attic story. There being iron bars his head got jammed and being perceived by one of the chairmen who attends at White's, the unfortunate man was extricated." He finally died on 1 June 1815. He is perhaps best known for his political caricatures lampooning statesmen, the French, and of course George III and the royal family. He also produced a number of satirical prints lampooning the aristocracy and royalty for their sexual predilections. Image 37 shows a buxom girl pushing a wheelbarrow of carrots along Bond Street, while looking over her shoulder at an older man, the Fourth Earl of Sandwich, who is tugging at her apron. He is slipping a coin into her pocket and clearly thinks he can buy her services. A more modern title might be 'Is that a carrot in your pocket or are you just pleased to see me…?' The Earl was a well-known womaniser, and his mistresses included Fanny Murray and Martha Ray, mentioned in Chapters Four and Seven respectively.

Gillray was merciless in lampooning the Prince of Wales – an easy target – see Image 39. It shows the corpulent figure of the Prince, picking his teeth with a fork. He is sprawled in a chair alongside empty bottles of wine, unpaid bills, and an overflowing chamber-pot. Everything paints an unsavoury picture of the Prince's dissolute life-style. Above his head is a parody of the coat of arms of the Prince of Wales, with a crossed knife and fork in the centre, and with the candles held in a wine glass and decanter. On the side table, alongside the jellies, is a small pot labelled 'For the Piles' , another labelled 'For a Stinking Breath', and a tub of pills and a decanter marked 'Velnos Vegetable Syrup.' No-one could accuse Gillray of being a sycophant. Given the willingness of the Prince to resort to litigation over defamatory remarks about his enormous girth (see the Leigh Hunt trial mentioned earlier) it is surprising that Gillray got away with it and avoided a spell in prison.

Nevertheless Gillray was treading on dangerous ground with some of his satires. He was no doubt confident that he could get away with showing the Prince in bed with his favourite mistress, but implying that the Prince had married Mrs Fitzherbert (as in a print entitled 'The Morning after Marriage') was quite a risk. After all, the Prince had denied as much to his father the King, and Gillray was therefore imputing dishonesty on the part of the Prince.

Other members of the royal family were also targets, as in Image 32 entitled *Fashionable Contrasts* and showing the large, clumsy feet of the Duke of York between the delicate ankles and tiny shoes of the Duchess. Gillray was commenting on the preoccupation of the British Press with the Duchess, endlessly going on about the daintiness of her feet – which were apparently all of six inches long. Gillray was fed up with the gushing comments about her foot size – and, after the print appeared, the sycophancy stopped immediately. However, the caricature went on to become one of Gillray's most famous prints, synonymous with 'unlikely coupling' and plays on the age-old joke about the size of the male member being linked to the size of the man's feet. Further caricatures parodying the royals and specific aristocrats on account of their misdeeds are shown in images 38–40.

THOMAS ROWLANDSON, 1756–1827

Thomas Rowlandson, a fine artist with more of an interest in gentle social satire than Gillray, was active from the middle of the 1780s and he often favoured pen and ink drawings before transferring the image onto a copper plate for printing. He had inherited money from a wealthy aunt, but then proceeded to gamble it all away, often sitting at the gaming tables for thirty-six hours at a stretch. Having spent his inheritance he had no choice but to make his career selling his prints and paintings. His output was prodigious and he often painted the same scene on several occasions. He rarely lampooned identifiable individuals, instead commenting on human frailties and foibles in general.

He knew that there was a ready market for crude and indecent images – what might be termed 'top shelf' images of fornication, erotica and general nudity. Image 21 entitled *Cunnyseurs* (mentioned earlier) is a case in point. It is thought likely that the future George IV was a collector of such 'free' prints, but if so they were all destroyed during the reign of Queen Victoria and are no longer to be found in the Royal Collection.

Towards the end of his life Rowlandson suffered ill health, dying at the age of 70 in 1827. In his will he left his estate of nearly £3,000 to Betsy Winter, the woman he had lived with for the previous two decades. As a bon viveur and chronicler of human excesses he was unrivalled, largely because he knew that the laugh was on him, as much as on the people he portrayed. In his lifetime he generated hundreds of images of everyday life, warts and all.

RICHARD NEWTON, 1777–1798

Richard Newton, who died at the age of 21, brought a youngster's eyes to the foibles of hookers and their clients. At the age of 18, he had been commissioned to draw the illustrations for Laurence Sterne's *Sentimental Journey through France and Italy* and just before he died he illustrated Henry Fielding's romp of a novel *Tom Jones*. He had taken over responsibility for running the print shop of William Holland when the latter was sentenced to prison for sedition in 1793, and it is thought possible that it was while visiting his employer in prison that Newton contracted what was termed 'gaol fever' (probably typhus) from which he subsequently died. Many of his drawings employ dreadful puns and lavatorial humour. *A peep into Brest with a Navel Review* illustrates his punning talents, shown in Image 43. Newton clearly had a dim view of the morality of parsons and clerics, as in his print entitled *Which way shall I turn me?* in which a vicar is torn between the pleasures of the flesh and the pleasures of the dining table (Image 44). Image 45 shows the world of the courtesan, as in *Launching a Frigate* with the brothel owner standing outside her house alongside a prostitute dressed up to the nines. Newton prepared the original drawing. It was then engraved by Thomas Rowlandson and was only published (by Thomas Tegg) some ten years after Newton had met his untimely end.

ISAAC CRUIKSHANK, 1764–1811, and GEORGE CRUIKSHANK, 1792–1878

Isaac was born in Edinburgh but spent his working life in London. He died after a drinking contest with friends, at the age of 55. Jointly with James Gillray, he worked to popularise the figure of John Bull as a symbol of Britishness. He also drew caricatures on the topic of the abolition of slavery, as well as taking frequent swipes at the excesses of the Age. Images 40 and 41 and Images 46 and 47 reflect his views on indecent fashions, whores and royal shenanigans.

George Cruikshank, son of Isaac, was a satirical caricaturist with a reputation for being 'the modern-day Hogarth' because of his work illustrating the writings of Charles Dickens. He had originally been apprenticed to his father, was married twice, and after his death was found to have fathered eleven children by his mistress. Staunchly patriotic, he lampooned the French mercilessly. His print entitled *Old Sherry*, lampooning the adulterous George IV and his far from blameless wife, appears as Image 50.

THEODORE LANE, 1800–1828

The son of a painter, Theodore Lane was born into a poor family in Worcester and was apprenticed in London at the age of 14. Within five years he was exhibiting at the Royal Academy. He came to public notice making water colours and painting miniatures, before graduating to painting in oils in 1825. In the same year he published thirty-six humorous prints under the title of *The Life of an Actor*, dedicating the book to George IV. He had thus already allied himself to the King's cause, and in his later prints poured scorn on the antics of Queen Caroline. Lane was merciless in depicting her friendship with the Italian Bartolomeo Pergami, a man of low birth with whom the Queen apparently lived while she was in exile in Europe. Images 48, 49 and 52 illustrate his effectiveness as a satirist. Tragically he died at the age of 28 when he fell through a skylight in Gray's Inn Road, leaving behind a widow and three young children. His death denied future generations the chance to see what he would have made of Queen Victoria and Prince Albert….

A host of other artists joined the party, often targeting the courtesans, the rakes and the madams who operated in London. It was a time for highly visual satire – and often it was very personal, with the targets easily identifiable. The more the prints sold, the more the public demanded new titles, and the more famous the people being satirised became. The caricaturists themselves became wealthy, happy to allow their skills to be bought by the highest bidder. Even the bile-filled Gillray was perfectly happy to pocket £200 as a secret annual 'pension' paid by the Tory party led by William Pitt, in exchange for the production of images taunting the Whig Opposition. After both Pitt and Fox died in 1806, Gillray went back to his previous practice of ridiculing both sides in equal measure. Similarly, George Cruikshank was so merciless in lampooning the Prince Regent that in 1820 he received a royal bribe of £100 for a pledge 'not to caricature His Majesty in any immoral situation.' Nevertheless, the sexual shenanigans of George IV continued to dominate the print shops, but it appears that the Prince adhered to the view that there was only one thing worse than being talked about – and that was not being talked about. Certainly he was an avid collector of caricatures featuring himself, and many remained in the Royal Collection until they were sold by George V to the Library of Congress over a hundred years later.

Chapter Six

Royal Scandals and Shenanigans

GEORGE I – an incarcerated wife, a murder and a brace of mistresses.

It has to be said: George Ludwig did not have a lot going for him when it came to qualities required to become King of Great Britain – except for one thing – he was a Protestant. Apart from that, he comes across as a heartless, unfeeling and vindictive man; someone who was perfectly willing to parade a mistress under the nose of his wife, and spend his time hunting and whoring, yet was prepared to lock his wife away for over thirty years, barred from seeing her children, because she had the temerity to take a lover. That lover was murdered, possibly with the knowledge of George Ludwig, and almost certainly by killers employed by George Ludwig's family.

When George had married his cousin Sophia Dorothea of Celle in 1682 he was 22 and she was 16. It was not exactly a love-match – she referred to him as 'pig-snout' and begged not to be forced to go through with the marriage. She fainted when she was first introduced to him. For his part, George was equally horrified, largely because he felt insulted by the fact that his bride was of illegitimate birth (although her parents did eventually marry each other). For some strange reason George's taste in women did not extend to this vivacious, good-looking young girl with a stunning figure. It was rumoured that his preference was for a somewhat short and portly paramour – another Sophia (Sophia Charlotte von Kielmannsegg). She was the married daughter of his father's mistress, the Countess Platten. The Countess was renowned for being particularly generous with her favours and there is no certainty as to which of her many lovers fathered Sophia, but the public were convinced that Sophia and George shared the same father. The relationship, if true, meant that George was having an incestuous relationship with his half-sibling.

George's marriage was arranged by the two prospective mothers-in-law purely for financial and dynastic reasons – George's mother was the Duchess Sophia of Hanover, and she was keen to get her hands on the very substantial dowry on offer, payable in annual instalments. As the duchess wrote to her niece:

One hundred thousand thalers a year is a goodly sum to pocket, without speaking of a pretty wife, who will find a match in my son George Louis, the most pig-headed, stubborn boy who ever lived, who has round his brains such a thick crust that I defy any man or woman ever to discover what is in them. He does not care much for the match itself, but one hundred thousand thalers a year have tempted him as they would have tempted anybody else.

The marriage was doomed. George treated his new bride with contempt, humiliated her in public, and was constantly arguing. But despite his 'extra-curricular activities' he managed to sire a son and a daughter by Sophia: George Augustus, born 1683, who went on to become King George II of Great Britain; and Sophia Dorothea, born 1686, later to become the wife of King Frederick William I of Prussia, and mother of Frederick the Great. However, Sophia was more and more abandoned by George – she had done her duty by producing a male heir, and he fell back on his other amorous pursuits. Faced with such a loveless environment, Sophia developed a friendship with a Swedish Count by the name of Philip Christoph von Königsmarck. The Count had a penchant for writing somewhat indiscreet letters to Sophia, and soon they became lovers. A huge number of particularly torrid letters fell into the wrong hands (in other words they were intercepted or stolen) and ended up with Sophia's father-in-law, and by 1694 the affair had become extremely public knowledge. George was incandescent with rage and physically attacked his wife, attempting to strangle her before he was pulled off by male attendants. His parting shot was that he never wished to see her again – and he never did.

Sophia and the Swedish count decided to elope, but their plans were intercepted. Having enjoyed one last tryst with his *inamorata*, the Count was ambushed and killed by members of the palace guard. Sophia was placed under house arrest and a 'kangaroo court' was held. It found her guilty of malicious desertion – a finding which had the dual advantage of ensuring that the dowry payments from her parents would be maintained, while avoiding those awkward questions about the paternity of her children which might have arisen if she had been publicly declared to have been an adulterer. In December 1694 the marriage was dissolved. Her children were then aged 11 and 8. They were taken away from her and she was banished to the Castle of Ahlden, never to see her offspring ever again. She remained, incarcerated at Ahlden, for thirty-three years until her death in 1726. When she lay dying with kidney failure she sent a letter to George, in which she predicted that he too would be dead within the year. Delivered posthumously, it cursed him from the grave, and a popular story has it that within a week of opening the letter, George was indeed dead.

All that was in the future when George ascended the British throne, but it explains why, when he first set foot on English soil on 18 September 1714 George brought with him two women who quickly became known by the nick-names of 'The Maypole' and 'The Elephant'. The 'Maypole' was his somewhat scrawny and wafer-thin *maîtresse-en-titre* – his official mistress, by whom he had three illegitimate children. They had met when she became a maid of honour to George's mother Sophia, the Electress of Hanover, in 1691. The 'Elephant' was Sophia von Kielmansegg, mentioned earlier as possibly being his illegitimate half-sister. The royal family denied vehemently that George slept with Sophia, but as far as the British public were concerned both The Maypole and The Elephant were royal mistresses, and stories were rife about the goings-on in the Royal household. As to the Elephant, Horace Walpole recalled:

...being terrified at her enormous figure... Two fierce black eyes, large and rolling beneath two lofty arched eyebrows, two acres of cheeks spread with crimson, an ocean of neck that overflowed and was not distinguished from the lower part of her body, and no part restrained by stays; no wonder that a child dreaded such an ogress, and that the mob of London were highly diverted at the importation of so uncommon a seraglio! ... indeed nothing could be grosser than the ribaldry that was vomited out in lampoons, libels, and every channel of abuse, against the sovereign and the new court, and chaunted even in their hearing about the public streets.

Sophia was the complete opposite of the willowy Maypole, who Horace Walpole termed 'long and emaciated.'

George was known to have a propensity for large women, or, as Lord Chesterfield put it: 'No woman was amiss if she was but very willing, very fat and had great breasts!' That still leaves the question: whatever did George see in the Maypole? The Maypole, more correctly styled Ehrengard Melusine von der Schulenburg, was loathed by the English court. She was hated for being dull and stupid, for having appalling dress-sense, for being avaricious, and for condoning incest (i.e. because it was believed that she shared the King's bed with his half-sister). She must have had something going for her though, since the King kept her as his mistress for almost forty years, and during that time she became an invaluable intermediary between the King and his Ministers. She grew rich on the sale of appointments, and incurred the wrath of Grub Street hacks who resented her meddling in British politics. As Robert Walpole remarked, she was 'as much Queen of England as any ever was, ... he [George I] did everything by her.' Above all though, she and The Elephant were closely linked with the scandal of the stock market crash in 1720 known as 'The South Sea Bubble'.

Both women appeared to have shared a common link – neither of them had enough money. In the case of Melusine she had her 'three nieces' to bring up and educate

– they were in fact her illegitimate children by George, but he never acknowledged them nor contributed significantly to the cost of their upbringing. In 1719 she had been given the title of Duchess of Kendal, and she needed to maintain appearances appropriate to her status. Meanwhile, Sophia was a widow bringing up five children – in a country where the cost of living was far higher than in her native Hanover, and where keeping up a lavish lifestyle, appropriate to what she saw as her entitlement, was extremely expensive. Both women were happy to be the recipient of bribes in the form of South Sea Company stock to the value of £15,000. In addition, two of Melusine's 'nieces' each received shares to the value of £5,000.

The South Sea Company entered into a guarantee with Melusine and Sophia that £120 would be paid for every point the stock price rose above £154. In 1719 the South Sea company had sought permission to convert some thirty million pounds of the British National Debt. Up until that time government bonds were not readily tradeable because there were problems redeeming the bonds, which were often for very large amounts which could not be sub-divided. The South Sea Company hit upon a clever wheeze whereby they would convert these un-wieldy, untradable bonds into low-interest, readily tradable bonds, and they set about bribing half the cabinet, including both Lord Stanhope and Lord Sunderland, to gain support for the scheme.

The Elephant and The Maypole were enthusiastic supporters of the proposal – small wonder since they had a vested interest in the success of the venture. Stock, which had stood at £128 in January 1720, was being valued at £550 when Parliament accepted the scheme in May. The price had climbed to £1,000 by August, before the crash caused the stock to plummet to £150 by the end of September. Many wealthy families became impoverished overnight. It was rumoured that the King had received payments from the Company, having been made a Governor of it in 1718. In the aftermath of the crash it became apparent that vast bribes had been paid to prominent people at Court, and both Sophia and Melusine were named in the House of Lords during a debate on the subject of bribery and corruption. Indeed the pair of them were most fortunate that Robert Walpole, entrusted with responsibility for clearing up the mess, shielded both the King and his royal appurtenances from the risk of prosecution.

Caricatures appeared, suggesting that the Duchess of Kendal had helped Robert Knight, the Treasurer of the South Sea Company, to escape abroad. More ridicule followed with the publication of packs of 'Bubble' playing cards, while a young William Hogarth produced his first satirical engraving *The South Sea Scheme* in 1721.

The Elephant, aka Sophia, was created the Countess of Leinster in 1721, becoming the Countess of Darlington and Baroness Brentford a year later. She died in 1725 and was buried in Westminster Abbey. Melusine, who went by the nick-name of 'the Scarecrow' in Germany and 'the Goose' in Scotland, died in 1743.

King George, then aged 65, had moved on to a new mistress – his first English one – a woman by the name of Anna Brett. Horace Walpole refers to her as being 'very handsome, but dark enough by her eyes, complexion, and hair, for a Spanish beauty.' The aristocracy was horrified to hear the rumour that she was to be elevated to the rank of Countess, since Mistress Brett (as she was derogatively called) was the daughter of a mere colonel with an infamous mother. No sooner had she started throwing her weight about at the Palace, making alterations and rubbing up the Maypole the wrong way, than news of the death of the King came through. She never did get her hands on a ducal coronet, and she disappeared from court and into obscurity.

The love-life of George I was to find echoes in subsequent generations of the royal family. His contempt and loathing for his wife, his willingness to parade his mistresses in public, his estrangement from his children – all were to be repeated throughout the ensuing century. When George I died, on one of his journeys back to his beloved Hanover, the death was met with a general indifference from the British public. As one newspaper article of the day put it 'The Devil has caught him by the throat at last'. There was to be no attempt to bring his body back to Britain, and he remains one of the few British monarchs to be buried on foreign soil.

GEORGE II – two mistresses, a short temper, and a military bore.

In many ways it was a case of 'like father, like son' with the first two Georges. Both had a similar attitude towards fidelity in marriage, both had disastrous relationships with their eldest sons. These were not the only similarities apparent at the time – as the writer Alexander Pope noted in his satirical blast against the decaying spirit of dullness which pervaded the kingdom in his poem *The Dunciad*:

> *Still Dunce the second rules like Dunce the first…*

Hardly the most complimentary reference to the newly-crowned monarch.

George II had arrived in England, like his father, in 1714 with an entourage which included his wife Caroline and his mistress. The latter was Henrietta Howard, and her story is an interesting illustration of the role and status of 'the royal mistress.' Her lot was not exactly a happy one – she had faced a life of genteel poverty after her father had been killed in a duel; she had hoped to find financial security and status by marrying Charles Howard, the younger brother of the Earl of Suffolk, but her husband turned out to be a cruel, dissolute drunkard, conspicuous for his extravagance and inability to manage money. At 30 years of age, he was fourteen years her senior when she married him. Desperate to find favour at court – and to avoid his creditors – the couple had headed for Hanover in 1713 and had been rewarded by Henrietta being made a Woman of the Bedchamber to Caroline, who shortly afterwards became Princess of Wales. At least that was paid employment, which is more than can be said for her secondary appointment, namely as mistress to the future George II. The man was a monumental bore, endlessly reminiscing about his prowess on the battlefield, and was notoriously short-tempered. No doubt Princess Caroline was delighted to have Henrietta to share the burden of her husband's company. For her part, Henrietta had the advantage of being somewhat deaf. Apart from that she was charming, intelligent, and very discreet. Jonathan Swift, writing his *Character of Mrs Howard* in 1727 had this to say about the omni-present 'wife of the left hand' (as mistresses were known):

> I shall say nothing of her wit or beauty, which are allowed by all persons who can judge of either, when they hear or see her. Besides, beauty being transient, and a trifle, cannot justly make part of a character. And I leave others to celebrate her wit, because it will be of no use in that part of her character which I intend to draw … from the attendance daily paid her by the ministers, and all expectants, she is reckoned much the greatest favourite of the court at Leicester-house: a situation which she hath long affected to desire that it might not be believed. There is no politician who more carefully watches the motions and dispositions of things and persons at St James's, nor can form his language with a more imperceptible dexterity to the present posture of a court, or more early foresee what style may be proper upon any approaching juncture of affairs, whereof she can gather early intelligence without asking it, and often when even those from whom she hath it are not sensible that they are giving it to her, but equally with others admire her sagacity. Sir Robert Walpole and she both think they understand each other, and are both equally mistaken.

In 1728 Mrs Howard managed to obtain a Separation Order from her cruel wastrel of a husband, although this left her totally reliant on the comparative pittance she received from being one of half a dozen Women of the Bedchamber. For twenty years she put up with the boredom linked to her somewhat degrading role as a menial servant, helping Caroline in her ablutions and assisting with her toilette. In the same way she put up with George, not just when he was living as part of his father's household at St James's Palace, but later when he moved to Leicester House and set up a rival court. By the time he became George II in 1727 the King seemed to be going through the motions with Henrietta – almost as if convention required him to keep a mistress and to spend the evenings with her. Writing some years later, Horace Walpole described their relationship:

> *No established mistress of a sovereign ever enjoyed less of the brilliancy of the situation than Lady Suffolk. Watched and thwarted by the Queen, disclaimed by the minister, she owed to the dignity of her own behaviour, and to the contradiction of her enemies, the chief respect that was paid to her, and which but ill compensated for the slavery of her attendance, and the mortifications she endured. She was elegant; her lover the reverse, and most unentertaining, and void of confidence in her. His motions too were measured by etiquette and the clock. He visited her every evening at nine; but with such dull punctuality, that he frequently walked about his chamber for ten minutes with his watch in his hand, if the stated minute was not arrived.*

Both of them must have found the convention extremely tiresome but it was a further four years before Henrietta could extricate herself from her royal paramour. Her escape came when her brother-in-law the Earl of Suffolk died. Whereas her estranged husband assumed the title of Earl (entitling her to be styled 'Countess') the late Earl's fortune was specifically bequeathed to Henrietta, with not a penny going to her husband. Even better fortune followed when her husband died, leaving her a free woman. Besides, a Countess could not be a mere Woman of the Bedchamber and, in 1731, she was promoted to being Mistress of the Robes. Soon, financial freedom enabled her to escape the cloying atmosphere of the Royal Court, and the public were astonished when she left the King and Queen in her wake and de-camped to Richmond where she built a fine Palladian mansion at Marble Hill. She had previously secured a royal pension of £2,000 a year. To the amazement of the public and amidst much newspaper comment, she married an MP by the name of George Berkeley. The year was 1735 and they enjoyed eleven happy years together before he died aged 57. This left Henrietta with her pension, but not much else, and even that was to end when George II died. Ironically she had 'bumped into' the King two days before he died, when her coach passed next to the royal carriage in one of London's narrow streets. The King stared blankly at her, apparently not even recognizing who she was. Her fortune spent and her royal pension having ended, her last years were spent in considerable poverty before she died in 1767.

George II's other acknowledged and official mistress was Amalie Sophie Marianne von Wallmoden, who shared the royal bed from the mid-1730s until the King's death in 1760. The pair of them feature in an etching dating from 1738 entitled *Solomon in his glory* held by the British Museum, showing the King sitting legs apart, while his mistress strokes his inner thigh. Amelie was born into a prominent family in Hanover and was described as being 'very well shaped, not tall, nor low; has no fine features, but very agreeable in the main.' She married one German, and then took another as a lover, bearing what was widely assumed to be the King's child in 1736, although he never acknowledged paternity. She was however elevated to the title of the Duchess of Yarmouth.

In 1739 Samuel Johnson had attacked the King's relationship in verse:

> *His tortured sons shall die before his face*
> *While he lies melting in a lewd embrace.*

This referred to the schism which had opened up between George II and his son Prince Frederick. Two years earlier Frederick had been banished from St James's Palace, and had set up a rival court which attracted many of those opposed to the King and his government. The antipathy between father and son was mutual. George II declared: 'Our first-born is the greatest ass, the greatest liar, the greatest canaille and the greatest beast in the whole world, and we heartily wish he were out of it.' Reflecting on the first time that he met his son's prospective bride, the King is supposed to have remarked 'I did not think that grafting my half-witted coxcomb upon a madwoman would improve the breed.'

The distaste for Frederick was shared by Sir Robert Walpole, who described the Prince as being a 'poor, weak, irresolute, false, lying, dishonest, contemptible wretch that nobody loves, that nobody believes, that nobody will trust.' Even the Queen (i.e. Frederick's own mother) described him as 'an avaricious, sordid monster.' Stories abounded about Frederick's love-life, giving rise to the opera *Vanelia: or the Amours of the Great* written by James Miller in 1732. It may not have been performed, but it contained over a score of songs similar to those in *The Beggars Opera*, all based upon an alleged affair between the young Prince and a lady named Vane.

The public were fascinated by the royal spat, with Frederick, for his part, describing his father as 'an obstinate, self-indulgent, miserly martinet with an insatiable sexual appetite.' No love lost there then! Frederick died in March 1751, possibly as a result of a burst abscess on the lung. Another version of his death suggests he developed septicaemia after being hit on the head by a cricket ball (giving rise to the witticism that this was the first case of play stopped reign …). His demise resulted in this epigram which appeared in Horace Walpole's *Memoirs of the last ten years of the reign of George II*, published in 1822:

Here lies Fred,
Who was alive and is dead:
Had it been his father,
I had much rather;
Had it been his brother,
Still better than another;
Had it been his sister,
No-one would have missed her;
Had it been the whole generation,
So much better for the nation.
But since 'tis only Fred,
Who was alive, and is dead,
There's no more to be said.

After the death of George II's daughter Louisa at the end of 1756, the King made this rather poignant comment:

This has been a fatal year for my family. I lost my eldest son – but I am glad of it …
Now [Louisa] is gone. I know I did not love my children when they were young: I
hated to have them running into my room; but now I love them as well as most fathers.

It somehow epitomises the failings of the Hanoverians in terms of family values. No-one regarded the King as 'father of the nation' or expected him to be an inspirational role model. In October 1760, George II died of an aortic aneurism, while seated on the close stool (i.e. the toilet). At that point the throne passed to his grandson George William Frederick, eldest son of the late Frederick, Prince of Wales.

GEORGE III – not a mistress in sight, but a prolific parent
The grandson of George II was 22 years old when he came to the throne. It is ironic that his reign coincided with an explosion in the trade of satirical prints. They mocked his avarice, they mocked his miserliness, they mocked his simple tastes, and his interest in agriculture, but the one thing they could not do was mock his family values and constancy to the woman who became his queen.

As a 23-year-old, he had met Princess Charlotte of Mecklenburg-Strelitz for the very first time on the morning of his wedding in September 1761, but appears to have been completely smitten with her. They had fifteen children together, nine sons and six daughters, and as far as is known the King broke with family tradition and never once took a mistress. Not that this stopped a curious story emerging in 1770. This was to the effect that, as Prince of Wales, he had secretly married 'a fair Quakeress' by the name of Hannah Lightfoot on 17 April 1759, at Curzon Street Chapel, and that they had two children together. In 1788 Samuel William Fores published a caricature entitled *The Fair Quaker of Cheltenham* showing the young monarch addressing his ardour to a young lady under the shade of an overhanging tree. Not a shred of evidence supported this wild allegation, but 'the story had legs' to the extent that in the course of the next century various spurious claims were put forward. Futile applications were made through the courts, seeking to declare the children of Queen Charlotte illegitimate, on the basis that the King had married her bigamously. It shows the willingness of people to publish (and read) scandalous stories about the Royals. The idea that 'truth should never get in the way of a good story' is nothing new.

But if the third George found wedded bliss, the same could not be said of his siblings. Take the sad case of his younger sister Caroline Matilda. Married at 15 by proxy to a man she had never met: a drunken, whoring, Danish king by the name of Christian VII, she was stuck in a foreign court where she did not speak the language and knew nothing of their customs.

SATURDAY 28.
    The marriage of her R.H. Princes*Carolina*
Matilda with the K.of *Denmark*, was appointed to be folemnized by proxy, at St *James's*,
the firſt of *October*, at half an hour paſt ſeven
in the evening; at which time none but peers
and peereſſes, peers eldeſt ſons,& peers daughters, privy counſellors and wives, and foreign
miniſters, are to be admitted. *Gaz.*

Her husband declined to stop visiting the local brothels, and in all probability gave her a nasty case of the Pox as a result. She sought treatment from a Dr Struensee who offered her rather more than just a cure. They became lovers, even though he was nearly twice her age, probably with the full knowledge and connivance of the King. She had a child by her lover, but in due course, pressure from disgruntled courtiers forced the mentally unstable King to take action against the happy pair. The ambitious but foolish doctor was tortured into making a confession, and was executed in 1772. The Queen was tried for adultery, convicted, divorced, sent into exile, caught scarlet fever, and was dead at the age of 23. And not once did her brother George III offer any sympathy or support. On hearing of her death, the King even barred her body from being returned for burial in Westminster Abbey.

The Q—n of D—n—rk conveying to Prison.

If he felt that his sister brought shame to the family, one wonders what George III must have thought of the antics of his other siblings. His brother the Duke of Gloucester went behind the King's back and secretly married Maria Walpole, the Dowager Countess of Waldegrave. She was an illegitimate granddaughter of Sir Robert Walpole (Image 63). Even that unsuitable marriage did not deter him from having children by his mistress Lady Almeria Carpenter.

Another brother, Henry Duke of Cumberland, was caught *in flagrante* with Lady Grosvenor in 1769. Lord Grosvenor was not amused, and sued the Duke for damages of £10,000 for criminal conversation – and won. Servants were brought forth to say that they had seen the bed 'very much tumbled, but not the bolster.' The evidence was damning, and the defence had to rely on the argument that Lord Grosvenor had been the first to break the marriage vows – a number of women (including whores from local brothels) came forward and gave evidence that he had slept with each of them 'as man and wife.' The case is mentioned later in relation to Lady Grosvenor, but it was the royal connection which produced the media frenzy. Evidence from royal servants revealed minute details about royal lifestyles – what time the Duke rose, where he took breakfast, what time he visited his club and so on, bringing these facts into the public domain. In many ways, this fascination with the day-to-day aspects of royal life has remained unaltered to the present day.

The court case was manna from heaven for the gossip-mongers of the day, not least because the lovers had been so indiscreet as to write particularly revealing letters about their affair. These letters had been intercepted by the cuckolded husband, and he had the foresight to have them copied so that they could be read out, in all their salacious details, in court. All this gave the judge the chance to pontificate that he hoped that the Duke would:

> ... *direct himself to nobler pursuits than the seduction of the wife of a Peer, and incline him to copy from a very near relation of his [meaning His Majesty] whose conjugal attachments, abstracted from his other virtues, not only ornamented the throne he filled, but shewed a bright example to his subjects in general.*

Within weeks, the public could buy 'Genuine copies of letters passing between His Royal Highness and Lady Grosvenor' together with a full transcript of the trial. The book became a best-seller. The Duke subsequently went on to marry a commoner, against the express wishes of the monarch. This led directly to the passing of the 1772 Royal Marriages Act which declared any marriage by a member of the royal family, without the consent of the monarch, to be illegal. The Prince's bride was the beautiful but far from virtuous Anne Houghton – a woman Horace Walpole described as being 'as artful as Cleopatra.'

But if his siblings disappointed the King with their inability to keep things buttoned up properly, nothing could have prepared him for the licentious and debauched behaviour of his own children. Later, the Duke of Wellington would describe the offspring of the king as 'the damnedest millstones ever hung around a government's neck', while the poet Shelley coined the phrase 'royal vampires' to describe the royal brood. None could rival the excesses of the Prince of Wales, later to become George IV.

THE PRINCE OF WALES – the satirist's dream
It is interesting to contrast the rather flattering formal portraits of a handsome young man, painted by artists such as Sir Thomas Lawrence, with the grotesque caricature shown as Image 39 made in 1792 by the acerbic James Gillray.

Aged 17, the Prince set his sights on seducing the young, married, but impecunious actress Mary Robinson. Negotiations were handled by Lord Malden (who also fancied her something rotten). As mentioned previously, Mary had appeared as 'Perdita' in *A Winter's Tale*, and the Prince used his Lordship to deliver a steamy correspondence between the Prince, calling himself Florizel, and the girl he called Perdita. The equivalent of the modern red-tops (especially the *Morning Post* and the *Morning*

Herald) quickly got wind of the intrigue – but were unable to work out whether Mary was having an affair with the Prince, or with Lord Malden, or even with both at the same time. Mary was showered with gifts from her royal admirer, and given a written bond in the sum of £20,000 payable when she was 21, as a sort of 'signing-on fee'. Eventually she gave in to his princely blandishments, and embarked on a hugely visible display of extravagance, with her own liveried coach, and all the latest fashions. Images 51 and 53 give two contemporary satirical views of the relationship, with *The Goats canter to Windsor* (Image 51) showing the Prince and his Perdita sitting atop a high gig. Three pairs of goats pull the vehicle, with Charles James Fox (shown by a fox's head) riding as postilion. The carriage is accompanied by three other riders on goats, the leading one being ridden (backwards) by the cuckolded husband Thomas Robinson. *Florizel and Perdita* (Image 53) is a composite portrait of the two lovebirds, and shows the despairing figure of George III on the left uttering the words 'Oh! My Son, My Son.' On the right a shelf held up by horns (the mark of the cuckold) supports the bust of Thomas Robinson, over the title 'King of Cuckolds'.

The Press were fascinated by her equipage – the *Rambler Magazine* gave a most fulsome description in its edition of 4 December 1783:

> *Mrs. Robinson now sports a carriage which is the admiration of all the charioteering circles in the vicinity of St. James's: the body Carmelite and silver, ornamented with a French mantle, and the cypher is a wreath of flowers; the carriage scarlet and silver, the seat-cloth richly ornamented with a silver fringe. Mrs. Robinson's livery is green faced with yellow, and richly trimmed with broad silver lace; the harness ornamented with stars of silver, richly chased and elegantly finished. The inside of the carriage is lined with white silk, embellished with scarlet trimmings. The Perdita has led a very splendid example to her impure sisters in the charioteering style, which few of them will be able to follow!*

This extract clearly demonstrate that whatever she did she made news, and whatever she wore made fashion.

But after less than two years the Prince did the equivalent of sending a text to end the relationship – he sent Lord Malden round with a message. It was a bolt from the blue, especially when the Prince made it clear that he had no intention of honouring his Bond. Mary had by then incurred debts of £7,000 and clearly faced the prospect of imprisonment since she had no way of satisfying her creditors. It was only when Mary threatened to release his love letters and demanded £25,000 to keep quiet that the Prince was persuaded to pay her a lump sum of £5,000 and a

Image 20. A Rake's Progress. (See pp. 20 and 59)

Image 22. The Rival Knights. (See p. 59)

Image 21. Cunnyseurs. (See p. 20)

Image 23. A Lobby Flesh-Monger. A young man negotiates a fee for the young lady. (See p. 25)

Image 24. The Covent Garden Frolick. Morning breaks, after a hard night on the town. (See p. 27)

Image 25. Nancy Parsons. (See p. 36)

Image 26. Kitty Fisher. (See p. 37)

Image 27. Grace Dalrymple Elliott. (See pp. 42 and 87)

Image 28. Frances Abington. (See p. 44)

Image 29. The Bird of Paradise. (See p. 40)

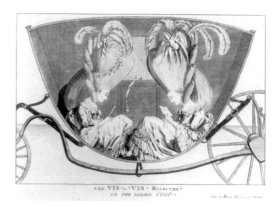

Image 30. The vis-à-vis bisected. (See pp. 31 and 42)

Image 31. The General Out-Generall'd. (See p. 52)

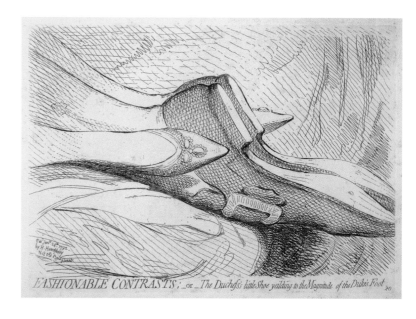

Image 32. Fashionable Contrasts. (See p. 70)

Image 33. The Light Guinea. (See p. 60)

Image 34. A Wink from the Bagnio. (See p. 54)

Image 35. The Beggar's Opera. (See p. 58)

Image 36. Very Slippy Weather. (See p. 69)

Image 37. Sandwich Carrots. (See p. 70)

Image 38. Contemplations upon a Coronet.
(See p. 112)

Image 39. A Voluptuary under the Horrors of
Digestion. (See pp. 70 and 85)

Image 40. The Devil to Pay. The future William IV sleeps soundly after a night with Dorothea Jordan. (See pp. 72 and 93)

Image 41. Symptoms of Lewdness. Mrs Fitzherbert and the Countess of Buckinghamshire share a box at the opera. (See p. 72)

Image 42. Fashionable Jockeyship. (See p. 88)

Image 43. A Peep into Brest. (See p. 72)

Image 45. Launching a Frigate. (See p. 72)

Image 44. Which Way shall I turn me. (See p. 72)

yearly payment of £500. In return she agreed to surrender the bond. She embarked on various affairs, both with Lord Malden and, it was rumoured, with Charles James Fox, before ending up in a tempestuous relationship with the dashing Colonel Banastre Tarleton, featured later.

The Prince's attentions had turned to Grace Dalrymple Elliott, a Scottish socialite mentioned in Chapter Four, and who had abandoned her somewhat older husband for a succession of wealthy and well-connected lovers. Her portrait by Thomas Gainsborough appears as Image 27. In 1782 she gave birth to a child, which she claimed was fathered by the Prince, but it is apparent that the father could have been one of a handful of suspects. Two years later, the Prince introduced Grace to the Duc d' Orleans and they quickly became lovers, leaving the Prince free to pursue other dalliances.

Next up was Lady Elizabeth Lamb, Viscountess Melbourne. In 1784 she had a son, George Lamb, who was generally assumed to be fathered by the Prince, although her husband dutifully acknowledged the child as his own. She was the inspiration for Sheridan's character Lady Teazle in *The School for Scandal*. By 1785 the Prince had fallen head-over-heels for Maria Fitzherbert. They married the same year, contrary to the provisions of the Royal Marriages Act, which meant that the union had no legal validity.

Maria is shown on the right in Image 41 in *Symptoms of Lewdness* with her friend Albinia, the Duchess of Buckinghamshire. Both ladies enjoyed high society parties and excursions to the opera, and the print shows them behaving with considerable indecency, breasts bared for all the world to see. Albinia was an unusual woman in the sense that she was the illegitimate daughter of an illegitimate mother, and yet ended up married to a Duke. This did not prevent her from running a crooked Faro bank, and eventually she was charged with running an illegal gaming house. Such minor matters did not preclude her being a confidante of Maria, who appears in the print wearing a miniature portrait of the Prince of Wales above her impressive décolletage.

A number of children were later borne by Maria, but these could not be regarded as legitimate royal offspring. Despite his constant philandering, Maria lived openly with the Prince until 1811, when the Prince, by then Regent, felt compelled to enter into a legal marriage with Caroline of Brunswick. However, during those years the Prince had innumerable affairs – one with the wife of a double-bass player at Drury Lane, another with Elizabeth Armistead (featured earlier), and another with a beautiful young singer called Mrs Anna Maria Crouch, to whom he gave a bond of £10,000.

The Press revelled in lampooning the debauched antics of the Prince and his cronies, especially as it was clear that there was no love lost between the King and his eldest child. In November 1788 the King was thought to be seriously ill and at his last gasp. This did not stop the Prince carousing with his drinking friends, Colonel George Hanger and the playwright Sheridan. Thomas Rowlandson shows the intoxicated trio bursting into the King's bedroom, with the Prince uttering the words 'Damme, come along, I'll see if the old fellow is ---- [dead] or not?' (Image 55)

The Prince was not exactly a one-woman-at-a-time-man. If for any reason he could not find a mistress available to satisfy his whims, he would eagerly set off for the local whore-house and take his pleasures with whoever was available. If he needed extra invigoration he could always rely on a spot of flagellation at the home of Mrs Collett in Tavistock Court, off Covent Garden. It seems that this particular predilection was shared with his younger brother the Duke of Kent (father to Queen Victoria). He was widely known to get his kicks from watching men under his command being flogged almost to the point of death. He too had a succession of mistresses before he 'settled down' with a wife, although in his case he did manage to keep the same mistress, called Madame de Saint-Laurent (born Thérèse-Bernardine Montgenet) for twenty-eight years.

In 1794 the Prince of Wales took up with Frances, Lady Jersey, daughter of the Bishop of Raphoe and by then an attractive 41-year-old grandmother. She helped persuade the Prince to finish with Mrs Fitzherbert (who was paid an annuity of £3,000 a year for her past loyalty) and to marry Caroline of Brunswick. Lady Jersey simply did not perceive the new Queen as being a threat to her ability to influence and control the Prince. Indeed she became one of the new Queen's Ladies in Waiting. Gillray's *Fashionable Jockeyship* appears as Image 42 and shows the Prince riding the cuckolded Earl of Jersey to the bedside of Frances Villiers, Countess of Jersey.

Poor Caroline, she really did have a tough time with the Prince. Her alliance was engineered for political reasons – she was Protestant, she was his cousin, and by marrying her the Prince hoped to get rid of his mountainous debts by pleasing his father the King. The engagement took place before they had even met each other. Wellington later remarked that Caroline was a woman 'of indelicate manners, indifferent character and not very inviting appearance' and reckoned that the match was prompted by Lady Jersey 'from a hope that disgust with a wife would secure constancy to a mistress'. If that was so, then her strategy worked. When the wedding took place on 8 April 1795 the Prince was so disgusted at the sight of his bride that he got utterly drunk and passed out at the side of the matrimonial bed. He loathed her for what he saw as her dirty, uncouth habits. It did not stop him performing his marital duties on at least one occasion, and nine months later, the Queen gave birth to a baby (the Prince's only legitimate child, and hence second in line to the succession). Immediately afterwards the Prince made a new Will, apparently leaving his estate to the woman he described as 'my wife' i.e. Maria Fitzherbert. To Caroline he bequeathed one shilling.

Caricaturists revelled at the hostility between the new queen and Maria Fitzherbert, with *The Rage* showing the pair squaring up to each other (see Image 54).

Image 46 shows Isaac Cruikshank's *Future Prospects*, with the Prince of Wales kicking over a tea table at which his wife Caroline sits with their baby Princess Charlotte. In the Prince's pocket there is a map of Jersey (a reference to his affair with the Countess) while the Earl of Jersey, sporting the cuckold's horns, is saying 'My wife is waiting for you in the next room.'

Within months of the royal wedding it was apparent to all that the union was doomed, and the gossip was not helped when Caroline started to be portrayed as the 'wronged woman', making her extremely popular with the public. The public had had enough of the philandering and grossly extravagant Prince. This was at a time when he was ostentatiously spending vast sums of money on refurbishing and furnishing Carlton House. During a time of national shortages, and war with France, the Prince appeared to have no semblance of sensitivity. His drunkenness, his whoring, his gambling and his excesses gave the Press and the Print Shops every opportunity to vilify him.

The Royal couple separated in 1795 and for ten years Caroline was rumoured to have had a succession of affairs. Admiral Sir Sidney Smith, Captain Thomas Manby, the politician George Canning and the artist Thomas Lawrence were all rumoured to have been lovers. Image 48 shows Queen Caroline accompanying Alderman Wood in a print entitled *A wooden substitute – any Port in a Storm*. Cavorting in the fields are rabbits and goats, both of which were regarded as symbols of carnal appetites.

In 1806 a 'secret' commission known as the 'Delicate Investigation' was set up to investigate the rumours of her adultery, but the 'secret' was soon revealed by the Press. The commission decided that there was insufficient evidence to show that Caroline had gone beyond being merely flirtatious. However, she was increasingly ostracized by high society, who preferred to side with the Prince, although the general public were far more inclined towards the hard-done-by Caroline. Her position became untenable and in 1814 she agreed to leave the country in return for an annual payment of a hefty £35,000.

By then the Prince had moved on to the good-looking but somewhat stout Isabella, Lady Hertford. She was the Prince's mistress from 1807 to 1819, and was then succeeded to the Prince's favours by Elizabeth, Marchioness Conyngham (see Image 52). The print shows the rotund George IV, dressed as his royal forbear Henry IV, about to be kissed by the well-rounded Marchioness.

Elizabeth was by then a voluptuous 48-year-old – a shrewd, calculating and greedy woman with a penchant for collecting jewels. Her behaviour led the public to award her the nick-name 'the Vice Queen'. The Prince was perfectly willing to indulge her, and showered her with gifts – he seemed childishly besotted with her. But she was never popular at court, being considered common and vulgar. She was the one by the Prince's side, and in his bed, when the Prince succeeded to the throne in 1820 on the death of his father George III. It cannot have been an easy time for her, because the new King was immediately embroiled in a fresh show-down with his estranged wife, the unloved and unlovely Caroline. While she was in exile she had entered a relationship with an Italian by the name of Bartolomeo Pergami – they were rumoured to be living openly together. They were an unlikely pair – she somewhat short and dumpy, Pergami tall and rather hairy. In *Dignity* (Image 49) the singularly unattractive Queen sits next to her bearded friend. A young man declines to sit at their table, with the words 'I shall not degrade myself and the service by sitting at the table with such a fellow as that.' The pair also appear in Image 56 in a print entitled *Installation of a Knight Companion of the Bath* showing the naked Queen in a scandalous bathroom scene, watched by servants who are peeping in through a partly-open door.

Cartoonists mocked them constantly, and the King was determined to end the humiliation by pressing for a divorce. He was, however, keen to avoid a court case in which salacious details of his own infidelities would be placed in the spotlight. The King had ordered a commission of enquiry which travelled to Milan and sought to interrogate the house servants in order to establish that adultery had taken place. The commissioners returned to London with two sacks of incriminating evidence and handed these in to Parliament. George IV called for the two green bags containing evidence of his wife's adultery to be placed before the House of Commons and House of Lords. Cruikshank, along with many others, saw this as 'the kettle calling the pot black' and shows the King as having a much larger 'sack of evidence' than his Queen (see Image 50).

The House conducted what was in effect a public trial of Caroline. All the messy details came out but the public was appalled at the hypocrisy of the situation. Tens of thousands signed a petition in favour of the Queen. Civil unrest was increasing, and the new King was hugely unpopular. The Bill before Parliament, stripping the Queen of her title, was dropped and instead Caroline was offered £50,000 per annum to resume her European exile. But when her husband planned his coronation, which took place on 19 July 1821 at Westminster Abbey, Caroline decided that, as she was technically still the wife of the new monarch, she should be recognized as such at this public ceremony. George IV banned her from the coronation. Nevertheless she turned up with her entourage and tried unsuccessfully to force access, finally being turned away at bayonet point. Although she was jeered by the watching hordes on account of her undignified behaviour, it did nothing to endear the new King to his subjects.

Later that same day Caroline fell ill. Rumours leaked out that she had been poisoned – and Caroline was convinced that this was the case. When she died, just three weeks later, the exact cause of death was unproved. Maybe she had cancer, or maybe the King had indeed given orders to be rid of her. What is clear is that there was an attempt by the establishment to prevent a funeral procession passing through the City of London, *en route* to the port of Harwich so that she could be buried in her native Brunswick. The public were having none of this insult to her memory, and tore down the barriers put up by the authorities. The mob insisted that the cortege should process through Westminster and central London, and in the chaos which ensued, the army charged the crowds with sabres drawn, attempting to disperse it. Granite setts from the roads were dug up and hurled at the soldiers, and two members of the public were killed. So much for a dignified end to a sad and tawdry story.

The King reigned for ten years – a decade in which he became more and more withdrawn from public life. All that eating and drinking had taken its toll: he had been grossly overweight for years, and by 1824 had a waist measurement of 50in. He suffered from gout as well as from breathing difficulties and possibly from laudanum poisoning. The extravagance and debauchery of the King made him almost universally despised – writers and commentators at the time were enraged by him because, as mentioned earlier, he sued one of their number, Leigh Hunt, for criminal libel and was awarded £500 damages. Leigh Hunt had called the grossly overweight Prince 'fat'. The description of him as an overweight lecherous drunkard and wastrel was not only self-evidently true, but the Press was also outraged that the courts were prepared to overlook the obvious, and to kow-tow to his Royal Highness in a most shameful way.

Meanwhile the middle classes were fed-up with their taxes being used to fund the King's reckless expenditure; the poor loathed him because he was cavorting at a time when they were starving as a result of the food shortages and rampant inflation which marked the period of the Napoleonic Wars. When he died in 1830 *The Times* reported that 'There never was an individual less regretted by his fellow-creatures than this deceased king'.

By then, he had already outlived his brother Frederick, Duke of York. He is remembered, not for being Commander-in-Chief of the British army, but for the nursery rhyme about marching his men up to the top of the hill, and marching them down again. Curiously, he was originally destined for the Church, having been made a bishop at the tender age of six months. But a life of drunken debauchery was more attractive to Frederick than anything religion could offer. He had married the smallpox-ravaged Princess Frederica of Prussia in 1791 but although they were technically married for nearly thirty years, the actual number of nights spent under the same roof could be counted on one hand. She preferred the company of her menagerie of monkeys, dogs and the odd kangaroo to that of her corpulent drunkard of a husband, and who can blame her?

After a number of mistresses, the Duke of York eventually moved in with the wonderfully corrupt Mary Anne Clarke, a lady who was renowned for having dispensed her favours amongst great swathes of the nobility. It may be ungallant to say that, having married a stone-mason, she resembled a foundation stone (always getting laid). She set about making money by using her royal connection to sell army commissions. She was not particularly discreet about it, and gave evidence before the House of Commons that the sale of commissions was done with the full knowledge of the Prince, who promptly resigned as Commander in Chief. Well, for a while, because eventually he was reinstated, thereby proving that you cannot keep a bad man down. Isaac Cruikshank had brought the scandal into the public domain with his scathing print *The Modern Circe* (see Image 57). It shows Mrs Clarke wearing the voluminous military cape belonging to the Duke of York, offering cover to a host of diminutive soldiers, civilians and clergymen, all with their arms out-stretched. They represent all the people who had been helped by her to benefit from the corrupt sale of commissions, ecclesiastical livings, and so on.

Mrs Clarke threatened to reveal the Duke's love letters, unless she was paid a small fortune to keep quiet. He paid up. Not inclined to brevity, in 1809 she published *The Authentic and Impartial Life of Mrs. Mary Anne Clarke, Including Numerous Royal and Other Original Letters, and Anecdotes of Distinguished Persons, Which Have Escaped Suppression, with a Compendious View of the Whole Proceedings, Illustrative of the Late Important Investigation of the Conduct of His Royal Highness the Duke of York, &C. &C. and a Curious Poem.* Other kiss-and-tell revelations led to her being hauled off to Court for libel: she was imprisoned for nine months. She withdrew to France and died in 1852 aged 76.

The Duke of York died childless in 1827. Three years later the King also died, largely unloved, and was succeeded to the throne by his younger brother William, Duke of Clarence.

WILLIAM IV – the sailor king.
It is difficult to be fair about the man who went on to become William IV: he had the same mistress, Dorothea Jordan, for twenty years, sired ten children by her, and then when pressure was brought to bear to produce a male heir, promptly ditched his 'wife of the left hand' in order to marry a woman eighteen years his junior.

He had started as he meant to go on: allegedly raping a maid in the employment of his mother the Queen when he was just 14. When his father, George III, decided that the navy would make a man of him, he was posted to the West Indies, whereupon he became an unrivalled expert on the goings-on in the brothels of Jamaica. He had a particular penchant for young black girls, a fact which did not pass the notice of James Gillray. *Nauticus* in Image 58 is fairly bland, with its comment that his lips were so kissable, but *Wouski* (Image 59) shows him in a hammock with his legs wrapped around an adoring native girl. Shown exhibiting a generous amount of cleavage, maybe she represents one of many who caused him to contract venereal disease. He spent his time whoring and drinking to excess, and even lived openly for a while with a known prostitute.

In time he fell for the charms of Dorothea Jordan. She was a famous actress, renowned for having the best legs in the business, with a string of lovers behind her. Her surname was actually 'Bland' and there is no evidence that there ever was a 'Mr Jordan'. The name was a godsend to the caricaturists, because a 'jordan' was another name for a chamber pot. Cue endless jokes combining lavatorial humour and sexual puns. Image 40 is a caricature by Gillray entitled *The Devil to Pay – The Wife Metamorphosed, or Neptune reposing after fording the Jordan.* It shows Dorothea relaxing in bed with the Duke. She exclaims 'What pleasant dreams I have had tonight. Methought I was in Paradise…' The Duke of Clarence sleeps contentedly. The chamber pot under the bed is inscribed with the far from complimentary words 'Public Jordan – open to all parties.' In a similar vein, *The Tar and the Jordan* (Image 61) shows the sailor prince crowned with a chamber pot, rushing past a group of complaining women, with the words 'Why, what a rout is here about a Damn'd crack'd bum-boat.' Another cracked chamber pot is being dragged along the street, tied to the Prince's wrist by a piece of string, while a startled flock of sheep run towards their drover.

In 1791 Dorothea moved in with the Prince at Bushy House, while still occasionally appearing on stage. In an era before birth control she seemed to spend much of her time producing royal bastards, all of them given the surname 'FitzClarence.' But all the royal dukes started to come under pressure to do the right thing and get married – none of them had produced a legitimate heir. So the Duke of Clarence got rid of Dorothea, offering her a yearly payment in return for her agreeing not to go on the stage. She accepted – she had little choice – and in return she was allowed custody of the daughters (but not the sons). Three years later she broke her side of the bargain, in order to try and raise money to help her spendthrift son-in-law. The Prince heard that she had resurrected her acting career, and tried to stop her annuity altogether and forced her to surrender custody of the girls. Dorothea fled to Paris in 1815 to avoid her creditors, and she died in utter penury just one year later.

Meanwhile William was scouring Europe looking for a suitable girl to marry – difficult, since many had either seen or heard of this un-prepossessing man with somewhat loathsome behaviour. He seems to have employed something of a scatter-gun approach to proposing marriage: eventually, after what were rumoured to be eighteen refusals, he found someone willing to take him on in marriage. She was Princess Adelaide of Saxe-Meiningen, unkindly described as being 'frightful, very ugly with a horrid complexion.' She had never met the groom when she arrived in Britain in 1818, to be confronted with the news that hers was to be part of a double wedding. The 'two-for-the-price-of-one' deal saw both William and his younger brother Edward, Duke of Kent, marry girls who between them spoke not one word of English. The wedding service and the vows were therefore printed in German, but with phonetic sub-titles in English.

Once he succeeded his brother to the throne, William actually achieved a measure of popularity – not because he was any good, but because he was seen as being not quite as revolting as his predecessor. When he died in 1837, *The Spectator* recorded the view that 'His late Majesty, though at times a jovial and, for a king, an honest man, was a weak, ignorant, commonplace sort of person'.

William was followed onto the throne by his niece Victoria. In practice she was the only legitimate offspring produced by the seven sons of George III. Apart from Edward, Duke of Kent, not one had a legitimate heir still living when William IV died. Charles Williams, caricaturist, had shown the Dukes of Clarence, Cumberland and Cambridge, together with their wives, in a cartoon called *A scene in the new farce called the rivals – or, A visit to the heir presumptive*. It came out in 1819, the year Victoria was born and is available in both the Royal Collection and at the British Museum. In it, the royal princes discuss their prospects of producing a male heir. ('I'll try again, and a boy too, I'll warrant' and 'Don't be in haste, I shall soon put you all out – my dear Duchess assures me it will be a boy. You will never have another one – it is all over at your house!' while another Duke exclaims '...our labour is all in vain...'

In the event, none of them produced a male heir and the crown passed to Queen Victoria in 1837.

One other brother is worthy of mention – George III's son Ernest. He was perhaps the most hated of the lot, suspected of rape, murder and more besides. The public loathed the Prince, and were prepared to believe that his depravity stretched as far as incest. His sister Sophia was widely rumoured to be pregnant in 1800. Cloistered away in the convent-like but hormone-charged atmosphere of the royal palace, she can rarely have come into contact with any other males, and perhaps this is how the rumour came about. It was suggested that she may have gone away to Weymouth to give birth to her child away from prying eyes – and that even her father, the King, was not told of her condition for fear that the news would trigger off one of his attacks of madness.

Stories emerged that the baby's father was an equerry by the name of Thomas Garth. He was thirty-three years her senior, with a large port-wine birthmark on his face, and sounded an unlikely bed-mate for the sickly Princess. He may just have been a 'fall guy', prepared to take the blame because he was willing to deflect the public from the scandalous truth that the real father of the child was her own brother, Ernest. It was alleged that Ernest had tried to rape Sophia on more than one occasion. However, it has to be said that much of the bile aimed at the Prince was politically motivated, always reaching a crescendo when he was in Britain, and diminishing when he returned to his beloved Hanover, where he became King in 1837. But the rumours about the Prince siring his sister's child gained currency in 1829 when a man claiming to be the offspring of the union came forward with letters which allegedly incriminated the royal family. His attempt at blackmail failed, but the story helped fuel the fire of gossip and public criticism of the Prince. Sophia for her part went blind and lived to the ripe old age of 70, while Ernest soldiered on until his death in 1851. He had been a thorn in the side of his niece Queen Victoria, claiming that the jewellery belonging to his mother Queen Charlotte should pass to him as the eldest surviving male heir. Victoria refused to hand over the jewels on the basis that they belonged to the Crown – the British Crown – and took great delight in wearing them ostentatiously on every possible occasion. It was only when her hated uncle died that she reluctantly returned the jewels to Hanover.

His death on 18 November 1851 was noted in *The Times* with the words 'the good that can be said of the Royal dead is little or none.'

In general, all that you can say of the royal brothers is that their love of fornicating was not at issue. Their tastes in women were varied and unconstrained, but no-one could accuse them of running their private lives in order to give a good example to the lesser orders. George III may have set out to give a good example, but his sons had no such inhibitions. And what was good enough for them was good enough for their coterie of hangers on – mostly aristocrats with the money and lifestyle to keep pace with their royal drinking partners.

Chapter Seven

Adulterous Aristocrats

Brooks' Club still has a record of the bet made in 1785 by Lord Cholmondeley with Lord Derby to the effect that 'Lord Ch…y' would join what would these days be termed the Mile High Club. There is no record of how close 'Lord Ch….y' got to winning his bet, or whether 'Mrs E…t' went along with the idea. She was Grace Dalrymple Elliot, with whom his Lordship had a lengthy affair. The wager demonstrates the very open nature of such conquests, as well as showing the popularity of ever more adventurous and obscure places where sex might take place.

> Laſt week, at Brooke's, Lord Ch—y offered to bet five thouſand guineas, that he would aſcend with Mrs. E——t in an Air Balloon, to the height of ſix thouſand feet, and perform in the aerial regions, the uſual ceremonial rites, paid at the ſhrine of the laughter-loving queen. The earl of D—— and ſeveral others accepted of the wager, thinking the experiment impracti-cable.

MARY ELIZABETH BOWES – like Mother, like son.

Mary Elizabeth Bowes was one of those figures the public loved to hate – somewhat unfairly. It was not her fault that her father had made an obscene amount of money out of coal-mining, or that he died when she was 11 years old, leaving her as one of the wealthiest heiresses in the whole of Europe. She is believed to have inherited a fortune estimated as being between £600,000 and £1,040,000 in 1760. Her father was a notorious rake and libertine, but Mary turned out to be far from frivolous – she loved botany and devoted much of her time and money to building glass-houses and studying plants, and growing exotic species. She was outspoken and was something of an intellectual. Various suitors were lined up for her but were turned down until, on her eighteenth birthday, she married the Earl of Strathmore. It was a magnificent affair – her trousseau alone cost £3,000. Her mother gave her a diamond stomacher costing £10,000 and other diamonds worth £7,000. In addition she had her pick from a green landau, a blue landau, a blue post-coach and a stone-coloured chaise, all of them with a full set of horses and liveried staff. The Earl quickly realized what a handful he had taken on board – why, she loved her cats and dogs more than him! Nevertheless, she bore him five children. The newspapers had a field day, in particular criticising her for her harsh treatment of the Earl's son, who she would beat regularly. One caricature entitled *Lady Termagant Flaybum* shows her, birch in hand, about to administer a beating which was apparently so frequent that it 'caused great annoyance to the neighbourhood' of their home at Forty Grosvenor Square.

The marriage was not to last long – the Earl was sickly and developed tuberculosis, but before he died in 1776, *en route* to Lisbon to try a cure in the warm airs of Portugal, he wrote a farewell letter home to his wife. It was largely devoid of any affection, but urged her to try and protect her inheritance by tying it up in trust for her children. For once in her life, it turned out that she did as she was told, and she assigned most of her life interests to trustees for the benefit of her children.

Aged 27, Mary sought solace in a relationship with George Gray. He was a nabob (an Englishman who had gone to India to make his fortune). Unfortunately Gray had lost whatever fortune he had, and was keen to marry the merry widow. She resisted his entreaties, but nevertheless managed to get herself pregnant by him not once but on at least three different occasions. In her diary she recorded the foul black liquid which she drank in order to terminate each of the pregnancies. She was happy, living at Chelsea, with her vineries and hothouses and had no wish to give up all her independence for married servitude.

And then along came Andrew Robinson Stoney, an Anglo-Irish adventurer. He was a thoroughly bad egg. It was not the first time he had set his sights on a wealthy woman as the means to riches. He pursued her, and ingratiated himself with her after a series of derogatory articles alluding to her affair with Gray (and others) appeared in the *Morning Post*. Who should rush to her defence, in print, but Andrew Robinson Stoney. In due course he even challenged the editor of the *Morning Post* to a duel, over Her Ladyship's honour. But it was all a put-up job – the critical letters, as well as the responses, were all written by Stoney. The duel was a sham, and the editor had been put up to it by Stoney.

Stoney pretended to have been run through by the editor's sword and staggered back to Mary to announce that he was dying for her, and her alone. Oh, and by the way, would she mind marrying him in order to satisfy his dying wish? What could the poor girl do? She agreed, and the recumbent body of the fatally wounded swain was brought into the church to gasp his wedding vows before he breathed his last. Only, he didn't die, and leapt from his bed as soon as the wedding had taken place, and proceeded to make Mary's life a living hell. He spent her money with wild extravagance; he forced her to sell her hothouses and rare plants; he beat her constantly, spied on her, raped her servants and forbade her to go out in any of her carriages. She was expected to sit down at table with a succession of her husband's mistresses. Eventually, he dismissed all her servants. Her letters were intercepted, and apparently her husband took to imprisoning her in a cupboard where she would be fed one egg and one biscuit per day. He also bullied her into writing her 'Confession' – an account of her past indiscretions, which he intended to keep so that he could blackmail her into subservience. Above all he was furious that Mary had heeded the advice of her first husband, and had put much of her fortune out of his reach. In 1784 Stoney went so far as to seize Mary's daughter Lady Anna Maria and send her to Paris. The young lady, being a ward in Chancery, had to be brought back by the Court.

The following year, Mary escaped and started divorce proceedings. This slow process took four years to finalise. With the divorce suit pending, her husband seized her and carted her off to Streatlam Castle. Her supporters gave chase. For eleven days the kidnapped Countess was incarcerated in her carriage, and beaten savagely. Eventually Stoney was overtaken at Darlington, and the poor woman was freed.

He was tried for assault and conspiracy to imprison his wife, and evidence that she had been tortured and mis-treated entered the public domain. Curiously, this did not particularly endear her to the public – especially when her action in putting her money out of her husband's reach became known. To some extent she was viewed as the maker of her own misfortune. But her husband was found guilty, fined £300, and sent to prison for three years. His final act of revenge was to get the 'Confessions' published – no easy feat since the newspapers refused to have anything to do with the vendetta (or at least, not until he had bought a fifty-one per cent stake in the paper, and compelled the editor to obey his orders). Thanks to the disclosures in her 'Confessions', Her Ladyship's reputation was in tatters, and never recovered. Ten years of litigation followed during which her ex-husband tried to lay claim to Mary's estate – small wonder that the uncertainty and worry nearly drove the poor woman mad. But eventually all claims were struck out, leaving Stoney destitute and friendless.

He was cast into prison, unable to pay his debts. For over twenty years he languished there under the jurisdiction of the Kings Bench. Prison however had its advantages – he hired a room within the confines of the jail, seduced a young girl called Polly, and kept her incarcerated inside this locked room, feeding her but once a day, and siring no fewer than five children by her. The unlovely, bullying, tyrant eventually died in June 1810. In an Age characterised by violence, depravity and greed, he was perhaps without equal. Thirty years after the brute died, the novelist William Makepeace Thackeray used his story in his novel *The Luck of Barry Lyndon.*

The story says much about the attitude of the Law towards domestic violence – it really had to be extreme before action could be taken. Here, the husband had compelled his staff to testify against Mary, stating that she willingly went along with the treatment. She was, after all, his property: he was, in law, her Lord and Master. Although it may be a fallacy to think that the law regarded it as a man's right to use the rule of thumb (i.e. to administer a beating as long as it was with a stick no bigger than the width of his thumb) the saying nevertheless indicates how the rights of a wife in the eighteenth century were far inferior to the rights of her husband.

Mary, known to all as the 'Unhappy Countess', had lived out her days with two of her daughters and a house full of dogs in eccentric isolation. She died at the age of 51 in 1800. She was buried in Westminster Abbey, apparently wearing full court dress, ready to meet her Sovereign Lord.

Her eldest son John, who later became tenth Earl of Strathmore and Kinghorne, was, like his mother, to feature prominently in the dinner-table gossip and printed tittle-tattle of the late eighteenth century. This was on account of his liason with Sarah, Countess of Tyrconnel. Born Sarah Hussey Delaval, Sarah was 'a bit of a goer,' much loved by the papers because she was witty, charming, attractive – and, some might say, promiscuous. As a wealthy young heiress she was snapped up by George Carpenter, the earl of Tyrconnel, but she quickly got bored with him and set her sights, and more besides, on the Prince Frederick, Duke of York. Contemporary accounts suggest that the Earl was flattered by the arrangement, and actively encouraged it. The public were fascinated by the whole affair, and *The Accommodating Spouse* reproduced as Image 60 shows the Earl leaving the marital bedroom in which the Prince has already stripped off his jacket and trousers. The Earl announces that he will not be back before breakfast, just as the Prince is hopping into bed with Sarah.

The Prince moved on to other pastures a year later, and Sarah settled for the bedroom charms of John, the aforementioned tenth Earl. John was a constant visitor at the family home of the Tyrconnels. Apparently the Earl of Tyrconnel was not worried by the arrangement, which saw the two men happily go off horse racing during the day, while John shared Sarah's favours at night.

In December 1791 the *Bon Ton Magazine* was able to report to its avid readers that Sarah had left her husband and had set up home with John at his home at Gibside, County Durham. This brazen display of living together outside of wedlock was unusual, and scandalised genteel society. Image 47 shows a print entitled *A luncheon at Gibside* with the lovers devouring a meal, and each other, while the Earl of Tyrconnel is riding past the open window wondering what is taking them so long.

The couple appear to have been genuinely in love, but their happiness came swiftly to a close when Sarah developed tuberculosis. She died in October 1800, and poor John found himself burying his lover just six months after he had buried his mother. It meant another trip to Westminster Abbey, and another corpse bedecked in lace and fine jewellery. He was devastated, although rumour had it that he sought comfort in the arms of Sarah's 19-year-old daughter. Keeping things in the family did not result in a long-lasting affair, and nine years passed before he finally 're-entered the amorous contest'. Being highly egalitarian, he fell for the charms of the daughter of his gardener, a 22-year-old by the name of Mary Milner. She bore him a son in 1811, and most unusually for the Georgians, he immediately admitted paternity. Nine years later, when he knew he was dying, he got up from his death bed to marry the ever-loyal Mary, hoping that his son would thereby be legitimated. He died sixteen hours later. To some extent it worked – the marriage legitimised the son under Scottish law but was ineffective so far as the (Irish) title and the English assets were concerned. John's brother therefore succeeded to the earldom, but at least Mary and her son were provided for out of the estate. The son, also named John, was educated at Eton and went on to become a great patron of the Arts. His home at Barnard Castle was purpose-built to house his splendid collection of fine and decorative arts, becoming the internationally significant Bowes Museum. A background history of debauchery and infidelity within the family thus led ultimately to a truly magnificent memorial.

LADY SEYMOUR WORSLEY – the lady with the twenty-seven lovers.
1781 must have appeared to have been quite a good year for Sir Richard Worsley, Seventh Baronet of Appuldurcombe. A military man and a Member of Parliament, he was serving in Lord North's government as Comptroller of the King's Household; he was a Privy Councillor – and Governor of the Isle of Wight, where his country seat at Appuldurcombe was situated. The renovations and improvements at this stately pile were to be his life's work – the gardens were later re-shaped by Capability Brown, and the house itself was to be stuffed with works of art and antiquities reflecting not one but two extensive Grand Tours.

True, his wife Seymour was a bit of a hot-head: he had married her in 1775 when she was a wealthy heiress at the tender age of 17. Her father had died when she was very young, leaving some £100,000 shared between Seymour and her elder sister. Sir Richard was 21, and she did her duty, bearing him a son and heir the following year, but they were not exactly soul-mates. She wanted the social whirl, the glamour, and to be in the public eye. She was also an outrageous flirt. She liked London parties, not being shut away on the Isle of Wight while her husband pursued his political and military career. He wanted military precision, order, and a chance to spend his wife's not inconsiderable fortune in amassing what he hoped would be the finest collection of sculptures from ancient Greece. It is possible that he also got his kicks from watching his wife in bed with other lovers.

It was a hot September day in 1781 when Sir Richard, accompanied by his wife and his close friend and neighbour George Maurice Bissett, travelled to Maidstone and decided to use the cold baths. The bathing areas were segregated – Seymour using one bath, the gentlemen the other. Afterwards, when they were changing, Sir Richard noticed a window which gave a view of the changing area used by his wife. He called Bissett over, gave him a lift up on his shoulders and shouted to his wife 'Seymour, Seymour! Bissett is looking at you!'

According to the subsequent evidence of Seymour's maid, Bissett continued to watch the naked Lady Seymour as she got dressed, for a full five minutes. Everyone then met up outside the baths, and went away in some merriment.

Subsequently, Lady Seymour gave birth to a daughter who was almost certainly fathered by Bissett. This did not worry Sir Richard unduly and he was happy to acknowledge the child as his own, in order to avoid public scandal. In fact he appeared to be quite happy to turn a blind eye to his wife's behaviour as long as it was kept private. But then the cat really got out of the bag: his wife eloped with Bissett, spending four nights with him at the Royal Hotel at Pall Mall in London, rarely leaving the bedroom except when asking for the sheets to be changed.

Humiliated, Sir Richard plotted his revenge – he wanted to expose his wife's infidelity and to punish Bissett. He declined to divorce his wife – or even to ask for a formal separation, and instead sued Bissett in the King's Bench Division for 'crim. con.' and sought damages of £20,000. The amount would have been enough to have destroyed Bissett. The figure was so high because it was intended to reflect the fact that Bissett was a man who was in a position of trust (he was a neighbour, a friend, and above all a junior officer in the same regiment as the baronet). He had abused that trust when he committed adultery with Lady Seymour and thereby 'damaged' her.

The problem was that Bissett was not the first to have 'damaged' her ladyship. By all accounts she was somewhat fast and loose when spreading her favours – and rather more besides. The newspapers were abuzz with stories that there were in fact another twenty-six paramours in the background. Bissett's case was therefore that she was already damaged goods. Not, of course, that many of the other lovers would wish to step forward and own up – after all, that could leave them open to crim. con. claims. However, five of her alleged lovers were prepared to give evidence in support of Bissett, not admitting their part in adultery, but giving their views on the wayward and scandalous conduct of Lady Seymour. One such witness was Viscount Deerhurst, who had been encountered by Sir Richard in his wife's bedchamber at four in the morning. He gave evidence admitting the encounter but declining to answer what he was doing there. He did however point out to the court that Sir Richard seemed disinterested – to the extent of allowing Lady Seymour to accompany the Viscount, on his own, when he left for Southampton a few days later.

More damning was the evidence from the hotel staff – there was only the one bed in the room which the lovers shared. Another witness was a Dr Osborne, who was called to explain the circumstances in which he had examined Lady Seymour. He claimed patient confidentiality – but then went on to say that Lady Seymour Worsley had consented to him disclosing that she had sought treatment for venereal disease. The Press had a field day, and suggested that she had contracted the disease from the Marquis of Graham (also a witness in the trial).

The gossip columns went into overdrive: twenty-six lovers in addition to Bissett, plenty of juicy details and gossip, and a tale of a man who dishonourably absconded with another man's wife! And then there was the bath incident – it was pointed out to the court that Sir Richard was a party to his own cuckolding. When Lord Mansfield addressed the jury before they withdrew to consider their verdict, he made it clear that the facts were not in dispute, stating 'This Woman, for three or four years, has been prostituted with a variety of people; that is extremely clear, and extremely plain.' Finally, the jury decided that the baronet had been wronged and set the damages, not at £20,000, but at one shilling. It gave rise to the print entitled *The Shilling, or the Value of a P[riv]y C[ouncillo]r's Matrimonial Honour* shown in Image 64.

The maid-servant, Mary Marriott, had made a statement giving full details of the incident, and the public were fascinated. Cartoonists such as Gillray led the ridicule with his print entitled *Sir Richard Worse-than-Sly exposing his wife's bottom, o fye!* Others followed, showing Bissett standing on the baronet's shoulders peeping through the window at the naked wife.

The humiliated baronet missed the important session of parliament the day after the trial, in which Lord North's Tory government faced a vote from the Whig opposition that 'the war on the continent of North America may no longer be pursued for the impractical purpose of reducing the inhabitants of that country to obedience by force.' Lord North had previously offered to resign but the King had insisted that he remain in office. The Whig motion was narrowly defeated – Lord North won by a single vote – but was apparently heard to remark before the vote was taken 'Oh! If all my Cuckolds desert, I shall be beaten indeed!'

Sir Richard withdrew from politics, and without his support North's administration soon collapsed and Sir Richard lost all his official posts. The war against the American colonies drifted towards an inevitable conclusion and Sir Richard's wife became one of the professional mistresses who existed in London relying on favours and occasional financial support from wealthy aristocratic friends. Bissett found himself a younger lover, but not before getting Lady Seymour pregnant again. Eventually she went to live in Paris, where the French seemed less censorious about her lifestyle. In 1788 Sir Richard agreed to enter into Articles of Separation in return for her promising to accept exile in France for four years – in practice she then got caught up in the aftermath of the French Revolution, and was trapped in Paris during the Terror. The baronet, who had spent the intervening twenty years building up his art collection, died in 1805. Ironically, he never did achieve his ambition of being the pre-eminent collector of Greek sculpture, having been pipped at the post by Lord Elgin and his marbles.

On Sir Richard's death the fortune which Seymour had brought into their marriage reverted to her. Now wealthy and living in Britain, she married a Frenchman and obtained a Royal licence for both of them to adopt her birth surname of Fleming. She died in 1818.

Gillray drew his *A peep into Lady W!!!!!'s Seraglio* shortly after the trial. It is shown as Image 65. Gillray doesn't just show the amorous lady in bed with one lover; he shows another leaving via the window and a further nine waiting their turn on the staircase. The suggestion that Her Ladyship enjoyed her pleasures like a common whore, a handful at a time, was scurrilously unfair and illustrates the casual disregard felt by the caricaturists towards the truth: once they had a victim in their sights, anything and everything was within bounds.

The inscription on the staircase is from Rowe's *The Fair Penitent* and reads: 'One lover to another still succeeds, another and another after that; and the last fool is as welcome as the former, till having loved his hour out he gives place, and mingles with the herd which went before him.' There was, of course, no suggestion that Seymour actually enjoyed all her twenty-seven lovers at the same time and place, but it made for an entertaining idea, and one which captured the public imagination.

THE NEW FEMALE COTERIE
When she was first publicly disgraced, Seymour became a member of an exclusive 'club' which customarily met every month at the very upmarket King's Place brothel run by Sarah Prendergast. The gathering was known as The New Female Coterie – although this was probably a name coined by Grub Street hacks. Denied social

acceptance elsewhere, this is where Seymour would have been able to catch up and gossip with other 'fallen women'. The club had been established by Caroline, Countess Harrington when she was blackballed by the original Female Coterie (an altogether more reputable gathering which would meet at *uber chic* Almacks). Caroline was a woman of great sexual desires and for many years had used Sarah Prendergast's premises as a rendezvous for her innumerable lovers. Curiously, the same brothel was frequented 'four times a week' by her husband, a notorious lecher. He was William Stanhope, Second Earl of Harrington, known to all as 'the goat of quality.' The New Female Coterie boasted membership by many of the great-but-no-longer-good, who would meet to have a good natter and get drunk on champagne and nostalgia. They included Penelope, Viscountess Ligonier. Attractive, witty and hungry for the love she could not find in her marriage to the somewhat dim-witted Lord Ligonier, she had embarked on a torrid affair with an Italian playwright called Count Vittorio Alfieri. Alfieri went on to write about the affair, and was challenged to a duel by the cuckolded Lord Ligonier. His Lordship injured Alfieri in the fight, which took place at Green Park, and went on to divorce his wife in 1771. She turned to Alfieri for support but found him unwilling to marry her because he knew full well that she had other lovers. Not only that, but she very publicly made it clear that she never regretted her 'indiscretions' – she deliberately set out to have an affair as a means of escaping from the tedium of a relationship where passion had run its course.

Another member of the New Female Coterie was The Honourable Catherine Newton. She had figured in a particularly infamous divorce case – a case where the lurid details of her repeated infidelities left little to the imagination. The details were published as *The Trial of the Hon. Mrs. Catherine Newton, Wife of John Newton… Upon a Libel and Allegations, Charging her with the Crime of Adultery with Mr. Isham Baggs, a Young Oxonian, 1782*. She was aged 16 at the time of her marriage to the 58-year-old John Newton in 1762, and the trial records show a history of her cavorting nearly-naked with a succession of stable lads, house servants and so on. Servants being servants, there were many willing to testify to the occasions when hands were seen placed on naked thighs, or that inappropriate assistance had been given when Catherine was being helped to mount her horse. House maids complained of having to re-make the beds several times each day, and there was much evidence of adjoining rooms not being locked, and of undergarments being found in inappropriate places. By the time young Master Baggs appeared on the scene Catherine's attentions to him were so obvious that even her old goat of a husband noticed. He kicked her out and she went back to live with her father in Wells, Somerset. Before long she embarked on an amour with a Captain Ackland, and became pregnant by him. Following her very public divorce she drifted to London and became part of the circle of disgraced ladies who sought support from each other's company.

One other member of the coterie was the beautiful Henrietta, wife of the First Baron Grosvenor. Despite the fourteen year age difference, she had married the man within a month of their first meeting, presumably unaware of his appetite for gaming and whoring. He is generally thought to have lost some £250,000 on the horses and at the gaming tables – a vast sum of money even for the gambling-mad eighteenth century. More to the point, he was one of the most debauched characters of the time, spending his time with a constant succession of whores. This left Henrietta with the view that what was sauce for the gander was sauce for the goose, and as mentioned earlier in Chapter Six, she embarked on an affair with George III's brother, Henry, Duke of Cumberland.

In the crim. con. trial which followed, Henrietta had tried to play down the significance of her affair by throwing as much dirt as possible at her husband, producing witness after witness from a variety of brothels across town. It worked in so far as it enthralled the readership of the newspapers which reported every word of the trial, but failed in the sense that her husband was awarded £10,000 in damages – a sum met by King George III, and hence ultimately by the British taxpayer. In the court case, Richard had sworn blind that 'from the time of his marriage he had always behaved towards his wife with true love and affection, and did all in his power to render her completely happy, and was and is a person of a sober, chaste and virtuous life and conversation….' Henrietta countered with tales of 'great neglect, indifference and dis-affection' and alleged that 'he held a criminal conversation and adulterous intercourse with divers [sic]strange women, leading a vicious lewd and debauched life … by visiting, corresponding with, and carnally knowing … prostitutes at … houses of ill-fame and reputation.' There were no half-way measures in this story.

The mud-slinging produced strong moral outrage at Henrietta's conduct (presumably the conduct of her lover and her husband was no worse than was to have been expected). She became the object of innumerable bawdy songs and faced hostility in the press. Even years later, when she publicly attended the impeachment trial of Warren Hastings, in the company of Lady Seymour Worsley, the *Morning Post* of 11 June 1788 commented on the irony, saying that 'The chaster part of the female company did not seem highly satisfied with these unexpected visitors.'

The legal separation from her husband left Henrietta with a paltry annual allowance of £1,200, and it seems that she may well have supplemented her income by 'a spot of freelance work' at Sarah Prendergast's seraglio. While her husband was alive, and was unable to divorce her because of his own adultery, she remained in social limbo until his death in 1802. Within a month his widow had become married to George Porter, Sixth Baron de Hochepied, and lived quietly and out of the public eye until her death in 1828.

THE GORGEOUS GUNNING GIRLS

When the Duke of Hamilton married Elizabeth Gunning in 1752 he was marrying into a family which had had been very much in the public eye for over three years. She was one of the two Gunning sisters who had captivated London society.

The Gunnings, Elizabeth and Maria, deserve a mention, not because they did anything scandalous, but because their story illustrates several important threads – the manipulation of the Press, the insatiable appetite for news of glamour and beauty, and the tragic consequences which often followed as a result of being a dedicated follower of fashion.

The sisters were born around 1730 into a well-connected but impoverished family which had moved to Ireland while the girls were still young. They may well have spent time in the Dublin theatres, which would explain why, when a ball was held in Dublin Castle in 1748 and hosted by Viscountess Petersham, they turned up wearing borrowed theatrical costumes. One went as Juliet, the other as Lady Macbeth. Thus attired they were introduced to the Earl of Harrington, Lord Lieutenant of Ireland. They appear to have made quite an impression on him, and their mother persuaded the Earl to provide her with a small pension – enough for her to pay for her to travel back to England with her two girls. She was clearly determined to propel her daughters into successful marriages, come what may, and when they arrived at their original home in Huntingdon she set about ensuring not just that the girls were seen at all the balls and social occasions, but that the local papers reported on the events and commented upon the beauty of her daughters.

By modern standards their looks may not seem anything special – but in the 1750s there was no doubting that their looks were considered sensational. Their fame built up to the extent that news of their beauty reached London – well-planned and well-publicised walks at Ranelagh Gardens ensured that by the time they were presented at the Court of St James on 2 December 1750 they were already famous. Reports in the Press suggest that the courtiers were standing on their chairs trying to catch a glimpse of them through the throng of admirers.

Horace Walpole took up the story of Elizabeth, the younger of the two sisters:

The Duke of Hamilton, hot, debauched, extravagant … fell in love with the youngest at a masquerade. At my Lord Chesterfield's house, the Duke of Hamilton made violent love at one end of the room, while he was playing at pharaoh at the other end; that is, he saw neither the bank nor his own cards, which were of three hundred pounds each: he soon lost a thousand. I own I was so little a professor in love that I thought all this parade looked ill for the poor girl; and could not conceive, if he was so much engaged with his mistress as to disregard such sums, why he played at all. However, two nights afterwards, being left alone with her while her mother and sister were at Bedford House, he found himself so impatient, that he sent for a parson. The doctor refused to perform the ceremony without license or ring: the Duke swore he would send for the Archbishop—at last they were married with a ring of the bed-curtain, at half an hour after twelve at night, at Mayfair chapel.

No licence was needed for the clandestine wedding in the Chapel; the date was 14 February 1752, which must have made it a Valentine's Day surprise for the bride, as well as for her mother and sister. She was now a Duchess. Her husband died in 1758 and shortly afterwards she re-married, to John Campbell, Marquess of Lorne. He became Duke of Argyll in 1770, thereby making Elizabeth a duchess twice over. She was a great favourite at Court, and in time George II awarded her the title of Baroness Hamilton of Hameldon in her own right. She bore her first husband three children, and her second one five, and died in 1790, her reputation untarnished in any way.

Her elder sister Maria was not quite so lucky in love. It started well enough – in 1752 she became a Countess by virtue of marrying the Sixth Earl of Coventry. The newly-weds travelled to Paris, but Maria felt uncomfortable there because she could not speak French. To add to her woes, her husband forbade her to wear rouge (then highly fashionable in France) and he publicly tried to wipe it off her face when she arrived at dinner wearing heavy make-up. When the couple eventually returned to England she was repeatedly mobbed whenever she appeared in public. Meanwhile her husband took up with one of the most famous courtesans of the day – Kitty Fisher. Once, while riding in Hyde Park, wife and mistress bumped into each other. An eye-witness by the name of Guistiniana Wynne reported:

…. Lady Coventry politely asked Kitty the name of the dressmaker who had made her dress. Kitty Fisher answered that Maria had better ask her own husband as he had given her the dress as a gift. The altercation continued with Lady Coventry calling her an impertinent woman, and Kitty replying that she would have to accept this insult because although Maria became her 'social superior' on marrying Lord Coventry, she was going to marry a Lord herself just to be able to answer back.

Poor Maria only lived a few more years; she died in 1760. She should have listened to her husband's advice about wearing make-up, but she did not, and paid the price for slathering on too much lead-based face powder. The skin eruptions caused by the lead meant even thicker amounts of 'paint' were applied, leading in time to blood poisoning and death at the age of 28. In the end, the vanity which had propelled her to the top of the social ladder caused her early death. As ever, beauty was not even skin deep.

LADY ANNE FOLEY

Lady Anne Foley was the third daughter of Maria Gunning and she was to hit the scandal sheets, in a way that would have horrified her mother, after her adulterous relationship with the Earl of Peterborough.

Losing her mother when she was 3 years old may have helped her wayward behaviour; being 'groomed' by a family friend called George Selwyn who was described at the time as 'singular' – a euphemism for an eccentric creep and very possibly a paedophile – may have made her worse. Whatever the reason, Lady Anne Coventry was never going to be happy with just one man in her life. In October 1778 she married. Her husband Edward Foley was the second son of a newly created baron. They appear to have had residences at numerous addresses including the family seat at Stroke Court in Herefordshire, at Weymouth Street, and at Somerset Street in the parish of Marylebone, and at various addresses on the South coast including Weymouth, Hastings and Brighton. His family were wealthy but his ability to spend money at the card tables far exceeded his assets. His wife felt neglected by her husband and sought out those who would offer rather more physical attention to her needs. On the occasions when she and her husband were at different addresses she does not appear to have been short of a bed companion. When she gave birth to a child, exactly nine months after the wedding, others might have assumed that Edward was the father, but she allegedly wrote to the Honourable Richard FitzPatrick saying 'Dear Richard, I give you joy. I have just made you the father of a beautiful boy…P.S. This is not a circular.' This might suggest that she was well aware that she already had a reputation for promiscuous behaviour.

No further mention is made of the infant, who appears not to have survived childhood. In 1781 she was introduced to the Right Honourable Charles Henry, Earl of Peterborough, by her brother Lord Deerhurst. The pair quickly became intimate – or as the subsequent divorce proceedings put it:

…she the Right Honourable Lady Ann Foley being of a wicked and lustful disposition, wholly unmindful of her conjugal vow; and not having the fear of God in her eye did…. carry on a lewd and adulterous correspondence with the said Lord Peterborough, in divers places, and on many occasions committed the foul crime of adultery with him.

At first Foley seemed oblivious to the affair but eventually decided that he could make a few bob out of the relationship, and sued for damages in crim. con. He only needed to prove one instance of adultery – 'the affair in the shrubbery' – but it was sufficient for him to win damages of £2,500 against Lord Peterborough. But when Foley then sued for divorce, he asserted various other occasions of adultery, including 'the amour at the oak tree' (where Ann was observed being rogered by the randy Earl of Peterborough while leaning up against the trunk of a convenient oak tree) the 'affair on the heath' (she did like her pleasures *en plein aire*!) and 'the case of the rocking carriage' (where it was noted that the carriage, although standing on the same spot, was observed to be in motion for upwards of an hour, in circumstances where servants were able to identify the occupants). Not only were the allegations sensational, but Foley ensured that they got maximum publicity by setting out all the lurid details in a well-received pamphlet. The case became a *cause célèbre* and the entire evidence heard at the trial at Doctor's Commons was published in a book. The preface included images of the oak tree incident, the frolic on the heath, and the rocking carriage just in case the public needed to get the picture more clearly.

The DRIVING SCENE.   *The* OAK TREE SCENE.   *The* FURZE BUSH SCENE.

An example of the lurid detail appears from the following trial extract:

...they walked together about fifty yards from where the carriage stood and then the said Right Honourable Lady Ann Foley laid herself down upon the grass, near some gorse, and then the said Lord Peterborough unbuttoned his breeches, and pulled up her petticoats, and laid down upon her; and they then and there had the carnal use and knowledge of each other's bodies, and thereby the said Right Honourable Lady Ann Foley committed the foul crime of adultery; and they continued on the ground together about ten minutes, during all which time they were plainly seen and observed....

Added humiliation was heaped on the parties when both Houses of Parliament discussed the affair before agreeing to the divorce.

Poor Anne: the Earl of Peterborough chose not to marry her, and he went away to lick his wounds and to stump up the £2,500. Anne did not remain single for long – she married an officer in the Fifteenth Hussars called Samuel Wright, went to live in Nottingham, and disappeared from public view.

She was not the only child of the gorgeous Gunning girls to attract the attention of Grub Street – her cousin Lady Elizabeth, Countess of Derby, was equally news-worthy.

ELIZABETH, COUNTESS OF DERBY – a truly scandalous affair, because *she* left *him*. Lady Betty Hamilton, daughter of Elizabeth Gunning and the Sixth Duke of Hamilton, had married the Twelfth Earl of Derby in 1774, and went on to give birth to three children. She was for a while one of the great arbiters of fashion, a style icon paired with the Duchess of Devonshire. But five years into her marriage she did the unimaginable – she embarked on a very public affair with the Third Duke of Dorset. Not only were the couple indiscreet, but she eventually walked out on her husband. Such brazen behaviour was unforgivable in the eyes of polite society.

The Duke was a well-known philanderer. On the plus side, he was a cricket-playing fanatic, which compared with the more typically aristocratic pursuit of horse racing was almost benign. He supported his own team, at a cost of a mere £3,000 a year (excluding what he spent on betting). On the other hand he had numerous affairs, besides the one with the Countess of Derby. One affair was with the Venetian ballerina Giovanna Zanerini who performed under the stage name of Giovanna Baccelli. She accompanied him openly when he went to Paris as the British Ambassador to France. He also had an affair with Elizabeth Forster. She eventually went on to become a great friend of Georgiana, Duchess of Devonshire, openly living in a *ménage à trois* with the Duke and Duchess and eventually succeeding Georgiana to the title of Duchess of Devonshire in 1809, three years after Georgiana died.

But it was the Duke of Dorset's affair with Elizabeth, Countess of Derby which scandalised society. When the Earl of Derby made no attempt to divorce his wife, the Duke lost interest in her. No-one thought any the less of him for his wayward ways – indeed he was even able to resume his friendship with the Earl of Derby once the affair had come to an end. Elizabeth, on the other hand, was forced to escape to the continent to avoid the opprobrium that followed, only returning once her husband's infatuation with the actress Elizabeth Farren became very public knowledge. The Countess eventually died aged 44, leaving the diminutive Earl of Derby to marry his actress lover just two months later.

ELIZABETH FARREN – an actress of many parts.
So, what of Miss Farren? She was the exception that proved the rule – not all actresses were prostitutes, just as not all prostitutes strutted their stuff on the stage. She was the daughter of a drunken surgeon-cum-apothecary from Cork, who had leanings towards the theatre. When he died, his widow was penniless and she returned to her home town of Liverpool with the young Elizabeth and her two sisters in tow. Mother and daughters appeared on the stage, and by the time she was 15, Elizabeth was showing enough promise to be employed at the theatre in Liverpool. In 1776 she moved to London where her attractive, slender figure, blue eyes, and fine manners gained her many admirers. She was especially well received for her portrayal of Miss Tittup in David Garrick's farce *Bon Ton or High Life above Stairs*. All went swimmingly for a year or two. She attracted a large male following including the likes of Charles James Fox, who very publicly lusted after her, until 11 July 1778 when she played Nancy Lovel in Colman's *Suicide*. This was a 'breeches' part, and Fox, in company of many other males, was rather looking forward to seeing her in tight trousers. It was after all, a time when the theatre was much like the modern pantomime with its principal boy, played by a girl, contrasting with the man playing a fat and florid female in a voluminous dress (think Widow Twankey). But horror of horrors, Miss Farren did not have the legs for the part! Or more accurately, she had a backside which positively drooped and Fox was vociferous in his disappointment. Her derriere was a disaster. No matter that the poor girl was magnificent as Miss Hardcastle in *She Stoops to Conquer* or that her Hermione was second to none – she would henceforth be remembered for her saggy posterior. In practice she managed very well without Fox's approbation, and although her name was linked romantically with other actors, notably John Palmer, she remained chaste as well as chased.

Her charm and good manners opened doors for her in London. She obtained the patronage of the Duke of Richmond, and was invited to give performances at private parties at his home in Whitehall. There she was to meet her most ardent admirer, the

Earl of Derby. As explained, he fell madly in love with her. The newspapers chose to portray her as a gold-digger, with scurrilous prints showing her eyeing up the ducal coronet (see *Contemplations on a Coronet* in Image 38) or plotting how to make the Earl marry her. In many prints she was shown as tall and scrawny, while the Earl is shown short and somewhat ugly – a rather unfair representation of the couple, but which served to show how their union was viewed by the public – as being completely ludicrous. Nonetheless, she got her ducal coronet when they married on 1 May 1797, following which she had a son and two daughters into the bargain. Her last performance on stage was as Lady Teazle in *The School for Scandal*, just a month after the death of the Earl's first wife. Cue many tears as she bade a sad farewell to the stage, before a large and appreciative audience. She died in 1829, aged 70, and was survived by her husband for a further five years.

CATHERINE TYLNEY-LONG – a quadruple-barrelled surname was never going to work.

When the immensely wealthy heiress Catherine Tylney-Long married a scion of the famous Anglo-Irish Wellesley family, her husband adopted her surname in addition to his own, becoming known as the Rt Hon William Pole-Tylney-Long-Wellesley. At 21, Catherine was attractive, lively and petite, but above all, she was loaded. She had inherited a vast fortune at the age of 16, estimated as giving her an income of £40,000 a year – and had spent five years trying to avoid fortune hunters. She then made the biggest mistake of her life, by marrying a man who would turn out to be one of the most profligate and odious men of the century. He was a nephew of the Duke of Wellington, and was reputed to have been turned down on the six previous occasions when he had proposed marriage to her. Unfortunately for her, her resilience failed her and she finally consented at the seventh time of asking. She had other suitors – notably the Duke of Clarence (later to become William IV) and cartoonists revelled in the Duke's embarrassment at being spurned in favour of the Irish ne'er-do-well.

The newspapers had a field day when the marriage took place in Piccadilly on 14 March 1812, reporting that after the ceremony:

...the happy couple retired by the southern gate ... where a new and magnificent equipage was waiting to receive them. It was a singularly elegant chariot, painted bright yellow, and highly emblazoned, and drawn by four beautiful Arabian grey horses, attended by two postilions in brown jackets, with superb emblazoned badges in gold, emblematic of the united arms of the Wellesley and Tylney families. The newly

married pair drove off, with great speed, for Blackheath, intending to pass the night at the tasteful chateau belonging to the bridegroom's father, and from thence proceed to Wanstead House, in Essex, on the following day.

Newspapers then, as now, seemed to concentrate as much on what everything cost as on what the bride wore. The same report advised that:

The dress ... consisted of a robe of real Brussels point lace ... placed over white satin. Her head was ornamented with a cottage bonnet of the same material, being Brussels lace with two ostrich feathers. She likewise wore a deep lace veil and a white satin pelisse trimmed with swansdown. The dress cost seven hundred guineas, the bonnet one hundred and fifty, and the veil two hundred, and she wore a necklace which cost £25,000.

If the day was the happiest of her life, things started to go downhill with ominous speed. No sooner had he had got his hands on his wife's money than William spent it with extravagant zeal. There were ostentatious parties at the family home at Wanstead which cost a fortune – and from which Catherine was excluded. And then there was the constant and unbelievably reckless gambling, on top of which vast sums were laid out in bribes to get William elected to Parliament. It was also decided to refurbish Wanstead, a magnificent Palladian mansion, at an estimated cost of £360,000. The papers reported that the couple were 'fitting up Wanstead House in a style of magnificence exceeding even Carlton House.'

In the course of a decade Catherine had to suffer in silence as her husband spent her entire fortune, forcing the couple to flee abroad to avoid their creditors – humiliating for a woman who had been given the accolade of being the richest woman in the land just ten years earlier. Worse humiliation followed when they reached Italy – William openly conducted an affair with one Helena Bligh, the wife of a captain of the Coldstream Guards. Catherine tried, unsuccessfully, to buy off her rival, but realising the futility of the exercise returned to Britain with her three children, determined to obtain a legal separation from her husband. Meanwhile Wanstead house had been put up for auction – the entire contents were sold but the house failed to attract a buyer and had to be sold 'one stone at a time.' The proceeds amounted to a miserable £10,000. William accepted no blame at all for the extravagance which cost his wife her entire fortune, always claiming that it was 'someone else's fault.'

Her health broken, Catherine died at the age of 35, entrusting the care of her children to her two sisters. Her death may well have been attributable to a nasty dose of the clap which her husband gave her, as there were indications that she developed an inflammation of the bowels caused by a venereal disease. A letter to one of her sisters hints at this. Her death triggered off a series of legal battles in which William tried to recover legal custody of his children.

Astonishingly for the time (when, as the natural father, he would always expect to be supported by the Courts) his case in Chancery failed – over and over again. Each case brought further salacious details of William's private life into the public domain. In particular he openly lived with Helena, his mistress, and when she came to live in London her husband Thomas Bligh decided that enough was enough, and he brought a suit of crim. con. against William. The public revelled in the gossip, and cheered tumultuously when the court awarded damages of £6,000 to the cuckolded husband. William retaliated by publishing accounts which sought to defend his adulterous behaviour, and heaping accusations of immorality on to the two Long sisters who had been given custody of the children by the Courts.

In November 1828 William married Helena, who by then had been exposed as a whore in the minds of the general public. It was a disastrous second marriage, and before long she was reduced to claiming Poor Relief from the parish. William eked out the last thirty years of his life in considerable poverty, dying in July 1857 while eating a boiled egg. The *Morning Chronicle* contained an obituary which described him as 'A spendthrift, a profligate, and gambler in his youth, he became a debauchée in his manhood … Redeemed by no single virtue, adorned by no single grace, his life has gone out even without a flicker of repentance…'

It has to be said: the boiled egg did the world a favour.

LAVINIA FENTON – aka Lavinia Beswick, aka Polly Peachum: the story of the showgirl and the duke, with a fairy-tale ending.
Sometimes it all worked out for the tart-with-a-heart. Sometimes she did get to meet the aristocrat who would whisk her away from all her boudoir games, and even make an honest woman of her … sometimes, but not often. One of the few was Lavinia – born to a prostitute called Fenton, but who adopted the stage name of Beswick in honour of her natural father, who was believed to have been a captain in the Royal Navy. After treading the familiar route of becoming a child prostitute and then a part-time actress, she got her big break in 1728 when she was cast in John Gay's *The Beggar's Opera*. In an inspired piece of casting, the character in the play who was 'no better than she oughta' called Polly Peachum, was played by … the girl who was no better than she oughta. Lavinia was perfect. She was a sensation in the part and she became an overnight celebrity – books were written, ballads were composed, her likeness was bought in

innumerable prints. And she came to the notice of the very much married Charles Powlett, Third Duke of Bolton.

He sat watching every performance, clearly besotted with the young star (she was twenty-three years his junior). The infatuation became obvious, but still the Duke came for his nightly dose of lust and adoration. Hogarth even painted a picture of the opera being performed, with the Duke watching, rapt, in a box right at the front of the auditorium. In the end, his wooing worked wonders – she set up home with the Duke, but only after he had, in effect, bought her services on an exclusive basis, with a large annuity. John Gay, writing to Jonathan Swift, claimed that the agreement involved her being paid £400 a year while they were together, and £200 a year if they ever parted. The Duke's wife, whom he had married fifteen years earlier, was childless and no doubt was not amused when the mistress produced three children in quick succession, all of them boys.

When the first duchess died in 1751 the Duke wasted no time in proposing to Lavinia and they were married before the year was out. Now a duchess, she outlived him by six years, dying in 1760. As far as can be seen, she had been faithful to the old boy during his lifetime but, when he died aged 68, Lavinia fell for the charms of an Irish surgeon called George Kelly, whose services she had sought when illness affected her during her stay at Tunbridge Wells. According to letters of Horace Walpole, she settled most of her money on her children and then made a will appointing the good doctor her sole executor and beneficiary. And with that she departed this world, having achieved far more happiness and success than would have been thought possible after such an inauspicious start.

AUGUSTUS HENRY FITZROY – a Prime Minister, a whore and two wives.
In April 1768 Augustus Henry Fitzroy, aka the Third Duke of Grafton, went to the opera – hardly newsworthy, except that he took with him as 'arm-candy' someone who was known to everyone in the audience – and it wasn't his wife. It was Nancy Parsons, one of the leading courtesans of the era, and a woman at the very top of her game. Their scandalous affair was noted in the notorious gossip column of the *Town & Country Magazine* called *Histories of the tête-à-tête annexed* where she was given the appellation of Annabella:

Annabella is now the happiest of her sex, attached to the most amiable man of the age, whose rank and influence raise her, in point of power, beyond many queens of the earth. Caressed by the highest, courted and adulated by all, her merit and shining abilities receive that applause that is justly due to them. She presides constantly at his

*sumptuous table, and does the honours with an ease and elegance, that the first nobility
in the kingdom are compelled to admire.*

And it was not as if the Duke's wife was dead – she had been chucked out of the
ancestral pile some three years earlier when the Duke installed Nancy as chatelaine.
Before long, Nancy was hosting dinner parties, and filling the role of social hostess.
The papers were agog, especially as the Duke went on to become prime minister. The
most vitriolic of his critics was someone writing under the pseudonym 'Junius', in
the paper called the *Public Advertiser* (originally known as the *London Daily Post and
General Advertiser*). 'Junius' mercilessly poked fun at the Duke's private life, including
a poem under the title of *Harry and Nan* (published in the *Political Register*) as well as
savaging him for his lack of leadership skills and political acumen, and for his failure
to uphold constitutional rights. Indeed so effective were the attacks on Grafton, and
on the corruption which marked some of his appointments to high office, that Grafton
resigned as Prime Minister in 1770 and gave up politics altogether. He also abandoned
the Church of England and to the great embarrassment of his friends, became a
staunch Unitarian (deeply unfashionable and not acceptable to the Establishment).

The fact is, the Duke was not really cut out for active politics – his passion was the
Turf. He kept his own pack of hounds and liked to hunt. He was an avid race-goer,
in particular for the races on Newmarket Heath, and he bet heavily. What he wanted
was a woman who shared his passions – but his wife, for all her looks, intelligence and
charm, certainly did not.

She was born Anne Liddell, the only child of Sir Henry Liddell, later Baron
Ravensworth. He had made a packet out of coal and owned extensive lands in and
around Durham. She had brought money to her marriage to the Duke in 1756 and
in time did her marital duty by producing the obligatory 'heir and a spare' as well
as a daughter called Georgiana. But her passion was gambling at cards, and holding
lavish parties, neither of which held any interest for her husband. They drifted apart
as her gambling debts increased. Anne objected to the mistresses he brought to the
house – by 1764 Nancy Parsons was in residence – and when she informed the Duke
that she hated him, she was told to pack her bags and leave. She did so, and the
couple were legally separated in January 1765. She kept her jewels and an allowance
of £3,000 a year, along with custody of Georgiana. The two boys were excluded from
the arrangement. As was normal in the eighteenth century, their upbringing remained
under the control of their father the Duke. Anne went off to the arms (and bed) of a
succession of lovers including the Third Duke of Portland. Their affair was public
knowledge and it was assumed that they would marry when circumstances permitted,

but to Anne's humiliation and distress, Portland went off and got engaged to Lady Dorothy Cavendish. He had omitted to inform the Duchess.

Anne had begun a correspondence with Horace Walpole and he introduced her to his friend the Earl of Upper Ossory. Within a short time they were lovers, and in 1768 news reached the ears of the Duke of Grafton that his estranged wife was pregnant. That was too much to bear, and he immediately set about divorcing her. Three days after that marriage came to an end, she and the Earl were married. Any hopes of taking up a public life were diminished when her ex-husband re-married – not to the ever-charming Nancy Parsons, who was to go on to become Viscountess Maynard, but to Elizabeth Wrottesley, who was Lord Ossory's cousin. Anne, understandably, preferred not to allow their paths to cross, choosing respectable rural retirement over anything which the Ton could offer. As Countess of Upper Ossory she kept out of the public limelight, dying in 1804 after being something of a muse for Horace Walpole over a period of some twenty-eight years. He wrote her more than 450 letters during this time, offering a wonderful snapshot of his views about the period in which he lived.

The Duke of Grafton's new wife was described as being 'not handsome, but quiet and reasonable, and having a very amiable character.' Elizabeth was just as keen a follower of equine matters as the Duke, and also bore him twelve children, of whom eight reached adulthood. Elizabeth died in 1822, having survived the Duke by eleven years.

In all, the stories of the women in the life of the Duke of Grafton give a fascinating insight into the way society treated scandal, especially aristocratic scandal. Anne, and also Nancy, were born survivors and they saw off the criticism thrown at them with dignity and quiet aplomb.

* * *

So, what do these snapshots of adulterous unions say about adultery in the eighteenth century? First (and no surprise here) that men generally fared better than women. Laws were made by men (there were no female MPs); laws were administered by men (there were no female judges) and the cases reflected the prevailing view that it was the carnal appetites of women which lay at the root of the problem. A man could commit adultery and keep his place in society, a woman could not. If an errant wife was legally separated from her husband, she lived in a sort of limbo, her character stained. Only if her husband divorced her could she re-marry and regain respectability. But these considerations only applied to the aristocracy – no-one else could afford to sponsor a

Private Members Bill through Parliament and so for the vast majority of the population divorce was never an option.

The rising numbers of what we now call the middle classes looked on with amazement at the antics of their supposed betters, aghast at the gambling and hedonism that marked the aristocracy. The backlash would come with the Victorians, but for the Georgians, they simply devoured the stories in the Press, and enjoyed seeing them ridiculed in prints, ballads and ditties.

Image 46. Future Prospects. The angry Prince of Wales seeks to escape domesticity, observed by his wife and baby daughter – and by the cuckolded Lord Jersey. (See p. 89)

Image 47. A Luncheon at Gibside. John Bowes is making a meal of Lady Sarah while her husband, the Earl of Tyrconnel, rides by. (See p. 99)

Image 48. A Wooden Substitute. (See pp. 72 and 89) **Image 49.** Dignity. (See pp. 72 and 89)

These unflattering pictures of Queen Caroline refer to the rumours that she was spreading her favours around.

Image 50. Ah, such a pair… Old Sherry. George IV and his wife, represented by sacks of evidence of their adulterous conduct. (See pp. 72 and 90)

Image 51. The Goats Canter to Windsor. (See p. 85)

Image 52. George IV as Henry IV. (See p. 72)

FLORIZEL AND PERDITA

Image 53. Florizel and Perdita. (See pp. 49 and 85)

Image 54. The Rage. Queen Caroline squares up to Maria Fitzerbert. (See p. 89)

Image 55. Filial Piety. It shows the carousing Prince, with friends, bursting in on George III, who is ill in bed.

Image 56. Installation of a Knight Commander of the Bath. Queen Caroline shares a bath tub with her swarthy Italian boyfriend. (See p. 90)

Image 57. The Modern Circe. Mary Clarke, mistress of the Duke of York, was notorious for selling army commissions. (See p. 92)

Image 58. Nauticus. The future William IV. (See p. 93)

Image 59. Wouski. The sailor prince enjoying life in Jamaica. (See p. 93)

Image 60. The Accommodating Spouse. The Duke of York hops into bed with Sarah, Countess of Tyrconnel. (See p. 99)

Image 61. The Tar and the Jordan. William, Duke of Clarence, runs away from gossip-mongers discussing his affair with Dorothea Jordan. (See p. 93)

Image 62. Tête-à-tête Nancy Parsons and the Duke of Grafton. (See p. 57)

Image 63. Tête-à-tête Lady Waldegrave and the Duke of Gloucester. (See pp. 57 and 84)

Image 64. The Shilling. (See p. 102)

Image 65. A peep into Lady W!!!!!'s Seraglio. (See p. 103)

Image 66. The Thunderer. (See p. 146)

Image 67. Teresia Constantia Phillips. (See p. 129)

Image 68. The loathsome Francis Charteris. (See p. 119)

Image 69. Quiz-zing a Filly. (See p. 148)

Chapter Eight

Sex Crimes – Rape, Bigamy, Murder, Suicide and Sodomy

FRANCIS CHARTERIS – aka 'The Rape-Master General'
Image 68 shows a mezzotint of Francis Charteris, one of the most loathsome creatures in Georgian history. Beneath the portrait are the heavily ironic words:

> *Blood!--must a colonel, with a lord's estate,*
> *Be thus obnoxious to a scoundrel's fate?*
> *Brought to the bar, and sentenc'd from the bench,*
> *Only for ravishing a country wench?*

For some people the word 'rake' is applied almost as a compliment – a recognition of hard-living and hard-drinking, with an almost heroic life spent on gambling and fornicating. But there was nothing heroic about Francis Charteris – he was not just a rake, he was a rapist, and a serial one at that. There are few men from the eighteenth century who come across as so totally devoid of decency and morality. Here was a thoroughly nasty piece of work – Swift described him as 'a most infamous, vile scoundrel.'

Redeeming features? None that anyone could see. He was born in 1675 into a wealthy aristocratic Scottish family. He joined the army and was chucked out on four occasions – most notably by the Duke of Marlborough who had him court-martialled for cheating at cards. Eventually he was dismissed by Parliament for accepting bribes. By then he had achieved the rank of colonel – a rank which he had purchased largely through his expertise at cards. On one occasion he fleeced the Duchess of Queensbury out of £3,000 by the simple expedient of playing cards with her after positioning her in front of a mirror, enabling him to see each hand of cards reflected in the glass.

He amassed money through bribery, fraud and blackmail as well as by dabbling on the nascent stock market. He was one of the few who did not get burned when the South Sea Bubble burst in 1720. He would lend money at an exorbitant rate of interest – sometimes 100 per cent – so it was small wonder that he reputedly had an income of £7,000 a year, as well as £100,000 invested in stocks and shares. He was a bully, a cheat and a con-artist, and a man who apparently thought he could have any woman he wanted, under some twisted idea of '*droit de seigneur.*' On one occasion in Scotland he raped a married woman at gunpoint, before running away to England to avoid capture. That meant that he was unable to return to the country of his birth, where he owned substantial estates, but in 1721 was able to petition the king (George I) for a pardon.

Armed with the pardon he clearly felt that he was free to commit rape with impunity – he revelled in the name 'Rape-Master General' and bragged of having had his way with some three hundred women. Nathaniel Mist, in his *Weekly Journal*, wrote: 'We hear a certain Scotch Colonel is charged with a Rape, a misfortune he has been very liable to, but for which he has obtained a *Nolle Prosequi*. It is reported now that he brags that he will obtain a Patent for ravishing whomever he pleases.'

Honour had no place in his repertoire – on one occasion when staying at an inn in Lancaster he reportedly persuaded a young servant girl to have sex with him on payment of a gold guinea. The next day, before departing, he told the inn-keeper that he had given the girl a gold coin and asked her to have it changed into silver – and that she had failed to deliver his change. The girl was searched, the gold coin discovered, and of course the word of Colonel Charteris was accepted, and the girl's protestations were in vain: he got his guinea back, and she got the sack.

One of the drawbacks of his notoriety was that it was well-nigh impossible to find female servants to work in his household, so when he needed a new servant-girl for his home at Hanover Square in London, he gave his name as Colonel Harvey. It was apparently part of a ritual, played out for the amusement of the somewhat fat 54-year-old colonel and his friends. Girls would be hired, raped, and then pushed out onto the streets.

As the Newgate Calendar put it:

His house was no better than a brothel, and no woman of modesty would live within his walls. He kept in pay some women of abandoned character, who, going to inns where the country waggons put up, used to prevail on harmless young girls to go to the colonel's house as servants; the consequence of which was, that their ruin soon followed, and they were turned out of doors, exposed to all the miseries consequent on poverty and a loss of reputation.

In October 1729 a young woman called Anne Bond was taken on as a maid-servant and was immediately besieged by the loathsome lothario. She resolutely declined the Colonel's demands for sexual favours. On the third day she overheard someone refer to her master as Colonel Charteris. Realizing who 'Colonel Harvey' was, she sought to leave his employment immediately. He responded by having her locked in her room. The next day, 10 November 1729, he sent for her demanding that she make up the fire. He then brutally raped her, after gagging her screams with his night cap. When she stated her intention to report the crime, he had her stripped and horse-whipped, alleging that she was a thief. She was thrown out with no possessions.

Brave girl – she made a complaint against Charteris and initially he was charged with the misdemeanour of assault with intent to rape. The Middlesex Jury upgraded the charge to rape – a crime which carried the death penalty. The case was referred to the Old Bailey and the trial started on 27 February 1730. By then the trial was the subject of huge Press attention. His defence team tried to besmirch Anne Bond's character, claiming that she was a prostitute and a thief. He claimed that the act was consensual, producing his household servants to give evidence that the girl was lying, and that they had heard no noises or screams at the time of the alleged offence. Charteris even produced a letter which his footman swore on oath came from the girl, but it was clearly a forgery. Three witnesses were produced to give evidence that Anne was a virtuous and religious young woman. The jury retired for just forty-five minutes to consider its verdict and, on 2 March, Charteris was found guilty and sentenced to death.

That should have been the end of the matter – he was carted off to Newgate prison and his goods were seized as being forfeit to the Crown. He was, it transpired, one of ten men sentenced to death by the court that day.

However, a campaign to pardon the appalling colonel got under way – it appears that he had 'friends in high places' not least with Robert Walpole, First Lord of the Treasury. More to the point, he seems to have been able to buy off Anne Bond with the promise of an annual sum of £800, enough for her to get married. She planned to open a public house, apparently to be named 'The Colonel Charteris Head.' The sum of £15,000 was reportedly spent on 'oiling the wheels of justice' (in other words, laid out in bribes). It worked. Six weeks after sentence was handed down, George II granted a Royal Pardon, and the man was set free. He then had the nerve to sue for the return of his goods – even though his conviction as a felon meant that the seizure was entirely lawful. He ended up having to sell shares to obtain the return of his chattels. Meanwhile the Press also alleged that he made a substantial 'thank you' gift to Sir Robert Walpole.

The public were outraged – the poor because it was a clear example that the rich could get away with anything, and the rich because he was a disgrace and a dishonest cheat. He was pilloried in the Press with books such as 'Some authentick memoirs relating to the life, amours … of Colonel Ch----s. Rape-Master General of Great Britain.' A ballad entitled *On General Francesco, Rape-Master General of Great Britain* was published and he became the subject of satirical attacks by popular writers such as Alexander Pope, John Arbuthnot and Jonathan Swift. Charteris returned to Edinburgh in ill-health, possibly as a result of illness contracted in prison. He died on 24 February 1732. The outraged citizens of Edinburgh saw no reason why he should receive the full sacrament – they chased away the clergyman conducting the funeral, and pelted the grave at Greyfriars with manure, offal and dead cats.

His conduct and unpopularity coincided with a campaign aimed at discrediting Walpole, who was seen as corrupt. The idea that 'the rich can get away with it' was echoed in John Gay's *The Beggar's Opera*, which cast the hero as a highwayman and posed the question: why do the poor get punished for their crimes, when the rich do not?

ELIZABETH CHUDLEIGH – bigamist.

The trial for the crime of bigamy by the Duchess of Kingston (born Elizabeth Chudleigh in 1721) was one of the sensations of the Georgian Age. The Press devoted endless column inches to the trial and its aftermath – to the lower orders it confirmed what they had always known: that their supposed social superiors were a load of lying degenerates. Many years later even *The Times* was moved to comment in June 1788 that 'Bigamy, it seems, is a greater crime than simple fornication or fashionable adultery.'

Elizabeth had risen from fairly humble origins – the family owned a small estate in Devon, but they were not wealthy. Her father had unwisely invested what family money there was (£1,000) in South Sea Stock, and when the Bubble burst in 1720 he lost the lot. Her father died when he was only 38, leaving the 5-year-old Elizabeth to be brought up in genteel poverty. Mother was forced to take in lodgers at her home in the newly-developed, but not yet fashionable, area of Mayfair in London.

Elizabeth's childhood seems to have involved little formal education. She was passed like a baton from the care of one country relation to another, until her mother used her friendship with the Earl of Bath to secure a position at Court for Elizabeth as maid of honour to Augusta, Princess of Wales. The year was 1743 and Elizabeth was 22. She desperately needed the annual sum of £200 which went with the position. When she wanted to shock she could be coarse and vulgar. For instance, she developed a reputation for flatulence at the dinner table, and took repeated pleasure on blaming it on the dogs. She was however a popular figure at Court – vivacious, bright and witty. One day at Winchester Races she encountered a young naval officer called Augustus John Hervey. The two fell impetuously in love, and Hervey proposed marriage almost immediately. His prospects were not good – his salary was a paltry £50 a year, and marriage would automatically mean that Elizabeth would have to abandon her position as Maid of Honour since married ladies were no longer considered to be maids. More to the point he was about to leave on a two-year tour of duty. A long engagement might have been prudent, not least because it would reveal whether his prospects were ever likely to materialise. He was the second son of the Earl of Bristol but his elder brother was alive, albeit in bad health, and it was by no means certain that Augustus John would ever inherit either the title or the money that would go with it. But the headstrong couple rushed into marriage, deciding to keep it a secret from the outside world. That way, she kept her position at Court, and he was able to avoid the risk of alienating his family. The wedding took place at Lainston in Wiltshire, on 4 August 1744, and he left to join his squadron, *en route* to the West Indies, two days later.

When the time came for Hervey to return to England, he found that his bride had not exactly been pining away during his absence. She had developed a close friendship with James, Sixth Duke of Hamilton, and her flirtatious behaviour had attracted a host of other admirers, none of whom were aware of her marriage. Proposals from both the Duke of Hamilton and the Duke of Ancaster had been turned down. Hervey was shocked and appalled at her reputation, and the couple did not even meet up for three months. It appears that Elizabeth was keen to see that her debts were paid by Hervey, but not so keen to have anything else to do with him. According to later reports, Hervey engineered a private meeting at his apartments by threatening to go public about the marriage if Elizabeth refused to see him. She turned up, was locked inside, and in the words of the time 'he would not permit her to retire without consenting to that commerce, delectable only when kindred souls melt into each other with the soft embrace.' In other words, he forced himself upon her. The report continued 'The fruit of this meeting was the addition of a boy to the human race.'

This was in 1747. In order to conceal the pregnancy Elizabeth discreetly moved to Chelsea where she could have the child, away from the prying eyes and ears of the Court. But the child, a boy, only lived a few months. The couple decided to separate a year after the birth, but, since the marriage was a secret, so was the news of the separation. From that point in time, Elizabeth could no longer look to Hervey for financial support and protection, leaving her in a most vulnerable position. Her impetuous behaviour and lack of decorum caused difficulties at Court – especially when she turned up at a masquerade ball at the end of April 1749, during the Jubilee celebrations of George II, wearing virtually nothing but a string of fig leaves around her waist.

Her fellow Maids of Honour were outraged at her bare-chested appearance. She went in the character of Iphigenia, who in Greek mythology was offered as a sacrifice to appease the gods offended by her father Agamemnon, and one of the guests remarked that she gave the appearance of being 'so naked ye high Priest might easily inspect ye

Entrails of ye Victim.' As *The Life and Memoirs of Elizabeth Chudleigh*, published in 1788, put it:

> ... *it has been asserted this lady appeared in a shape of flesh-coloured silk so nicely and closely fitted to her body as to produce a perfect review of the unadorned mother of mankind, and that this fair representative of frailty ... had contrived a method of giving as evident tokens of modesty, by binding her loins with a partial covering, or zone, of fig-leaves.*

The King was, as might be expected, far from disinterested in her appearance and asked if he might touch her breast, only to be met with the response that Elizabeth knew of something softer – and promptly placed the King's hand on his head. His Royal Highness was enchanted by the near-naked nymph, and the gossip-mongers had a field day. Clearly she had the opportunity to become a royal mistress, but for Elizabeth this prospect did not feature in her long-term quest for security. Besides, the Hanoverian kings could be notoriously parsimonious when it came to mistresses.

Instead she befriended the shy but rather well-connected Evelyn Pierrepont, Second Duke of Kingston-upon-Hull. A cousin of Lord Bute (future Prime Minister) he was considered one of the most handsome men in England. Not for him the outrageous extravagances of Court – his interests were simple: fishing and cricket. Surprisingly, Elizabeth was happy to share these passions and by 1752 it was noted that the pair were an item. Their union meant that Elizabeth was able to spend money like water. A fine new house was built in London – called initially Chudleigh House, but later renamed Kingston House. Parties for their rich and influential friends were held, and Elizabeth was granted a fair amount of personal freedom, travelling on the continent, where she became a particular friend of the Electress of Saxony. When in England with the duke she was content to spend her time fishing and sharing his other interests – she even arranged a ladies cricket match in his honour.

The question of her marital status became an issue. Hervey had settled in England and wanted a divorce, which could only be obtained by a private Act of Parliament. Such a step would inevitably mean public gossip and adverse comments in Parliament. If granted, the divorce would have meant that on any remarriage she would be seen to be 'second hand goods'.

Elizabeth therefore objected to the whole idea of a divorce and instead petitioned the Ecclesiastical Court for a declaration that she had never been married. The onus was on Hervey to prove that the marriage had taken place – but whereas servants were produced to say that they had heard of the wedding, no-one would testify that they had been present at the ceremony. Elizabeth swore blind that there was no such wedding. On 10 February 1769, sentence was pronounced, 'that the said Elizabeth Chudleigh was and now is a Spinster, and free from all matrimonial contracts and espousals with the said Augustus John Hervey.' A month later, on her forty-eighth birthday, Elizabeth married the duke.

Oddly, polite society turned against the couple. Everyone *knew* that she had been married, and whereas it was one thing to be the Duke's mistress, received at Court and by the great and the good, it was another to be seen as a flagrant bigamist. Elizabeth found herself shunned, and she and her husband retreated to their country estates. All was well for a few years, but the Duke suffered a series of strokes and died in 1763. Under his will, everything passed to his widow, on condition that she did not remarry. Enter the jealous relations, outraged at either having to wait, or worse still, having to be cut out of their inheritances altogether.

Elizabeth set out for the continent. She was received with the courtesies due to a duchess by the Pope, Clement XIV. Meanwhile, March 1775 saw her first, and therefore legal, husband succeed to the Earldom of Bristol, making her the Countess of Bristol. It was not a title she wished to be known by.

Later in 1775 she was forced to return to England because the Duke of Kingston's nephew, Evelyn Meadows, brought proceedings against her based on the fact that she had married bigamously. He wanted to show that the Will should be set aside, either on the basis that there was no marriage, or that Elizabeth had used undue influence. In vain Elizabeth sought to have the hearing set aside by virtue of the earlier decision of the Ecclesiastical Court. In vain she tried to get George III to intervene, or to help her get the case transferred to the House of Lords. All this was duly reported in the papers of the day. Worse still, the actor play-wright Samuel Foote tried to put on a play called *A Trip to Calais*, in which the thinly disguised figure of the Duchess was represented by a coarse, avaricious woman named Kitty Crocodile. His purpose may have been no more than to extort money from Elizabeth – he reportedly turned up at her house and read aloud passages to the mortified lady, and demanded £2,000 in return for agreeing not to have the play published. By all accounts Elizabeth tried to outflank Foote by using her influence with the Lord Chamberlain, who was happy to have the play banned. Outraged, Foote took the story to the papers. Matters were made worse when Elizabeth responded to a letter written by Foote – he simply published the exchange of letters, which brought the entire saga out into the open. The whole story became public property.

The bigamy trial in April 1776 was a sensation: Elizabeth was unwell and therefore escaped being locked up in the Tower prior to the trial. She was effectively put under house arrest instead. 350 tickets were printed granting entrance to the court – even Queen Charlotte turned up one day. The general consensus was that Elizabeth would be found guilty – and there was much conjecture as to whether she could be sent to a penal colony, given that Britain was by then at war with her American colonies.

Witnesses who had previously denied the wedding suddenly appeared out of the woodwork and agreed that they had been present at the ceremony. Others, who might have helped Elizabeth, simply declined to give evidence or went on long holidays abroad. The result was inevitable – she was found guilty, probably not helped by the fact that in 1759, before her bigamous union, she had taken the extraordinary step of registering the original marriage in the Parish Church at Lainston. Quite why she had done this was unclear – maybe it was a safety precaution in case the Duke did not marry her, perhaps she wanted to be able to fall back on the idea of being a Countess if and when Hervey became Earl. Whatever the reason, it hardly helped her case, although she personally addressed the court for three quarters of an hour. The decision of the Lords was unanimous – 119 peers took it in turns to give a verdict of guilty. Only her rank (i.e. as Countess of Bristol) spared her from imprisonment. Instead she fled to the continent, her fortune intact but her reputation in tatters.

Within days, pamphlets giving lurid details of the trial appeared not just in London but across the country. One ran to thirty-two pages and was published by Joseph Harrop, printer and proprietor of the *Manchester Mercury*. He sold it for three pence, or offered it for free to subscribers of his newspaper. In effect it was the forerunner of the free supplements which accompany today's gossip magazines.

The run-in with Samuel Foote led to a secondary scandal, which was to ruin the actor-playwright. Elizabeth employed the Reverend William Jackson as her secretary. He wrote articles in the *Public Ledger* suggesting that Foote was a homosexual. Foote successfully sued for libel, but the Reverend, probably bankrolled by Elizabeth, and using the *nom de plume* of Humphrey Nettle, published a lengthy attack on Foote under the title of *Sodom and Onan*. It contained a recognisable portrait of Foote, together with an illustration of a large naked foot. The satire attacked Foote as a sodomite, using language which was neither subtle nor appropriate for a man of the cloth. Foote responded by re-writing *A Trip to Calais* as *The Capuchin*, with Reverend William Jackson lampooned as 'Dr Viper'. The bitter exchange of vitriol was followed by criminal charges being brought against Foote in late 1776. He appeared before the Kings Bench to answer allegations, made by his former footman John Sangster, that Foote had attempted to commit an unnatural act upon his person twice in May 1775. Lord Mansfield heard the case, and concluded that the whole thing was a conspiracy to blacken Foote's character, and Foote was acquitted. But the damage had been done, and Foote died, a broken man, shortly afterwards. He was 57.

On the back of the bigamy trial the Meadows family sought to have the Will set aside. A suit in the Court of Chancery would inevitably take many years, and during this time Elizabeth drifted from one European court to another. To her great consternation, she was not an honoured guest at Maria Theresa's court in Vienna, thanks in part to the intervention of the British Ambassador. She found greater favour at the court of the Russian Empress, and bought an extensive estate near St Petersburg which she named Chudleigh. She also had residences in Rome and in Paris, finally dying in the French capital in 1788, still legally the Countess of Bristol but denied the title of Duchess of Kingston. The Meadows family descended on her assets like vultures, reclaiming what they saw as rightfully theirs. News quickly crossed the Channel and, in death, the bigamist Elizabeth became famous once more, with pamphlets and newspapers reviving public interest in her scandalous life. One book ran to 252 pages and bore the title *Authentic Particulars of the Life of the Late Duchess of Kingston During Her Connection with the Duke: Her Residence at Dresden, Vienna, St. Petersburgh, Paris and Several Other Courts of Europe, Also a Faithful Copy of Her Singular Will.*

Was she a gold digger, a callous woman who lied through her teeth and enjoyed a status to which she had no entitlement? Or was she simply a woman who genuinely did not regard herself as being married (whatever the letter of the law) when she had spent so little time with Hervey as man and wife? Perhaps she had simply convinced herself that she was entitled to regard the order from the Ecclesiastical Court as binding. Having been raped by Hervey, who can blame her? Certainly she appears to have been a loving and devoted partner to the Duke – he was clearly the love of her life, and vice versa. In the event it did not really matter – the public were able to indulge their appetite for scandal, gossip and intrigue, and the case sums up much about Georgian attitudes and hypocrisy towards marriage, infidelity, the courts and money.

SALLY SALISBURY – beware of a whore with a knife.
Right at the start of the Georgian period a young prostitute called Sally Pridden hit the headlines. She had been born in Shrewsbury in 1690, the daughter of a bricklayer, and she used the name 'Salisbury' because she reputedly resembled Lady Salisbury. She rose to the dizzy heights of being a famous courtesan thanks in part to her ready wit, droll sense of humour and quick repartee. And also because she was willing (and apparently able) to sell her virginity to eager customers on no fewer than twenty-six occasions. Her entry into the world of prostitution received a huge boost when she was taken under the wing of the notorious bawd Mother Wisebourn. The introduction to

the famous 'abbess' was subsequently described in detail: she was made to stand naked while an intimate inspection was carried out. As a contemporary report stated, Mother Wisebourn 'felt every limb one by one, touch'd her to see if she was sound, as a jockey handles a Horse or Mare' while checking that she had the right demeanour to pass the test of appearing pure and innocent. In time she was to claim to have had a string of aristocratic lovers, ranging from Lord William Bentinck, Charles Fitzroy, the Duke of Richmond and his half-brother the Duke of Albans, to Lord Bollingbroke and Lord Cardigan. Indeed she even claimed that the Prince of Wales (later to become King George III) had been her lover.

Her downfall dated from the night of 22 December 1722. She had turned up at the Three Tuns Tavern in Chandos Street, rather the worse for drink and possibly suffering from delusions brought on by drug-taking, and there she met her lover John ('Jacky') Finch. He came from a well-respected family – his elder brother was a lord. They argued, especially over the fact that Finch had bought opera tickets and given them to Sarah's younger sister Jenny. Sarah was convinced that Finch was trying to have his wicked way with Jenny and in a fit of rage picked up a knife and stabbed him close to the heart. He was not expected to live, but miraculously recovered, and swore forgiveness. It did not stop Sally being dragged off to face a charge of attempted murder. She was found guilty of assault, but was acquitted on the more serious charge, was fined £100 and sentenced to a year in Newgate prison. There she caught 'gaol fever' (i.e. typhoid) and died in February 1724. The *London Journal* remarked that 'the famous Sally Salisbury died on Tuesday… of a consumption … preceded by a fever, so that she was reduced almost to a skeleton.' A more flippant obituary appeared some years later in the *Weekly Oracle* (1735):

> *Here lies flat on her Back, but unactive at last*
> *Poor Sally lies under grim Death;*
> *Through the course of her Vices she galloped so fast*
> *No wonder she's now out of Breath.*
> *The goal of her Pleasures she drove very hard*
> *But was tripped up e'er half way she ran;*
> *And though everyone fancied her life was a Yard**
> *Yet it proved to be less than a Span.*

*'Yard' it must be remembered, was slang for an erect penis.

TERESIA CONSTANTIA PHILLIPS – bigamy.

Teresia Constantia Phillips – or 'Con' Phillips as she was generally known – was a woman who tended to do things to excess. As a 'courtesan to the nobility' she was the mistress of a surprisingly large number of people who were rich and famous. As a wife she got through rather more husbands than was seemly, marrying five times. She may have been a serial bigamist, and was also a woman who gave her backing to one of the most famous sex-shops in the country (the shop known as The Green Canister, mentioned previously, where customers could buy condoms, dildos and other erotica). She is also regarded as an important figure in the development of the autobiography. Her *An Apology* was published in serial form (there were eighteen parts or instalments) with several editions appearing in print between 1748 and 1760.

An Apology may well have been intended as a kiss-and-tell memoir designed to earn Con a few pounds from blackmail, at a time when her traditional income was declining. It also gave her a chance to get her own back at the men who had used her, and at the chicanery of a legal system which had failed her. *An Apology* became a popular work – even though no publisher could be found to take the risk of being linked to its publication. Con therefore had it printed herself, and signed each copy as a sign of its authenticity.

She was raped as a teenager, allegedly by Lord Chesterfield, leading her to a life in the sex trade. It was a life marked by debt and frequent litigation, punctuated by trips to and from the Caribbean. In the 1740s, Grub Street castigated her for her loose morals, and its hacks derided her conduct, all of which made her famous to the extent that mezzotints of her portrait were bought in their thousands. *An Apology* makes it clear that she was well aware that at least one of her trips to the altar was bigamous, but felt that the public was entitled to hear her side of the story. She had been used by men, and was perfectly willing to use them in return. Marriage certainly helped her precarious finances, but when she died, in Jamaica in 1765, she was destitute and friendless. *The Gentleman's Magazine* of that year contained a lengthy and somewhat critical obituary, but also reflected that she had been 'mistress of the revels' on Jamaica, a post which apparently gave her the right to a benefit on stage twice a year, each one earning her an estimated 100 guineas. She was 59 when she died, and apart from the opprobrium which bigamy brought her name, she was never convicted of a criminal offence as a bigamist. Her portrait appears as Image 67.

LORD BALTIMORE – a kidnapper, a rapist, a liar – but a free man.

The thirty-nine years which Frederick Calvert, Sixth Baron Baltimore, spent on this earth were not exactly useful or commendable. He inherited his title, and vast swathes of Maryland, when he was 20. He took no interest whatsoever in his colonial heritage, instead preferring to swan around Europe visiting Turkish brothels and hitting on the idea of coming back to Britain to convert his stately pile into a Turkish-style seraglio, where he could keep his harem of mistresses. In 1753, at the age of 22, he married Lady Diana Egerton, daughter of the Duke of Bridgewater. He was described at the time as 'a disreputable and dissolute degenerate' and also as being 'feeble in body, conceited, frivolous, and dissipated...' His marriage was a disaster and they separated in 1756. He lived openly with a number of mistresses and became father to a small tribe of offspring. In 1758 it was rumoured that he had insisted on taking his wife out for a drive in her carriage, but that the phaeton had overturned. The one certain thing was that the poor lady died as a result of her injuries. Foul play was hinted at but no charges were brought.

Even with his harem of willing concubines under his roof, he yearned for new conquests and it looks as though some of his friends were perfectly willing to assist in procuring them for him. He took a fancy to a young God-fearing Quaker girl called Sarah Woodcock. She was a virtuous young innocent living in London with her father, while working in a millinery shop. Lord Baltimore saw her, took a fancy to her, and lured her to his home under false pretences. Once there she was imprisoned and threatened with violence unless she gave in to his Lordship's advances. Too scared to eat or drink in case she was being poisoned, she was kept a prisoner for four days until, weak and broken in spirit, she was raped by Lord Baltimore. He kept her in his house for a whole fortnight, raping her constantly, before her desperate father heard of her plight, and of her whereabouts, and secured a writ of *habeas corpus.*

Lord Baltimore's trial at Kingston Assizes was a sensation. He claimed that Sarah consented, and indeed that she had been free to go at any time. Basically his defence was no more than: 'It is her word against mine, and I am Lord Baltimore, son of a very distinguished father, and that should be good enough for the jury.' Amazingly – it was sufficient, and after eighty minutes of deliberation the jury acquitted him of all charges, as well as dismissing the cases brought against two of his employees who had been accessories.

Innocent in the eyes of the law maybe, but the newspapers generally sided with the humble milliner and savaged Baltimore for being an aristocratic debaucher who had behaved abominably and then tried to hide behind his rank and privilege. He suffered further embarrassment when Sarah Watson, one of the former members of his harem, published her memoirs under the title of *Memoirs of the Seraglio ... by a Discarded Sultana* (London, 1768). It contained many salacious details, eagerly lapped up by the public, including the suggestion that although he kept eight mistresses Lord Baltimore was not actually able to satisfy even one of them.

He was driven into exile by all the adverse publicity, and died of a fever contracted in Italy. For him it really was a case of 'See Naples and die'. His body was returned to England and he was buried at Epsom. Reflecting on the case, the *Newgate Calendar* commented 'What shall we think of a man, of Lord Baltimore's rank and fortune, who could debase himself beneath all rank and distinction, and, by the wish to gratify his irregular passions, submit to degrade himself in the opinion of his own servants and other domestics?'

Others might think that degrading himself in the eyes of his servants was nothing compared to the wrong he did to a terrified Sarah Woodcock.

MARTHA RAY – death at the opera.

Of all the people who one might expect to 'seduce 'em and leave 'em' the Earl of Sandwich was a real paradox when it came to Martha Ray. He was, after all, a member of Dashwood's notorious Hellfire Club, which met at Medmenham Abbey and specialized in bringing in whores by the cartload for general orgiastic enjoyment. Years earlier he had seduced a young girl who went on to become the illustrious whore called Fanny Murray. He was also, over a period of time, Postmaster General, First Lord of the Admiralty and Secretary of State for the Northern Department. This powerful figure with a reputation for gambling, whoring – and inventing the sandwich – met Martha Ray when she was a 16-year-old girl training to be a milliner, in a shop on Tavistock Row, off Covent Garden. The girl had a fine singing voice and had an ear for music. Instead of debauching her and moving on, the Earl paid for her to go to France so that she could further her musical education and become proficient on the harpsichord, and also to acquire a grounding in etiquette, fine manners and other social graces. She returned and became, to all intents and purposes, the wife of the good Earl. Except that he already had a wife; one who had been declared insane and was living with her sister in apartments at Windsor Castle. Undeterred by such niceties, Martha took up residence at the Earl's home in Westminster and at the family seat at Hinchingbrooke, and got her feet under the table to the extent of producing at least five (and possibly as many as nine) children. The Earl accepted these mini-Sandwiches to the extent that he appeared to like them rather more than his legitimate issue.

The problem faced by Martha was that she had no security whatsoever – the Earl could chuck her out at a moment's notice. Also, he was twenty-four years older than her, and if he died she would be homeless, penniless and a social outcast. She decided to take up a career on the stage, in musical roles, in order to be financially independent – and although the Earl was not in favour of the idea he had little say in the matter because he was heavily in debt following rather too many losing streaks at the gaming tables. Martha became well-known in operatic circles, and on the night of 7 April 1779 had gone to see a musical starring Margaret Kennedy called *Love in a Village* at The Royal Opera House at Covent Garden. She went in the company of her great friend, the singer Caterina Galli, because the Earl had work commitments and was unable to attend. As Martha was leaving the theatre to alight her carriage a man stepped forward brandishing two pistols. He fired at her head at point blank range and she died instantly. The assailant then put the other pistol to his head and tried to pull the trigger. Notwithstanding his army training (he was an ex-army captain) he missed, which left the man frantically trying to club himself over the head with the pistol butt … not an effective way to try and commit suicide. The assailant was detained and turned out to be the 26-year-old Reverend James Hackman, a man besotted with the deceased ever since he had met her at Hinchingbrooke as a guest of the Earl. He had apparently proposed marriage to Martha, and been turned down out of hand. He then decided that she would be bound to change her mind and look favourably on his proposal if he left the army and became a vicar. Once he had become the Reverend James Hackman he renewed his pursuit and was again repulsed. The deranged man then developed the fixation that Martha was having an affair with someone else – possibly George Hanger, Fourth Baron Coleraine. He watched Martha go into the opera house and had popped home to pick up the two pistols. When he was arrested he was carrying two letters, one addressed to his brother-in-law which pretty well amounted to a confession, and the other a love letter to Martha.

The death was a shattering blow to the Earl – the first he knew of the incident was when her carriage returned to his doorstep, minus any passenger. He apparently 'wept exceedingly' and lamented 'I could have borne anything but this.' Martha was only 37 years old when she died; two days later she was buried at Elstree parish church, still dressed in the robe she was wearing when she was shot. Within days of the funeral, Hackman was on trial for his life. Oddly, he pleaded 'not guilty', claiming that he only intended to kill himself. The second pistol rather indicated otherwise, and the verdict of 'guilty' was returned without hesitation. Justice was swift – the trial followed just five days after the shots had been fired, and the trip to the gallows at Tyburn followed just a couple of days later. Before he was hanged, Reverend Hackman sought forgiveness from the Earl, and apparently was given it although the Earl stated that Hackman had 'robbed him of all the comfort in the world.' After the hanging, Hackman's body was cut down and taken away for dissection at Surgeon's Hall.

The public were fascinated at the crime of passion, the sad tale of a man so besotted by love that he killed the object of his desire. As *The Newgate Calendar* later noted: 'this shocking and truly lamentable case interested all ranks of people, who pitied the murderer's fate, conceived him stimulated to commit the horrid crime through love and madness. Pamphlets and poems were written on the occasion, and the crime was long the common topic of conversation.' One year after the shooting the events surrounding the murder formed the basis of a novel by Herbert Croft entitled *Love and Madness*.

The Earl never really recovered, retiring from public office two years later. He brought up the children of his union with Martha, and died in 1792.

EARL FERRERS – murderer.
The story of the unlovely Laurence Shirley, who was to become Earl Ferrers, is one of arrogance, cruelty, dissolute living and ultimately murder.

His grandfather, the First Earl, had sired no fewer than fifteen sons and twelve daughters (by two wives) and looking after that lot rather diminished the fortunes of the earldom. Nevertheless the title included family estates in Leicester, Derbyshire and Northamptonshire. Laurence's father was the tenth son, and Laurence inherited the title in 1745. It is worth mentioning that there appears to have been a strain of madness in the family.

At the age of 20 he had turned his back on a University education (Oxford) and had gone to Paris where he displayed a talent for every excess, especially drinking, gambling, fighting and whoring. He returned to England and initially set up home with a Mrs Clifford, by whom he had four daughters. Requiring a son once he succeeded to the earldom, he married a 16-year-old girl called Mary Meredith in 1752, but without giving up his mistress. For the young bride it must have been horrific. Her husband was twice her age and was violent when drunk (which was often). She must have been humiliated by his womanising. It was a time when the rich (particularly the males, and especially the nobility) could do more-or-less what they wanted. As it turned out, the one thing they could not do was 'get away with murder'.

All the more amazing that in 1758, Mary succeeded in petitioning Parliament for a formal separation from the Earl, on the basis of his cruelty. Horace Walpole noted in a letter that year to his friend Sir Horace Mann:

The most particular thing I know is what happened the other day: a frantic Earl of Ferrers has for this twelve-month supplied conversation by attempting to murder his wife, a pretty, harmless young woman, and everybody that took her part; having broken the peace, to which the House of Lords tied him last year, the cause was trying again there on Friday last.

Parliament not only took the unusual step of awarding a formal separation, which must have cost Mary's family a fortune in legal fees, but also declared that the Earl's assets should be controlled by trustees and that the trustees should pay Mary rents and profits from the family estates. Laurence must have been furious at having to watch as he lost control of his affairs. Initially he had been keen to recommend his steward John Johnson as rent collector to the Trustees – John had worked for him loyally for some years and was good at book-keeping. Maybe he thought he could lean on John to 'cook the books.' However, it appears that over time the Earl grew to distrust the steward. Perhaps this was inevitable, given John's role as go-between, serving the Earl but paying his rents to the Earl´s estranged wife.

On Sunday 13 January 1760, Earl Ferrers went to his home at Stanton, about two miles from Ashby-de-la-Zouch in Leicestershire, and ordered the unfortunate Mr Johnson to come to him on the Friday following, at three o'clock in the afternoon. The steward arrived as requested and waited to be summonsed to the Earl's quarters. The Earl was still eating his lunch. After the meal he sent Mrs Clifford and her young daughters for a long walk and arranged for all five of the male servants to depart on sundry errands. This left only the three housemaids, an old man and a young boy in the house. He then called Mr Johnson into his study, locked the door and, according to *The Newgate Calendar*:

> *... being thus together, the Earl ... ordered him to kneel down. The unfortunate man went down on one knee; upon which the Earl, in a tone of voice loud enough to be heard by the maid-servants without, cried: "Down on your other knee! Declare that you have acted against Lord Ferrers. Your time is come — you must die." Then, suddenly drawing a loaded pistol from his pocket, he presented it and immediately fired. The ball entered the body of the unfortunate man, but he rose up, and entreated that no further violence might be done him; and the female servants at that time coming to the door, being alarmed by the report, his lordship quitted the room.*

The Earl agreed that a doctor could be sent for, and went off for a drink or two in his private quarters, emerging worse for wear some hours later. He refused to let the doctor take the dying man away to his own house. The doctor patiently waited until the earl retired to bed, and rigged up an easy chair with poles so that the dying man could be carried away in a makeshift sedan. He died the following morning at nine o'clock.

Come the morning and the Earl declined to give himself up – half-dressed he rode off on his horse, but a few hours later was confronted by an angry crowd and despite being armed with a blunderbuss, a brace of pistols and a dagger, was disarmed and taken before the magistrates.

The Earl was entitled to insist that his trial should take place before his peers in the House of Lords – not for him the humiliation of being tried as a common criminal. He was permitted to drive in his landau, pulled by six horses, to London where his trial started in Westminster Hall in April. The Earl was not permitted to have a defence counsel when he appeared before his peers and was required to conduct his own case. His chosen defence required him to prove that he was insane, but unfortunately for the Earl, the more lucid and eloquently he conducted his defence, the more he proved that he was perfectly sane. He was found guilty – and at that stage he indicated a regret at having pleaded insanity, saying that he intended to kill his victim, and showing no remorse. Murder carried an automatic death penalty. The avid readership of the trial reports loved the idea of a peer of the realm getting his just rewards, and ensured that when sentence was carried out, it was witnessed by tens of thousands of onlookers.

In vain the Earl pleaded to be dispatched in the manner of a nobleman, that is to say by being beheaded by a swordsman. But that penalty only applied to treason, and the Earl was forced to accept that he would end up in the hangman's noose, just like any other common felon. He was however entitled to travel from his place of imprisonment (the Tower) to Tyburn in his own landau, accompanied by a guard of lancers. A huge crowd was in attendance on 5 May 1760 to see the hanging and the journey to Tyburn took nearly three hours. The Earl was attired in his best white suit, richly embroidered with silver, (the one he wore at his wedding) saying 'This is the suit in which I was married, and in which I will die.' A specially made set of gallows had been put up, furnished with black silk cushions for his Lordship's comfort.

He was the last member of the House of Lords to be hanged. It was considered to be his duty as a nobleman to die in a proper and dignified manner – he did his duty, but probably only for the first and last time in his life.

JOHN DAMER – suicidal debts.
From the *Bath Chronicle*:

> Yesterday morning, about four o'clock, a Noble-
> man (well known on the turf) retired from a gaming-
> table near Pall-Mall, with the lofs of 70,000l

The death of John Damer at the Bedford Arms, Covent Garden on 15 August 1776 provides an interesting insight into Georgian attitudes to many things – fashion, debt, gambling, marriage and prostitution. At the date of his demise he had lost £70,000 pursuing his gambling addiction – the equivalent of well over five and half million pounds in modern money. He was also a most devoted follower of fashion, reportedly changing his outfit three times a day. His tailor's bills alone must have been ruinous. When he died, his wardrobe of clothes were reportedly worth £15,000.

The German traveller and writer von Archenholz describes the man's departure from this world as follows:

The conduct of the Hon Mr Damer, only son to Lord Milton was … extraordinary, and gave rise to a thousand melancholy reflections. Young, handsome, tenderly beloved by his father, nearly adored by the ladies, and with all the honours and dignities of the state within his reach he conceived a sudden disgust to life. Having repaired to a bagnio he commanded twelve of the most handsome women of the town to be brought to him, and gave orders that they should be supplied with all manner of delicacies. Having afterwards bolted the door he made them undress one another and, when naked, requested them to amuse him with the most voluptuous attitudes. About an hour afterwards he dismissed them, loaded with presents, and then, drawing a pistol from his pocket immediately put an end to his existence.

Well, his departure from this world clearly showed a certain flair. Others give different versions of the sad death – Boswell's 'Johnson' has him eating three buttered muffins, immediately before committing suicide and knowing that he would not be around to suffer the indigestion which would inevitably follow. *The Gentleman's Magazine* for that month rather lamely gave the cause of death as 'lunacy'.

The one thing which was certain is that John Damer could not face the financial burden of his gambling debts – nor the unhappy marriage which he had entered into with Anne Conway seven years earlier. She, poor woman, was saddled with his debts, because her father-in-law insisted that she should accept personal responsibility for them. She did however go on to become a fine sculptress. She was taken under the wing of Horace Walpole, who was a great admirer of her works. And indeed when he died he left her his extraordinary stately pile at Strawberry Hill at Twickenham.

Anne exhibited her works at the Royal Academy on no fewer than thirty-two occasions, sculpting the great and the good ranging from His Majesty the King, to Horatio Nelson. Her representation of the god Apollo, as a 10ft high statue, was to be seen in the foyer of the Drury Lane Theatre.

Caricaturists delighted in showing her sculpting the godly nether regions – they knew that the public would be scandalised at the idea of a female getting so 'up close and personal' with the male form. It was however considered entirely acceptable for a man to be painting or sculpting a female nude – a reminder of the misogynistic attitudes prevailing in the Georgian era. But Anne also enjoyed a reputation as a bit of a cross-dresser – she was frequently seen wearing male clothing – and she set tongues wagging because of her fondness for female company, especially with the actresses Sarah Siddons and Elizabeth Farren, and with the writer Mary Berry. Rumours circulated of her 'Sapphic' tendencies, with the diarist Hester Thrale dismissing Anne contemptuously with the comment that she was 'a Lady much suspected for liking her own Sex in a criminal Way.' In print, *A Sapphick Epistle* appeared in 1771, portraying her as a lesbian. She died in 1828, at her house in Grosvenor Square and was buried in the Kent village of Sundridge, along with her apron and her array of sculptor's chisels and mallets, and the ashes of her beloved dog.

Chapter Nine

Rakes, Roués and Romantics

Rake:

Noun: a fashionable or wealthy man of immoral or promiscuous habits.
Synonyms: playboy, libertine, profligate; degenerate, roué, debauchee, dissolute man,
loose-liver; lecher, seducer, ladies' man, womaniser, philanderer, adulterer.
Informal: lady-killer;
Dated: gay dog, rip, blood;
Archaic: rakehell

JAMES BOSWELL, 1740–1795

On the basis of the opening definition, even James Boswell, biographer of Dr Samuel Johnson, deserves the title of rake. He had been born in Edinburgh in 1740. His father, a Scottish judge, wanted him to be a lawyer, whereas young James felt drawn to the world of journalism and the stage. In 1762 he came down to London and kept a journal of his stay – and as you might expect from a 22-year-old set loose in a city awash with lewdness and depravity, he revelled in his sexual encounters, and faithfully recorded many of them in his Journal. It is not the bragging which make the incidents endearing – it is the underlying male hypocrisy in his attitude towards prostitutes and prostitution, venereal disease and the use of condoms.

After a mere week in London, on 25 November 1772 he wrote:

I had now been sometime in town without female sport. I determined to have nothing to do with Whores as my health was of great consequence to me. I went to a Girl, with whom I had an intrigue at Edinburgh but my affection cooling, I had left her. I knew she was come up [to London]. I waited on her and tried to obtain my former favours; but in vain. She would by no means listen. I was really unhappy for want of women. I thought it hard to be in such a place without them. I picked up a girl in the Strand and went into a court with intention to enjoy her in armour [i.e. wearing a condom]. But she had none. I toyed with her. She wondered at my size, and said "If I ever took a Girl's Maidenhead, I would make her squeak." I gave her a shilling; and had command enough of myself to go without touching her. I afterwards trembled at the danger I had escaped. I resolved to wait cheerfully, till I got some safe girl or was liked by some woman of fashion.

An encounter with a London prostitute the year before had left Boswell with a venereal disease, hence his determination not to catch anything again. But the condoms, which he variously described as 'machines' and 'armour' had the disadvantage of needing to be moistened with water before use. A further fortnight passed, his passions unassuaged. He writes:

… I am surrounded with numbers of free-spirited Ladies of all kinds; from the splendid Madam at fifty guineas a night, down to the civil nymph with white thread stockings, who tramps along the strand, and will resign her engaging person to your honour for a pint of wine and a shilling.

In practice he had no need to resort to either, because he had met a girl who he called Louisa. She was 'a handsom [sic] Actress of Covent-Garden Theatre' and having described meeting her on 14 December he then spends the next month recounting how he tried to get her into bed. His seduction techniques appear to have worked and, on 12 January, he describes arranging for them to take a Hackney Carriage to an Inn where they checked in as 'Mr and Mrs Digges'. That night he proudly records that he rose to the occasion at what he describes as 'a most luscious feast'; declaring 'Five times was I fairly lost in supreme rapture.' But James omitted to use a condom, believing the girl to be clean – oblivious of the fact that he was as likely to infect her as the other way round. However, she was not as clean as she made out, and James describes a number of painful encounters with the medical profession before he was ready to re-enter the market-place. Louisa was replaced entirely by one-night stands. On 25 March he writes:

As I was coming home this night I felt carnal inclinations raging thro' my frame. I determined to gratify them. I went to St. James's Park and … picked up a Whore. For the first time did I engage in Armour which I found but a dull satisfaction. She who submitted to my lusty embraces was a young Shropshire Girl only seventeen, very well-looked, her name Elizabeth Parker. Poor being. She has a sad time of it!

The following week, on 31 March, he wrote:

At night I strolled into the Park and took the first Whore I met, whom I without many words copulated with free from danger, being safely sheeth'd. She was ugly and lean and her breath smelt of spirits. I never asked her name. When it was done she slunk off. I had a low opinion of this gross practice and resolved to do it no more.

Two weeks later he broke that resolve, recording on 9 April that he 'then came to the Park and in armorial guise performed concubinage with a strong plump good-humoured girl, called Nanny Baker.'

Four days later he recalled another incident:

I should have mentioned last night that I met with a monstrous big Whore in the Strand, whom I had a great curiosity to lubricate as the saying is. I went into a tavern with her, where she displayed to me all the parts of her enormous carcase; but I found that her Avarice was a large as her A- – - ; for she would by no means take what I offered her. I therefore, with all coolness pulled the bell and discharged the reckoning, to her no small surprise and mortification, who would fain have provoked me to talk harshly to her, and so make a disturbance. I was so much in lewd humour, that I felt myself restless, and took a little girl into a Court; but wanted vigour: So I went home resolved against low, street debauchery.

By 10 May his vigour had been restored sufficiently for him to record:

At the bottom of the Hay-market I picked up a strong jolly young damsel, and taking her under the Arm I conducted her to Westminster-Bridge, and then in armour compleat did I engage her upon this noble Edifice. The whim of doing it there with the Thames rolling below us amused me much. Yet after the brutish appetite was sated I could not but despise myself for being so closely united with such a low Wretch.

Exactly one week later:

I sallied the Streets and just at the bottom of our own, I picked up a fresh agreeable young Girl called Alice Gibbs. We went down a lane to a snug place; and I took out my armour, but she begged that I might not put it on, as the sport was much pleasanter without it; and as she was quite safe. I was so rash as to trust her, and had a very agreeable congress.

The week later saw London celebrating the King's birthday. 'It was the King's Birth-night and I resolved to be a Blackguard and to see all that was to be seen.' writes the randy diarist, and, dressing himself as a lower-class of person, he went out on the town:

4 June, 1763 I went to the park, picked up a low Brimstone, called myself a Barber, and agreed with her for Sixpence, went to the bottom of the park, arm in arm, and dipped my machine in the Canal, and performed most manfully. In the Strand, I picked up a profligate wretch and gave her sixpence. She allowed me entrance. But the miscreant refused me performance. I was much stronger than her; and volens nolens [in other words whether she wanted or not] *pushed her up against the Wall. She however gave a sudden spring from me; and screaming out, a parcel of more Whores and Soldiers came to her relief. "Brother Soldiers" (said I) "should not a half-pay Officer r–g–r for sixpence? And here has she used me so and so." I got them on my side and abused her in blackguard stile, and then left them. At Whitehall I picked up another girl to whom I called myself a highwayman, and told her I had no Money; and begged she would trust me. But she would not.*

On 18 June, 1763 the journal records:

At night I took a street-walker into privy Garden, and indulged sensuality. The wretch picked my pocket of my handkerchief; and then swore that she had not. When I got home, I was shocked to think that I had been intimately united with a low abandoned perjured pilfering creature. I determined to do so no more; but if the Cyprian fury should seize me, to participate my amorous flame with a genteel Girl.

By then, Boswell had just made the acquaintance of Dr Johnson, a man he instantly admired. Later, in 1791, Boswell would write a biography of Johnson, entitled *Life of Samuel Johnson*. The good doctor convinced him that 'promiscuous concubinage is certainly wrong. It is contributing one's share towards bringing confusion and misery into Society.' He was, so he says, a changed man. 'Notwithstanding of the Reflections, I have stooped to mean profligacy even yesterday. However, I am now resolved to guard against it' he wrote, but within the fortnight his resolve crumbled:

3 August, 1763 I should have mentioned that on Monday night [two days earlier], *coming up the Strand, I was tapp'd on the shoulder by a fine fresh lass. I went home with her. She was an Officer's daughter, and born at Gibraltar. I could not resist indulging myself with the enjoyment of her. Surely, in such a Situation, when the*

Woman is allready abandoned, the crime must be alleviated, tho' in strict morality, illicit love is allways wrong.

He wrote no more of amorous conquests in his Journal. That is not to say he became a celibate monk, but that he no longer wished to record something which he accepted was anti-social and bad, not simply for his own health, but for the health of society.

WILLIAM HICKEY, 1749–1830

Hickey was a contemporary of Boswell, and, like Boswell, published memoirs giving a remarkable insight into eighteenth century life – not just in London, but in India where he had spent his working life as a lawyer. His *Memoirs*, although written in the years leading up to 1810, were eventually published between 1913 and 1925. He was the seventh son of a successful Irish lawyer, and went to Westminster School in London. He was, however, expelled for his dissolute behaviour, not least in keeping a mistress. On one occasion he describes being given a guinea by one of his father's friends, resolving to spend it at the theatre and in making love to his mistress. As he says:

Having discovered the residence of my wanton little bedfellow, Nanny Harris, I directly went to her lodgings … there I was, a hopeful sprig of thirteen, stuck up in a green box [at Covent Garden]. From the theatre she took me home to supper, giving me lobster and oysters, both of which she knew I was very fond of, and plenty of rum punch.

Things got out of hand when he started training as a lawyer – he lived way beyond his means, gambled and drank to excess. Nanny was never 'an exclusive relationship' and in 1765, aged 16, he records that his main concern in life was running after the maid servants, including one named Nancy Dye, 'a fine little jade.'

His Memoirs go on to give details of how he and a group of extravagant young men 'of his own stamp' took rooms together. His description of roistering life in Covent Garden brothels is set out in Chapter Three. Hickey went on to describe how he passed his evenings and nights in 'theatres, taverns and brothels, amidst abandoned profligates of both sexes, and in every species of folly and intemperance'.

He was of course living way beyond the means of a solicitor's articled clerk. Over a period of some seven months he augmented his income by fiddling the accounts at his father's office, but having embezzled some £500, was caught and sent in disgrace to India to atone for his sins. His Memoirs recount his life in India, and in Canton. On occasions he returned to England, giving an opportunity to resume his association with the low life of London. It was an opportunity which was pounced on eagerly, and expensively. Once more he ran up debts, and borrowed money on the strength of his father's credit. Once more he helped himself to client's money held by his father's firm, and once more he was caught. This time his father announced that he wished to banish his son for ever, making it clear that he never wanted to see him again.

However, the father relented after a short while and agreed that William should be sent to Jamaica to practice Law. His stay there lasted less than two years. He was then packed off back to India, where he remained until his retirement in 1808, apart from a two-year spell back in London while preparing a petition to Parliament. Hickey never married, but in addition to his countless affairs he did have a number of long-lasting relationships. One of these was with a Charlotte Barry, who adopted the name 'Hickey' until her death in 1783. Another was Jemdanee, one of his Indian mistresses. He was devoted to her – they had a son but he died in infancy. However, it is for his 'intrigues' that he will be remembered, including his affair with one of the most famous courtesans of the day called Emily Warren. Reynolds had painted her as 'Thais' and commented on her 'faultless and finely formed' figure. As previously mentioned, she was the mistress of Hickey's friend Bob Potts, but when William bedded her he complained that she was unfeeling and unresponsive. To her, it was just a job.

William Hickey died in the Spring of 1827, and was buried at St John the Evangelist, Smith Square, Westminster.

GEORGE HANGER, 1751–1824

Writing about his life, George Hanger summarises it as follows:

I was early introduced into life, and often kept both good and bad company; associated with men both good and bad, and with lewd women, and women not lewd, wicked and not wicked; in short, with men and women of every description, and of every rank, from the highest to the lowest, from St. James's to St. Giles's; in palaces and night cellars; from the drawing-room to the dust cart. Human nature is in general frail, and mine I confess has been wonderfully so.

No regrets there then, from a man who eventually became Fourth Baron Coleraine, having succeeded to the title after his equally dissolute brothers William and John passed on. William had figured in one of the *Histories of the tête-à-tête annexed* in the *Town & Country Magazine* of 1772 with the celebrated actress Sophia Baddeley. For his part, George seemed to have kept James Gillray in business single-handed, with the National Portrait Gallery listing some twenty of his caricatures.

Other caricatures include one by Rowlandson showing him as a lecherous box-office lounger chatting up a pair of young ladies in the theatre foyer, and one where he was apparently floored by an irate fishwife who he pushed out of the way while accompanying the Prince of Wales on a trip to Plymouth.

He had made the army his career, and amazed his army colleagues by going off and marrying a gypsy girl. All was well until she ran off with an itinerant tinker – for her, a lucky escape. George became a macaroni, spending huge sums on his immaculate wardrobe. As befits a true rake, he is rumoured to have fought three duels by the age of 21, although one suspects that these were over his own honour rather than over the honour of some affronted lady.

His army career, both in Britain and America, seems to have been marked by more action in the bedroom that ever took place on the battlefield and it is as a womaniser that he became famous. However, he served throughout the American Revolutionary War, transferring to forces under the command of Sir Banastre Tarleton as a major and as commander of its light dragoons. He himself claimed to be the best shot in the British Army. He returned to England in 1784 and joined the 'Prince of Wales set' being made equerry to the Prince. However his finances were in a mess and he served time in the debtor's prison before raising enough cash to start a business. Seeing him 'in trade' astonished his friends, especially as he chose to be a coal merchant. He was, no doubt, the best dressed coal merchant in the land.

He was one of the closest friends of the Prince of Wales, and had a reputation for being a ladies man *par excellence.* He was also extremely eccentric. One time he made a £500 wager on a ten mile road race between turkeys and geese. Hanger lost the bet when the twenty turkeys dropped out after three miles. Eventually the Prince tired of his exploits, finding them 'too free and coarse.'

Hanger wrote a rambling autobiography in 1801 and in it put forward the view that marriage was a device invented by a priesthood with 'no authority whatever in Scripture.' He thought marriage was quite unnecessary, but that if you had it you should also allow polygamy because otherwise 'it would lead to fornication, adultery and whoredom'. He also saw fit to lecture 'the Cyprian ladies' on what he described as the:

> *…three predominant passions which reign in the female breast, -- gambling, intriguing, and drinking. The courtly dame of St. James's, the city belle, the St. James's and St. Giles's Cyprian, are equally addicted to them. In general, they are linked thus: they either drink and intrigue, or game and intrigue; for drinking does not suit with those who play for large sums. Some there are, the most perfect of the female sex, in whom all*

the three cardinal virtues unite, and are equally predominant: there are very few that are not influenced by two, and scarce any without one, of these craving passion.

He died in 1824 at the age of 74 leaving behind a woman described by him as his wife. By all accounts he had omitted to marry her, and no mention of her appears in his obituary notice in *The Gentleman's Magazine*.

BANASTRE TARLETON, 1754–1833

Hanger had been a close friend and army colleague of Banastre Tarleton, another of the 'set' with which the Prince of Wales mixed. Ban, as he was known in Britain, had been born in Liverpool to wealthy parents – his father was the mayor, and the family had built its fortune on the slave trade and its associated businesses of rum and tobacco. He was one of six children, but not the eldest. He was therefore expected to find a career in the army, which he did most successfully. Although his first commission was purchased for £800, all his subsequent promotions were on merit, and he was made up to lieutenant-colonel in 1782. Later he was member of parliament for Liverpool, and ended up as a general and a baronet. His exploits in the American War of Independence made him a national hero – whereas he was reviled in America and given the soubriquet 'Butcher of the Carolinas and 'Butcher Ban'. The phrase 'Ban's quarter' grew to mean giving no quarter at all. As history is written by the victors, suffice to say that nowadays he would be seen as an advocate of 'total war', and a 'scorched earth' policy.

Whatever his fighting prowess he was always rumoured to have made more bedroom conquests than military ones. The man was ludicrously good looking, as attested to by the portrait of him by Sir Joshua Reynolds, held by the National Gallery in London, with his tight trousers, green jacket and plumed hat; he was always described as being handsome, a charmer and a ladies' man. He hit the party scene with a vengeance when he returned after the American war. He was a regular attendee at dinners, balls, the theatre and so on, and was invariably the centre of female interest. The gossip mongers had a field day trying to keep up with his amorous conquests, and he was featured in the *Tête-a-Tête* histories of the *Town & Country Magazine* as 'the intrepid patriot' having an affair with a Miss Emily Webb.

Emily was the daughter of a prominent solicitor, and she succumbed to Ban's charms and moved in with him. As the *Town & Country Magazine* coyly remarked, 'they sleep under the same roof, and the colonel has not been once at the war office for some time.' Other well-publicised affairs took place, with the magazine reporting that 'he certainly did not confine his amours to those private intrigues which *honour* stamps with secrecy; for we find him roaming at large with .... the Bird of Paradise, and the Arm---d.' In other words, he enjoyed the company of those eminent Toasts of the Town described previously, namely Gertrude Mahon and Elizabeth Armistead.

By this time the Prince of Wales had finished his relationship with 'Perdita' that is to say, Mary Robinson, and she had been taken under the protection of Lord Malden. She was at the height of her fame, a beautiful and popular figure, and Lord Malden was immensely proud of having captured her affections. Rashly he boasted to Ban that her loyalty and faithfulness were unbreakable, a challenge which Ban rose to immediately. He bet Lord Malden that he could seduce her – and promptly won the bet. As can be imagined, the lady was much displeased when she subsequently heard that she had been the subject of such a wager, but extraordinarily she forgave Ban and entered into a relationship with him which lasted fifteen fiery years.

Image 66 is of the print called *The Thunderer*. In it James Gillray shows Tarleton outside a brothel with the Prince of Wales (identified by his plumed ostrich feathers). Above the front door of the brothel is an effigy of Mary Robinson as a whirligig, legs apart, and with the words 'This is the Lady'll kiss most sweet. Who'd not love a Soldier?' The door bears the inscription 'The Whirligig – Alamode Beef, hot every Night' – in other words, 'she was a dish regularly enjoyed by military personnel'.

That Mary loved Ban to distraction is not at issue, and she wrote poem after poem pouring out her love for him on those occasions when they argued and split up. Over and over again they re-united, always to the horror of Ban's mother, who thoroughly disapproved of the young hussy. It got to the stage that Ban's gambling and horse racing debts had got so out of hand that he was faced with the debtor's prison unless he could raise immediate funds. His mother agreed to provide finance on condition that he gave up his mistress. At first he refused, but eventually worn down by family and financial pressures, he agreed to the split and to travel to France. What he did not know is that his loyal mistress, by then pregnant with their child, would ride to try and head him off at Dover, with £300 in her pocket to pay his debts. She, poor thing, guessed his port of departure wrongly – he was headed for Southampton, not Dover, and he crossed the Channel unaware of her devoted gesture. Worse still, Mary suffered a miscarriage during the journey and the resulting botched midwifery left her semi-paralysed below the waist. When Ban heard, he came to her immediately and for a time the on-off relationship continued. It has to be said that Ban was not as faithful a partner as Mary perhaps deserved. There is a birth record to show that he fathered at least one child, called Banina, with an un-named woman, and rumours also abounded that he had an unhealthy interest in Mary's 18-year-old daughter.

After one final split in 1798 Tarleton went and married Susan Bertie, the illegitimate daughter of the Fourth Duke of Ancaster. He was 44 and she was 20, but more to the point she was an heiress with a fortune of £20,000. Mary was devastated at the betrayal and wrote a novel called *The False Friend*, clearly alluding to Tarleton, describing him as 'A Being, who lived only for himself, who, wrapped in the flimsy garb of vanity, and considering every woman a creature formed for his amusement, marked each succeeding day with a new crime....'

He died, riddled with gout rather than guilt, in 1833.

RICHARD BRINSLEY SHERIDAN, 1751–1816

A man practically born on stage (his father was a Dublin actor-manager and his mother a playwright) Richard Brinsley Sheridan went on to become a successful playwright, an MP, a brilliant orator, a theatre manager and, as a confidante of the Prince of Wales, a gambler, a heavy drinker and a womaniser. Four years after leaving Harrow school the 21-year-old Sheridan had fought a duel over the love of Elizabeth Ann Linley, with a man called Captain Thomas Mathews. Although married, Mathews had been pursuing Elizabeth and when he placed an advertisement in the Bath Chronicle which defamed Elizabeth, the young Sheridan had no alternative but to defend her honour and to challenge Mathews to a duel. The pair met in Henrietta Street, Covent Garden, but the sword fight was bloodless because Mathews lost his sword. He was forced to sign an apology and retract his allegations against Elizabeth, who was already famous both for her beauty and for having an exquisite singing voice. However, that was not the end of the matter, because Mathews then demanded another duel. They fought again, at Kingsdown near Bath, and this time the ferocious encounter left both men bloodied and injured. Both swords were broken in the duel, but the fight continued for some time before Mathews fled from the scene. Sheridan recovered, and then eloped with Elizabeth to France. When they returned he married Elizabeth, and promptly banned her from ever singing again in public.

Theirs was a tempestuous relationship, and while Sheridan achieved considerable fame and success with *The Rivals* and *The School for Scandal* (published in 1775 and 1777 respectively) his wife went on to have various affairs. Sheridan had bought a share in the Drury Lane Theatre, but in 1780 he gave up writing for the theatre and stood as member of parliament for Stafford. He was alleged to have paid the 'usual' bribe of five guineas to each of the burgesses in return for their votes, and therefore had to spend his maiden speech defending the allegation of bribery. His staunch support for Charles James Fox brought him into contact with the Prince of Wales and before long he was an accomplice in many of the escapades which brought the Prince into the spotlight. Sheridan was not particularly good at holding his drink; he was a poor businessman, and at times a heavy gambler. He was consistently living beyond his means, but the one thing that he and his wife had in common was that they loved holding fashionable parties at their London home. They spent much time living apart, and he had a number of affairs. He did not seem unduly worried when his wife became pregnant, apparently by her lover Lord Edward FitzGerald. Elizabeth died three months after giving birth to the baby (Mary) but Sheridan honoured his promise to his dying wife to the effect that he would look after the infant. Mary was a sickly child and she too died, in 1793.

Sheridan re-married two years later. His loyalty to the Prince was rewarded when he was made Receiver-General to the Duchy of Cornwall in 1804 and became Treasurer to the Navy in 1806. However, he continued to live beyond his means and made no attempt to settle his debts. Being an MP protected him from enforcement proceedings, but when he failed to secure re-election in 1812 the circling vultures closed in with a vengeance. He died impoverished in July 1816. As one writer said at the time: 'the more nearly he approached towards poverty, the more grossly did he abandon himself to sensual indulgences'. A more general view is that he squandered his talents, both as a playwright and as a parliamentary orator, because of his failure to control his finances and of his determination to 'keep up an appearance equal to that of his opulent associates'. In truth, you needed to be wealthy to be a real rake, and simply sharing life's excesses with the Prince of Wales was never going to be enough to make him a true roué. However, as Sheridan put it: 'In marriage if you possess anything very good, it makes you eager to get everything else good of the same sort'.

WILLIAM DOUGLAS, aka 'Old Q' 1724–1801

William Douglas was a man of various names and titles. As a 7-year-old he inherited an earldom when his father the Second Earl of March died. In 1786 he became Fourth Duke of Queensberry on the death of his cousin, and as an old man was always known as 'Old Q'. He became a somewhat revolting roué with a penchant for young girls, and spent his entire adult life gambling ferociously and whoring relentlessly. Famously, he spent most of his money on prostitutes and champagne. Image 69 shows him with his quizzing glass in hand, inspecting a young filly – not necessarily equine.

At the age of 28, Earl March developed such a passion for a Miss Frances Pelham that he deliberately bought a house next door to where she lived in Arlington Street, and had a bow-window constructed so that he could spy on her as she came and went. She was the daughter of the Chancellor of the Exchequer. Her brother, the Hon Henry Pelham, disliked March intensely and opposed any form of contact between his sister and the Earl. By the time her brother died, and she was free to marry whom she pleased, Frances discovered that the Earl had transferred his attentions elsewhere. Mortified, she turned to the faro tables and lost both her fortune and her reputation.

March had a particular penchant for Italian lovers – mostly opera singers and dancers – and had affairs with Teresina Tondino, the Contessa de la Rena, La Zampirini and the Marquesa Fagniani.

When he was in his mid-sixties he proposed marriage to the young daughter of his next door neighbour in Piccadilly, a Miss Gertrude Vanneck. Her father, Sir Joshua Vanneck, refused to consent to the union, even though the Duke was immensely wealthy and proposed three times. At other occasions he managed to seduce Lady Jane Stuart, the diarist Lady Mary Coke, Lady Henrietta Stanhope, and Lady Anne Conway. In his old age, Queensberry always wore dark green when he appeared in public, in winter carrying a large muff. Seated behind him in his carriage there would always be two servants, while his groom, Jack Radford, would follow on horseback ready to take notes and to deliver messages to any desirable young girls who took the old duke's fancy. Old Q took to recruiting young girls through the offices of procuresses such as the notorious Mother Windsor, and then re-enacting *The Judgement of Paris*. In the original classical Greek myth the goddesses each took it in turns to bestow a different 'gift' to tempt Paris. Old Q altered the script somewhat, so that the goddess-whores had to tempt him with a variety of carnal delights – a temptation to which he always succumbed. He also took to bathing in milk, believing that the restorative powers would enable him to perform more effectively in bed. The story went around that no-one would buy milk in Piccadilly in case it had already been used by Old Q.

He is believed to have fathered at least one child, a daughter Maria (known as Mie Mie) who was born in 1771; her mother was his mistress the Marchesa Maria Fagniani. Mie Mie certainly went on to have an odd upbringing. As an infant she was brought up by George Selwyn, one of the weirdest men of the age. In his public life, he served as a member of parliament for forty-four years without once troubling to make a single speech in the House. In his private life, he was a member of the notorious Hellfire Club, and would appear at public executions dressed as a woman. He had an obsessive interest in death in general, and in corpses in particular, allegedly bordering on necrophilia. Nevertheless he managed to persuade the girl's mother to allow him to foster the child, to whom he became inordinately devoted. Selwyn left Mie Mie an inheritance of £20,000 when he died. The girl was also left a vast inheritance (£100,000) by Old Q, and as a 21-year-old she married Lord Yarmouth, eventually becoming the Marchioness of Hertford.

SIR JOHN LADE, 1759–1838
Sir John was one of the inner circle of friends of the Prince of Wales, and was his riding instructor. The man was a superb horseman, but one who gambled and lost

heavily. His escapades on and off the race track made him a legend, and when he was not riding horses he was pursuing loose women. He is mentioned in Chapter Four as the rescuer of Gertrude Mahon, with whom he conducted an affair in the late 1770s. Oddly, when he came to choose a wife he selected a girl who was not a high class courtesan, but someone who had risen from the stews. His bride was Letitia, and she was rumoured to have been a cook in one of London's brothels. By all accounts she did rather more than just cook for the punters, one of them being the Duke of York. Her sexual appetite was legendary, with contemporary reports speaking of her being able to 'withstand the fiercest assault and renew the charge with renovated ardour, even when her victim sinks drooping and crestfallen before her.' By reputation she never 'turned her back against the most vigourous assailant.' She also swore like a trooper – so much so that the phrase 'swears like Letty Lade' entered the vocabulary.

Letty was a brilliant horsewoman, much like Sir John. Together they would attend sporting fixtures such as race meetings and boxing tournaments. She herself raced at Newmarket, and, like John, was regularly to be seen striding around wearing jockey's colours and carrying her riding whip. What made her a source of scandal in polite society was her carnal reputation, and her earlier association with the notorious highway robber called Jack Rann. Known to all as 'Sixteen string Jack' because of the coloured ribbons he wore from the top of his stockings, he was another fine horseman who regularly attended the same race meetings as Sir John. Letty had been rumoured to have been Jack's mistress (before she met Sir John). Jack met his fate at the gallows in 1774, and her name was always tarnished by her association with him.

Sir John conducted a lengthy affair with Letty before 'making an honest woman of her' in 1787. They seem to have been a perfect match for each other, and held riotous dinners with their rakish friends at their homes at Cant's Hill and Brighton. Their portraits were painted by Sir Joshua Reynolds, and the Prince of Wales commissioned George Stubbs to paint a picture of her to hang in his private quarters. The picture is impressive, and shows Letty riding side-saddle while her horse rears onto its hind legs *en levade* – a difficult manoeuvre requiring great skill and balance.

Gambling losses eventually took their toll and the couple faded from public scrutiny. Sir John spent time in the debtor's prison before the Prince Regent came to his rescue with a pension of £500 a year. The royal pension was still being paid, by Queen Victoria, up until his death in 1838. By then he had out-lived Letitia by thirteen years.

CASANOVA, 1725–1798

Casanova, who also went under the title of the 'Chevalier de Seingalt' visited Britain in 1763 and had some interesting things to say about the country, its customs, and its women. There was rather more to him than just being a randy old rake – he was a polymath, an intellectual, a man who invented a lottery system for the French, was a writer of mathematical works, an astrologer and a spy. He also translated *The Iliad* into his native Venetian dialect and wrote a science fiction novel. And in between all that, he seduced a large number of apparently very willing and happy ladies.

Towards the end of his life, when he was employed as a librarian in a remote castle in Bohemia he wrote his autobiography covering the first forty-nine years of his life, entitled *The Story of my life by Jacques Casanova de Seingalt*. Of the English he says: 'the people have a special character, common to the whole nation, which makes them think they are superior to everyone else. It is a belief shared by all nations, each thinking itself the best. And they are all right.'

Arriving in London he quickly found lodgings ('Thus in less than two hours I was comfortably settled in a town which is sometimes described as a chaos, especially for a stranger. But in London everything is easy to him who has money and is not afraid of spending it').

Of English life he wrote:

there is no playing cards or singing on Sundays. The town abounds in spies, and if they have reason to suppose that there is any gaming or music going on, they watch for their opportunity, slip into the house, and arrest all the bad Christians, who are diverting themselves in a manner which is thought innocent enough in any other country. But to make up for this severity the Englishman may go in perfect liberty to the tavern or the brothel, and sanctify the Sabbath as he pleases.

When he came to London the problem was that he did not speak English – and the whores did not speak Italian or French. He got a friend to translate a notice which he put up in his window, advertising the availability of rooms to let in the house he had rented, to a young lady. The actual wording was:

The landlord of the second and third floors probably occupies the first floor himself. He must be a man of the world and of good taste, for he wants a young and pretty lodger; and as he forbids her to receive visits, he will have to keep her company himself.

The Press got wind of the notice and guessed the reason behind the proviso against having any visitors – he intended to monopolize the young lady himself, and it was not so much a 'room to let' as an offer of employment. Casanova was amazed that the Press should write so freely and so openly: 'Such matters as these' [i.e. gossiping about

the notice he had put up offering accommodation and speculating as to his intentions]
'give their chief interest to the English newspapers. They are allowed to gossip about
everything, and the writers have the knack of making the merest trifles seem amusing.
Happy is the nation where anything may be written and anything said!'

The advertisement worked – a girl he called 'Mistress Pauline' responded, was
interviewed, and 'got the job'. True to form, they became lovers, but never on an
exclusive basis.

Casanova was to write:

> *I also visited the bagnios where a rich man can sup, bathe, and sleep with a fashionable
> courtezan, of which species there are many in London. It makes a magnificent debauch
> and only costs six guineas. The expense may be reduced to a hundred francs, but economy
> in pleasure is not to my taste.*

On another occasion he describes an unsatisfying and expensive encounter with a
prostitute:

> *It was one evening when I was at Vauxhall, and I offered her twenty guineas if she
> would come and take a little walk with me in a dark alley. She said she would come
> if I gave her the money in advance, which I was fool enough to do. She went with me,
> but as soon as we were alone she ran away, and I could not catch her again, though I
> looked for her all the evening.*

He does not appear to have been a great admirer of English food and drink, writing:

> *One day I was invited by a younger son of the Duke of Bedford to eat oysters and drink
> a bottle of champagne. I accepted the invitation, and he ordered the oysters and the
> champagne, but we drank two bottles, and he made me pay half the price of the second
> bottle. Such are manners on the other side of the Channel. People laughed in my face
> when I said that I did not care to dine at a tavern as I could not get any soup. "Are you
> ill?" they said, "soup is only fit for invalids".*
>
> *The Englishman is entirely carnivorous. He eats very little bread, and calls himself
> economical because he spares himself the expense of soup and dessert, which circumstance
> made me remark that an English dinner is like eternity: it has no beginning and no end.
> Soup is considered very extravagant, as the very servants refuse to eat the meat from
> which it has been made. They say it is only fit to give to dogs. The salt beef which they*

use is certainly excellent. I cannot say the same for their beer, which was so bitter that I could not drink it.

Time and a dissolute lifestyle was beginning to take its toll on the middle-aged libertine. At the age of 38 he met and fell for the charms of a lovely 17-year-old London courtesan named Marie Anne Genevieve Augspurgher, known as *La Charpillon*. She toyed with him for some weeks and then rejected him. (He later wrote in his Memoirs: "It was on that fatal day…that I began to die.") Other rejections followed. Worse, he caught a dose of the clap and left Britain to resume his European travels, feeling decidedly under the weather and much poorer than when he arrived. His memoirs remain one of the great autobiographies of all time. As Casanova put it: 'Worthy or not, my life is my subject, and my subject is my life.'

THE BARRY FAMILY – Hellgate, Cripplegate, Newgate and Billingsgate
Two centuries before 'Watergate', the Barry family were having a monopoly of '-gates'. Four poor little rich kids – daughter Caroline, born 1768; Richard born in 1769; Henry born in 1770; and Augustus in 1773. Their father was the Sixth Earl of Barrymore but unfortunately he died when Richard was just 3 years old, passing the title to him. Their mother Emily (the daughter of the Earl of Harrington) died eight years later. So these four wealthy and well-connected orphans were left in the occasional care of their grandmother. Granny, aka the Countess Harrington, packed Richard off to Eton, reputedly with the sum of £1,000 in his pocket for spending money, but then, somewhat inconveniently, she too died. Caroline and her feral brothers seemed to have been left to grow through adolescence and into maturity without close adult guidance – apart from the poor Reverend Tickell of the Berkshire village of Wargrave. He was nominally in charge of the Barry brood, but he appears to have had an uphill struggle to keep in control. As a trio of debauchers, rakes, profligates, gamblers and foul-mouthed ill-tempered brattish aristocrats these boys really took the biscuit.

Richard, the Seventh Earl, went on to become a close friend of the Prince of Wales, earning himself the name of 'Hellgate'. His younger brother Henry was born with a club-foot and, in the days before political correctness, was known by all as 'Cripplegate'. That left Augustus, who somehow or other grew up to become a Reverend, but was the most profligate gambler of them all, and he was given the moniker 'Newgate' because, supposedly, that was the only one of the debtors prisons he had not been sent to. And Caroline? Well, she used such foul language that the Prince of Wales gave her the nick name of 'Billingsgate' – because she swore like a fishwife!

By the age of 16 Hellgate had already won a wager of £1,000 at Newmarket. He loved racing, frequently riding his own horses to victory, and he developed a passion for boxing. When he returned to Wargrave in the school holidays he and his mates would terrify the villagers by taking over the reins from the carriage drivers and racing through the village, smashing windows with their whips. By the age of 18 he was developing his own racing stud, keeping a hunting pack in his own kennels, and building a reputation as a hell-raiser. Rumour had it that he had spent or lost £300,000 by the time he hit 21. But he stayed just on the right side of being a pain in the neck to the Wargrave residents by entertaining them all lavishly, providing food and drink at numerous sporting activities in the village. He loved dramatic performances and built a theatre in Wargrave, at a cost of some £60,000, so that plays could be put on. The Seventh Earl and his friends were naturally given key parts to perform.

As a prankster he had no equal, setting up a blistering pace by forming clubs for every occasion: there was the 'Two o'clock Club', which met at that hour of the early morning to hold court and impose ludicrous punishments on any member committing a perceived misdemeanour. There was the Bothering Club, the *Je ne sais quoi* Club, the Warble Club and so on. The latter had the very sensible rule 'that if any member has more sense than another, he be kicked out of the club'.

By now he was gambling heavily – sometimes winning as much as £25,000 on a single boxing match, sometimes losing a fortune on horse races. He liked odd challenges – such as a man–against–horse over thirty yards, with a turn round a tree at the midway point, but he consumed his assets with relentless impetuosity and was in danger of being adjudged bankrupt. Rather to everyone's amazement he married – but not for money. In 1792 he eloped with the 17-year-old Charlotte Goulding, the daughter of a sedan chair man. Like her husband, she too was a bare-knuckle boxer.

He stood for parliament – probably as a way of thwarting his creditors – and joined the army, being appointed Captain in the Royal Berkshire Militia. War with France and the threat of invasion meant that he was required to keep his musket loaded at all times – and when he was in his carriage escorting three French prisoners-of-war into custody the musket went off accidentally. The ball lodged in his eye and, at the age of 23, Hellgate drew his last breath. The date: 6 March 1793.

His title was taken over by Cripplegate – another person who saw it as his duty to ensure that the Prince of Wales maintained his life of debauchery, scandal and intrigue. The Eighth Earl reportedly had a fine singing voice, but became better known for his pranks – kidnapping young women, then leaving a coffin standing upright outside their front door before knocking loudly – just to see the horror in the face of the servant coming to answer the call.

He was forever quarrelling and challenging others to duels – and then enlivened proceedings by always conducting the duel while totally naked. In 1795 he decided to get married, but like his elder brother chose as his bride a girl without means, called Anne Coghlan – she was in fact the beautiful daughter of a local tavern-keeper. His debts continued to mount and he died in France at the age of 56 in 1823, probably of a stroke. He was penniless as well as childless, so the Earls of Barrymore died out (younger brother Newgate had already perished). That just left 'Billingsgate', who called herself Baroness de Barry, after her marriage to Louis Pierre Francis Malcolm Drummond, Comte de Melfort. Needless to say, such a family provided an easy target for satirists such as James Gillray and Isaac Cruikshank, and they were rarely out of the news.

PERCY BYSSHE SHELLEY, 1792–1822

Born in Sussex in 1792 and drowned in Italy thirty years later, the poet Shelley had a short but eventful life marked by numerous affairs and controversies, An atheist, a vegetarian, a political radical and an advocate of free love, he offended rather a lot of people in his lifetime, and many of his writings disappeared from view during the more morally repressed Victorian era.

He had been sent to Eton where he was bullied mercilessly (he would not accept 'fagging', he didn't like sport, and he had a rather high-pitched voice). On going up to Oxford he managed to get chucked out in only a year, for publishing a pamphlet expounding atheism. The authorities were horrified, as was his father, who urged him to give up his radical ideas and his 'somewhat progressive' views on love and promiscuity. Percy rebelled, and eloped to Scotland to marry a 16-year-old girl called Harriett who had a crush on him. She had been regularly threatening suicide, and insisted that her elder sister (aged 28) move in with them. That must have been awkward for Percy, who disliked the sister intensely, but it became the first of numerous 'threesomes' in his life.

Percy quickly became rather more interested in an English teacher called Elizabeth Hitchener whose ideas inspired him to write his first epic poem – *Queen Mab* – about a utopian society. The Shelleys had a child, Elizabeth Ianthe, but by the time Harriett got pregnant again her husband had fallen for the charms of a well-educated and ferociously intelligent girl called Mary. The object of his new passion was the daughter of Mary Wollstonecraft, the famous feminist author of *A Vindication of the Rights of Women*. Mary Wollstonecraft had died giving birth to her daughter, leaving the young Mary to be brought up by her father William Godwin, author of a radical work called *Political Justice*. He was much respected by Percy, but if he thought that Godwin would be thrilled when Percy decided to elope to Europe with Mary, as he did in 1814, he was much mistaken, especially as the pair took with them Godwin's step-daughter Clara Mary Jane Clairmont (known as Claire). Mary and Claire were step-sisters, both aged 16 at the time. Together the trio toured France, Switzerland, Germany and Holland before running out of money and returning to England. By then, Mary was pregnant. Harriett was also expecting, and she gave birth first, to Percy's son Charles, in November 1814. Mary produced a daughter three months later, but the infant died after a few weeks. Mary quickly fell pregnant again and had another child in 1816, which they called William. Harriett meanwhile had decided to get a legal separation, and to rub salt in the wound applied for sole custody of her children on the basis that Percy was an unfit parent.

Percy's grandfather had died in 1815, leaving him a legacy of £1,000, and this enabled Percy to set off once more for Europe with Mary, again with Claire in tow. Claire was in love with George Byron and she introduced him to their group, and they all spent the summer in Switzerland. They returned to the depressing news that Mary's half-sister Fanny had committed suicide. A few weeks later, Percy's wife Harriett chose a similar fate, drowning herself in the Serpentine in London's Hyde Park. This left Percy and Mary free to marry, which they did in 1817. The court however refused to allow Percy custody of his children – his views on free love horrified the authorities and it was decided that the children were better off with foster parents.

Percy and Mary settled in Marlow, Buckinghamshire, and became friends with the poets John Keats and Leigh Hunt. Shelley's attempt at publishing a work entitled *Laon and Cythna; or, The Revolution of the Golden City* about incestuous love proved too much for his publishers, although it did re-appear in a modified form a year later. In 1818 the Shelley's decamped for Italy, moving around from city to city, but were beset with problems as first their son William and then their daughter Clara Everina succumbed to illness and died. In December 1818 the birth of a girl called Elena Adelaide Shelley was registered in Naples, with the mother given, not as Mary, but as a 'Marina Padurin.' Some observers speculated that the actual mother was Claire Clairmont, or possibly the family nursemaid. The child died just over a year later. By then Mary had given birth to a son Percy Florence Shelley (later, Sir Percy). The parents had moved from Naples to Florence and Pisa and then on 8 July 1822, less than a month before his thirtieth birthday, Shelley and a couple of friends decided to sail across the Gulf of Spezia. While returning from Livorno in his sailing boat, the 'Don Juan', a storm overtook the craft and all on board were drowned, although stories persisted that Shelley had either been bumped off because of his political views, or as a result of a botched robbery at sea. His body washed ashore and was cremated on the beach, in order to comply with quarantine regulations. Mary did not attend the funeral. *The Courier* reported: 'Shelley, the writer of some infidel poetry, has been drowned, *now* he knows whether there is God or no.'

LORD BYRON, 1788–1824

A brilliant poet, but a man whose love affairs scandalised the Regency period, George Gordon Noel Byron had to endure a club foot, a father who deserted him, a mother who was mentally unstable, and a nurse who sexually abused him when he was 9 years old. It was small wonder that he turned out to be so unconventional. He became Sixth Baron Byron when he was 10, and was sent away to Harrow, where as a young teenager he dabbled in sexual encounters with both genders. In 1805 he went up to Trinity College, where he found time to attend wild parties, pursue a variety of sexual conquests, and to indulge his love of gambling, boxing and horse racing. In 1811 he took his seat in the House of Lords, and embarked on a passionate affair with the married Lady Caroline Lamb. It was she who dubbed him 'mad, bad and dangerous to know'. Byron became an overnight sensation with the publication in 1812 of the first two cantos of his epic poem *Childe Harold's Pilgrimage*. Thereafter he turned his attentions to Jane Harley, Countess of Oxford, before moving on to an alleged affair with a girl called Augusta, who was his own half-sister and who had married the previous year. In the spring of 1814, Augusta gave birth to a daughter who was christened Elizabeth Medora Leigh. It was widely rumoured that Byron was the father. He then rebounded into a marriage with Anne Isabella Milbanke. The wedding, in January 1815, was followed by the birth of a child called Augusta Ada. The marriage barely lasted the year before his wife left him, taking their daughter with her. Apparently she could not cope with her husband's debts, his heavy drinking, his bisexuality – and the allegations of his incestuous relationship with Augusta.

In 1816 Byron left for Switzerland where he met up with Shelley – and Claire Clairmont, who gave birth to his daughter, Allegra, in 1817. When his friends returned to England, Byron stayed in Europe and travelled to Italy, writing *Don Juan* and generally enjoying himself with a bevy of female beauties along the way. At one stage he fell in love with an Italian countess, a married woman by the name of Teresa Guiccioli. She was, at 19, eleven years younger than him. They had met just three days after her wedding to the Count, and they immediately fell in love, prompting Byron to settle in Ravenna between 1819 and 1821 while they conducted their very public affair.

In 1823 he decided to throw in his lot with Greek freedom fighters, who wanted to liberate Greece and overthrow the Ottoman Empire. Byron poured money into equipping the Greek navy, taking command of a group of fighters, and generally being heroic. However, he caught an infection, and died of his illness (probably sepsis) in 1824, aged just 36. His embalmed body was brought back to England, but was denied a burial at Westminster Abbey – as would have been customary for a man of his standing and fame. Apparently the powers-that-be at Westminster felt that his immoral behaviour made him an unfit candidate for burial in their Abbey. Nevertheless, tens of thousands of people came to view his body when it lay in state for two days in London, before being taken away to be interred in the family vault near Newstead Abbey in Nottingham. He may have been considered a great hero in Greece, but it was 145 years before even a plaque with his name on was put up in Poets' Corner – and then only after a campaign which lasted over sixty years. In the nineteenth century, society was simply not prepared to accept Byron as a national hero. Others had their peccadilloes and were forgiven, but in the case of Lord Byron he was considered to be just too depraved, too immoral, and not in any way repentant. Had he been born fifty years earlier, the world might have turned a blind eye, but by the 1820s the British public was moving away from accepting the notoriously profligate behaviour of the aristocracy towards the more moral, more repressed, and less flamboyant world of the Victorians.

The pendulum was about to swing: sex continued, scandal continued and satire continued, but the openness of the Georgians was replaced by Victorian hypocrisy and censure.

Glossary

A Selection of Sexual Terms

(G) indicates that the explanation is from the 1811 *Dictionary of the Vulgar Tongue*, by Francis Grose.

Madams
Abbess (or Lady Abbess); Bawd; Buttock broker (Cant); Covent Garden abbess; Gap-stopper; Go between; Mother/ Mother of the maids.

Pimps
Cock pimp; Panderer; She-napper; Squire of the placket.

Prostitutes
Academician; Bat; Biter; Bunter; Buttock; Crack; Covent Garden nun; Cyprian Corps; Dasher; Demi Rep; Doxy; Drab; Dress Lodger; Drury Lane vestal; Convenient (Cant); Fashionable impures; Flash mollisher; Flower seller; Harlot; Hedge whore; Hoydon; Impure; Laced mutton; Lady of easy virtue; Ladies of the First Quality; Mab; Madam Ran (Cant); Merry arse Christian; Mob; Moll; Nymph; One of us/one of my cousins; Spell; Thaiis; Quean; Pintle-merchant; Piper's wife; Public ledger; Punk; Receiver-General; Squirrel; Star gazer; Strumpet; Tail; Three penny upright; Trumpery; Unfortunate women; Woman of the town; Woman of pleasure.

Nine descriptions of women with loose morals:
1. Demanders for Glimmer or Fire
2. Bawdy Baskets
3. Morts
4. Autem Morts
5. Walking Morts
6. Doxies
7. Delles
8. Kinching Morts
9. Kinching Coes

Bullies
Bully back; Flash man.

The customers
Corinthians ; Flogging cully; Keeping cully; Mutton monger; Top diver.

Premises
Bagnio; Buttocking shop; Cab; Cavaulting School; Corinth; Flash Panney; House of Civil reception; Nanny house; Nugging house; Nunnery; Pushing school; Punch-house; Seraglio; School of Venus; Smuggling Ken; Snoozing Ken; Vaulting school.

Homosexuality
Back Gammon player; a He-strumpet; an Indorser; Madge culls; a Miss Molly; Windward passage; Queer cull.

Sexual organs – male
Blind boy/blind visitor; Hair splitter; Nutmegs; Roger; Pego; Plug tail; Silent flute; Sugar stick; Tallywags (or Tarrywags); Thomas/Man Thomas; Tools; Twiddle-diddles; Whirligiggs; Yard.

Sexual organs – female
Cock alley; Cock Lane; Crinkum Crankum; Cunny; Dumb glutton; Fruitful vine; Hat/Old hat; Madge; Money; Muff; Notch; Pitcher; Quim; Water-mill.

The sex act
Blanket Hornpipe; Clicket; to grind; Moll Peatly's Gig; Mutton; Nub; to Occupy; to roger; to bull; Strapping: (Cant); to swive; Two-handed put.

Terms associated with venereal disease
Covent Garden ague; Clap; Crinkums; Dropping member; Drury Lane ague; Dumb watch; Fire ship; Flap dragon; French disease; French gout; Frenchified; Flapdragon; Job's dock; Notch; to nap; Nimgimmer; Peppered; Pissing pins and needles; Pox; Sauce; Scalder; Shanker; Spanish gout; Tetbury portion; Venus's curse.

Miscellaneous
Apple dumplin shop: A woman's bosom (**G**)

Bubble: A cheated person or dupe

Burning shame: A lighted candle stuck into the parts of a woman, certainly not intended by nature for a candlestick (**G**)

Buttock-ball: A dance attended by prostitutes (**G**)

Cantharides: Aphrodisiac

Dutchess: A woman enjoyed with her pattens on, or by a man-in boots, is said to be made a dutchess (**G**)

Electuaries and Eringoes: Aphrodisiacs

Flyer: To take a flyer; to enjoy a woman with her clothes on, or without going to bed (**G**)

Fustilugs: A dirty slattern. (**G**)

Pucker water: Water impregnated with alum, or other astringents, used by old experienced traders to counterfeit virginity (**G**)

Socket money: A whore's fee, or hire; also money paid or a treat, by a married man caught in an intrigue (**G**)

Short-heeled wench: A girl apt to fall on her back (**G**)

Van-neck: Miss or Mrs Van-Neck; a woman with large breasts; a bushel bubby (**G**)

Whore's curse: A piece of gold coin, value 5s 3d, frequently given to women of the town by such as professed always to give gold, and who before the introduction of those pieces always gave half a guinea. (**G**)

Whore's kitling, or Whore's son: A bastard (**G**)

Whore-monger: A man that keeps more than one mistress. A country gentleman, who kept a female friend, being reproved by the parson of the parish, and styled a whore-monger asked the parson whether he had a cheese in his house; and being answered in the affirmative, 'Pray,' says he, 'does that one cheese make you a cheese-monger?' (**G**)

Wife in water colours: A mistress, or concubine (**G**)

Bibliography

Alexander, David: *Richard Newton and English caricature in the 1790s*, Manchester, Manchester University Press, 1998

Anon.: *The Life of Miss Anne Catley*, London,1888 (available in digital format online via Internet Archive at https://archive.org/details/lifemissannecat01unkngoog and via Nabu Press, 2012)

Baker, Kenneth: *George IV, a life in caricature*, London, Thames and Hudson, 2005

Baker, Kenneth: *George III, a life in caricature*, London, Thames and Hudson, 2007

Bleackley, Horace: *Ladies Fair and Frail – sketches of the demi-monde during the Eighteenth Century*, London, Bodley Head, 1909 (and available in digital format via Internet Archive at https://archive.org/details/ladiesfairfrails00blea)

Boswell, James: *London Journal 1762-1763*, London, Penguin Classics, 2010.

Bricker, Andrew: *Libel and Satire: The Problem with Naming*, (online via Academia.edu at https://www.academia.edu/8193433/_Libel_and_Satire_The_Problem_with_Naming).

Cleland, John: *Memoirs of a Woman of Pleasure* London, 1748, Halcyon Classics, 2010

Clergue, Helen, and Roscoe, Edward Stanley: *George Selwyn: His Letters and His Life*, London, T. Fisher Unwin, 1899. (Also in digital format via Internet Archive at https://archive.org/details/georgeselwynhis00clergoog)

Cruickshank, Dan: *The Secret History of Georgian London: How the Wages of Sin Shaped the Capital*, London, Random House Books, 2009

Gonzales, Don Manoel: *Voyage to Great Britain, containing an account of England and Scotland* London, 1745

Gonzales, Don Manoel: *'London in 1731'* London, Cassell's National Library, 1888 and available as an e-book via Project Gutenberg at https://www.gutenberg.org/ebooks/2822)

Grose, Francis: *The Dictionary of the Vulgar Tongue*, London, S. Hooper, 1785. (1811 edition also in electronic format via Project Gutenberg at https://www.gutenberg.org/ebooks/5402)

Hanger, George: *The Life, Adventures and Opinions of Colonel George Hanger, written by Himself*, London, Johnson & Stryker, 1801 (available in digital format from Internet Archive at https://archive.org/details/lifeadventuresop01cole

Harvey, AD: *Sex in Georgian England*. London, George Duckworth & Co., 1994.

Heard, Kate: *High Spirits, The Comic Art of Thomas Rowlandson*, London, Royal Collection Trust, 2013

Hickey, William: *The Memoirs of William Hickey*, London, Hurst & Blackett, 1913-25, 4 Vols (via Internet Archive at https://archive.org/details/memoirsofwilliam015028mbp).

Hickman, Katie: *Courtesans*, London, Harper Collins, 2003

Linnane, Fergus: *Madams: Bawds & Brothel Keepers of London* London, The History Press, 2005.

Peakman, Julie: *Lascivious Bodies: a sexual history of the eighteenth century*, London, Atlantic Books, 2004

Robinson, John Robert: *Old Q' a Memoir of William Douglas, 4th Duke of Queensberry*, London, Sampson. Low, Marston, & Co, 1895 (available via Internet Archive at https://archive.org/stream/oldqamemoirwill00robigoog#page/n9/mode/2up

Rubenhold, Hallie (Ed): *Harris's List of Covent Garden Ladies*, London, Random House, 2005. (*Harris's List is* also available in digital format for 1788 via Project Gutenberg at http://www.gutenberg.org/cache/epub/42075/pg42075.html

Seingalt, Jacques Casanova de: *The Memoires of Casanova*, London, 1894 and in digital format via Project Gutenberg at https://www.gutenberg.org/ebooks/2981

Steele, Elizabeth: *The memoirs of Mrs Sophia Baddeley, late of Drury Lane Theatre,* London, 1787 (available in digital format via Internet Archive at https://archive.org/details/memoirsofmrssoph56stee).

Thomson, Mrs AT: *The Wits and Beaux of Society,* New York, 1861. (In digital format through Project Gutenberg at http://www.gutenberg.org/ebooks/18020)

Walpole, Horace: *The Letters of Horace Walpole, Earl of Orford,* London : R. Bentley, 1840 (in digital format through Gutenberg Project at https://www.gutenberg.org/ebooks/4609)

Wilson, Harriette; Blanch, Lesley (Ed): *Harriette Wilson 's Memoirs: The Greatest Courtesan of Her Age,* London, John Murray, 1957

Accreditation for images used in this book:

My sincere thanks to all the museums, libraries, and galleries who have allowed the reproduction of images throughout this book and in particular to René Levaque for his generosity.

Cover image and page ii: *Love in her eyes sits playing.* Mezzotint by J.R. Smith, after Matthew William Peters. © British Museum

Image 1 A Bagnigge Wells Scene, or no resisting Temptation published by Carington Bowles, 1776. Lewis Walpole Library, Yale University. lwlpr00112

Image 2 Retail Traders not affected by the Shop Tax from 1787. Library of Congress PC3-1787

Image 3 A St Giles's Beauty published by Carington Bowles in 1784. Lewis Walpole Library, Yale University. lwlpr05402

Image 4 and 5 Progress of a Woman of Pleasure by Richard Newton.

Image 6 St James's and St Giles's by Thomas Rowlandson, 1794. Lewis Walpole Library, Yale University. lwlpr08182

Image 7 Dividing the Spoil, St James's and St Giles's by Isaac Cruikshank, 1796. Lewis Walpole Library, Yale University. lwlpr09823

Image 8 Plate One of *A Harlot's Progress,* by William Hogarth, 1732. Lewis Walpole Library, Yale University. lwlpr22337

Image 9 The Whore's Last shift, by James Gillray, 1779. © National Portrait Gallery. NPG D12977

Image 10 The Merry Accident (with Kitty Fisher). Library of Congress. PC 2 Merry Accident

Image 11 Six stages of mending a face by Thomas Rowlandson, 1792. Lewis Walpole Library, Yale University. lwlpr07475

Image 12 Crim. Con. Temptations with the prices affixed by Isaac Cruikshank, 1796. Lewis Walpole Library, Yale University. lwlpr08758

Image 13 Cross-examination of a Witness in a case of Crim. Con. published by SW Fores, 1818. Library of Congress PC3 – 1818

Image 14 Flagellation engraved by John June, 1752. Library of Congress PC 3 – 1752—Flagellation

Image 15 Harris's List of Covent Garden Ladies, 1773. Wikimedia

Image 16 Harris's List or Cupids London Directory by Richard Newton, 1794. Library of Congress PC 3 – 1794

Image 17 Dressing for a Masquerade by Thomas Rowlandson, 1790. Lewis Walpole Library, Yale University. lwlpr06896

Image 18 A Lesson Westward Robert Dighton, 1782. Yale Center for British Art, Paul Mellon Collection. B1986.29.371

Image 19 The Beauty Unmask'd by Henry Morland, 1770. Lewis Walpole Library, Yale University. lwlpr02861

Image 20 Plate Three from Hogarth's *A Rake's Progress,* 1732-3. Sir John Soane's Museum.

Image 21 Cunnyseurs by Thomas Rowlandson. Via Wikimedia Commons.

Image 22 The rival knights or the Englishman in Paris by Thomas Rowlandson. Via Wikimedia Commons.

Image 23 A Lobby Flesh-Monger treating with a Saleswoman for a Prime Piece published by W Dent, 1790. Library of Congress. PC3 – 1790

Image 24 A Covent Garden Morning Frolick by Louis Philippe Boitard. Yale Center for British Art. B1977.14.15826

Image 25 Mrs. Horton, later Viscountess Maynard (formerly Nancy Parsons) painted by Sir Joshua Reynolds. Metropolitan Museum of Art, Fletcher Fund. 45.59.3

Image 26 Kitty Fisher painted by Nathaniel Hone, 1765. © National Portrait Gallery. NPG 2354

Image 27 Grace Dalrymple Elliott, by Thomas Gainsborough, 1778. Metropolitan Museum of Art, bequest of William K. Vanderbilt. 20.155.1

Image 28 Frances Abington as Prue painted by Sir Joshua Reynolds in 1771. Yale Center for British Art, Paul Mellon Collection. B1977.14.67

Image 29 The Bird of Paradise- the name given to Gertrude Mahon. Print by Carington Bowles. Lewis Walpole Library, Yale University. lwlpr04723

Image 30 Vis a vis bisected, or the Ladies Coop by M Darly. Library of Congress PC 1 – 5373

Image 31 The General Out-Generalled, or, first come, first served 1808. Library of Congress. PC 2 – General out-generalled

Image 32 Fashionable Contrasts or the Duchess's little shoe yielding to the Magnitude of the Duke's Foot by James Gillray, 1792. Yale Center for British Art. B1977.14.21012(20)

Image 33 The Light Guinea, or, the Blade in the Dumps Lewis Walpole Library, Yale University. lwlpr03817

Image 34 An Evening's Invitation, with a Wink from the Bagnio published by Carington Bowles in 1773. Lewis Walpole Library, Yale University. lwlpr03558

Image 35 The Beggar's Opera, with Captain Macheath upbraided by Polly and Lucy, by G S Newton, 1826. Yale Center for British Art. B1973.1.42

Image 36 Very Slippy Weather by James Gillray, 1808. Lewis Walpole Library, Yale University. lwlpr10996

Image 37 Sandwich Carrots, dainty sandwich carrots by James Gillray, 1796. Lewis Walpole Library, Yale University. lwlpr08790

Image 38 Contemplations upon a Coronet by James Gillray, 1797. Lewis Walpole Library, Yale University. lwlpr08927

Image 39 A voluptuary under the Throes of Digestion by James Gillray, 1792. Library of Congress. PC 1 – 8112

Image 40 The Devil to Pay: the Wife metamorphos'd, or Neptune reposing after fording the Jordan by James Gillray, 1791. Lewis Walpole Library, Yale University. lwlpr07247

Image 41 Symptoms of Lewdness, or, a peep into the boxes by Isaac Cruikshank, 1794. Lewis Walpole Library, Yale University. lwlpr08317

Image 42 Fashionable Jockeyship by James Gillray, 1796. Lewis Walpole Library, Yale University. lwlpr09830

Image 43 A peep into Brest by Richard Newton. Lewis Walpole Library, Yale University. lwlpr08335

Image 44 Which way shall I turn me by Richard Newton. Lewis Walpole Library, Yale University. lwlpr08336

Image 45 Launching a Frigate by Richard Newton. Lewis Walpole Library, Yale University. lwlpr11127

Image 46 Future Prospects, or, symptoms of Love in High Life by Isaac Cruikshank, 1796. Lewis Walpole Library, Yale University. lwlpr09828

Image 47 A luncheon at Gibside by Isaac Cruikshank. Lewis Walpole Library, Yale University. lwlpr07450

Image 48 A wooden substitute – any port in a storm by Theodore Lane. Metropolitan Museum of Art, Harris Brisbane Dick Fund. 17.3.888-235

Image 49 Dignity by Theodore Lane, 1821. Metropolitan Museum of Art, gift of Adele S Gollin. 1976.602.1

Image 50 Ah! Such a pair was never seen so justly form'd to meet by Nature – Old Sherry by George Cruikshank. Library of Congress. PC 1 – 13735

Image 51 The Goats canter to Windsor, or, Cuckold's Comfort published by J Wallis in 1784. Lewis Walpole Library, Yale University. lwlpr05446

Image 52 King Henry IV showing King George IV as his regal predecessor, by William Heath, 1829. Lewis Walpole Library, Yale University. lwlpr13027

Image 53 Florizel and Perdita published in 1783. Lewis Walpole Library, Yale University. lwlpr05237

Image 54 The Rage by W Hintin, 1794. Lewis Walpole Library, Yale University. lwlpr08390

Image 55 Filial Piety by Thomas Rowlandson, 1788. Lewis Walpole Library, Yale University. lwlpr06500

Image 56 Installation of a Knight Companion of the Bath attributed to Theodore Lane, published by George Humphrey, 1821. Wikimedia

Image 57 The Modern Circe, or, a sequel to the Petticoat by Isaac Cruikshank, 1809. Library of Congress. PC 1 – 11252

Image 58 Nauticus by James Gillray, 1791. Lewis Walpole Library, Yale University. lwlpr07241

Image 59 Wouski by James Gillray, 1788. Yale Center for British Art. B1977.14.21012(5)

Image 60 The accommodating spouse; Tyr-nn-es delight! – coming York over her; – or what you like by James Gillray, 1789. © National Portrait Gallery. NPG D12999

Image 61 The Tar and the Jordan by Richard Newton, 1797. Yale Center for British Art. B1981.25.1471

Image 62 Histories of the tête-à-tête annexed – Nancy Parsons and the Duke of Grafton. Lewis Walpole Library, Yale University. lwlpr02768

Image 63 Histories of the tête-à-tête annexed – Lady Waldegrave and the Duke of Gloucester. Lewis Walpole Library, Yale University. lwlpr02755

Image 64 The Shilling, or, the value of a P(rivy) C(ounsell)or's Matrimonial Honor. Published by Hannah Humphrey, 1782. Lewis Walpole Library, Yale University. lwlpr04908

Image 65 A peep into Lady W!!!!'s Seraglio by James Gillray, 1782. © National Portrait Gallery. NPG D12984

Image 66 The Thunderer by James Gillray. © National Portrait Gallery. NPG D12981

Image 67 Teresia Constantia Phillips Mezzotint by Robert Sayers, after Joseph Highmore. Princeton University Library.

Image 68 Colonel Francisco i.e. Francis Charteris by George Francis, 1730. National Portrait Gallery. NPG D1263

Image 69 Quiz-zing a Filly by James Gillray, 1795. Lewis Walpole Library, Yale University. lwlpr08553

Index